LIGHT ON KUNDALINI YOGA

- For you

CLEMENS BIEDRAWA

1st Edition

DEDICATION

This book is dedicated to the true YOU and the Goddess who dwells in this heart. She is all and all that will ever be. It is dedicated to everyone who is searching for the true ground of existence. It is dedicated to the heart, which is thirsty for the nectar of being. This manual is for you, because you are all.

And of course most intimately, this book is also dedicated to the people who guided me on my path, Alex, Julie, all my teachers and my three beautiful children, Noah, Issael and Nils.

ACKNOWLEDGMENTS

I want to acknowledge the great contribution of Dr. Mark Dyczkowsky, Christopher Wallis and Sir James Mallinson to the understanding of Yoga—a lot of the knowledge, and some rare translations that are cited in this manual were available only due to their tireless research and hard work. I further acknowledge all yogis, seekers and true souls.

Table of Contents.

Sit straight with your being erect.

Settle yourself in the cavity of your heart.

There is a luminosity inside of yourself, which expands from your heart through the world.

You are that body of your inner luminosity. it is your very self.

Breathe in and settle in your heart – All is you.

Breathe out and expand this heart throughout the world – You are all.

This is your love relationship.

INTRODUCTION

Dear Reader,

I am a practitioner of yoga who has been fortunate enough to extensively journey through the practice of yoga, and also to be taught Hatha and Kundalini Yoga from an authentic Indian lineage.

I have spent many years providing teacher training in Hatha and Kundalini Yoga in Austria and France. This book began as a handout to help my students grasp the knowledge they were receiving and to give them a set of practical guidelines to follow during their training. However, it has since evolved into an exploration of the secrets of Indian mysticism and the roots of yoga. In this book, we will explore the history, philosophy, and practice of yoga in the light of its historical sources and scriptural heritage. I chose this path not because I am interested in digging through the ashes of the past, but because I want to search for the fire that is hidden within. The goal is always to truly animate one's body, heart, and spirit. After all, what is now ashes wishes to be fire once more.

We all have the responsibility to elevate our own unique fire from the past and make it shine as a light for everyone else.

I hope that every seeker can profit from this precious gift which offers a gentle way of understanding Kundalini Yoga – perhaps in such a way as you have never understood it before.

May the goddess bless you.

PRESENTATION OF THE TEXT

This is a manual about yoga and the Indian culture behind it. As small changes can lead to completely different meanings, a great deal of emphasis will be placed on the correct pronunciation and spelling of Sanskrit words. As an example the word for the heart chakra, *anāhata* means 'unstruck', while the word *anahata* means 'not uninjured', 'not unwashed'. To avoid ambiguity and errors caused by the romanisation of words, italicised Devanagari transcripts (IAST) occur throughout the book, to help familiarise the readers with the actual Sanskrit terms and help them grasp the wide semantic range of each word.

Nevertheless this book is intended for a more general readership rather than for scholars of Sanskrit. Therefore, at the end of this book, I have added a glossary explaining some of the terms. I have also left some originally Sanskrit words in English as they are now in common use, such as Kundalini Yoga (*kuṇḍalinīyoga*), Hatha Yoga (*haṭhayoga*), and many more. I have no academic background in Sanskrit, nor am I a native English speaker. I am simply a dedicated yogi.

Please, enjoy this book from the fullness of your heart.

By concentrating on the lotus of the heart, there arises a
state of sorrowless joy, which is infused with inner light.
Such a state anchors the mind in a state of freedom.

Yoga-sūtra-bhāṣya (1 : 36)

YOUR SAṂKALPA

WHAT IS YOUR HEART'S INTENT?

If you do not know it, now it is the time to discover it. Write it down just here.

WHAT IS YOGA?

yogaś citta-vṛtti-nirodhaḥ

Pātañjalayogasūtra, (1:2)

In all its forms, yoga is the answer to humankind's fundamental questions. The West sought answers in science, while the East turned to spirituality.

What and why am I? Why is there a reality? What is its meaning? What is its nature? Who is the individual within it?

The West examined matter and measured it. The East contemplated experience and explored it. Yoga is a phenomenological science that concerns itself with the phenomenon of experience. Measurable reality is subordinate to internal experience. This approach is valid if one considers that all reality must first pass through the experiencer before it can become meaningful.

The yogas are an investigation into one's own nature and that of the existence that lies within. Furthermore, they offer a path from which to realise one's true nature beyond the phenomena of transitory experience.

Yājñavalkya defines yoga as the union of the individual self with the supreme soul. Patañjali describes it as the stilling of the patterns of consciousness. Abhinava Gupta defines it as the realisation of one's eternal nature. All of these definitions are correct and useful – the only differences being in the method of practice rather than the final goal. Yājñavalkya offers us the science of *kuṇḍalinī* as a means to elevate the individual soul. Patañjali teaches us purification of mind to reach final stillness, and Abhinava Gupta offers us tantra as a way to connect with the heart of all, and realise one's own true and ever-expanded being.

In all of its definitions and forms, yoga is an investigation of one's eternal being. Yet it transcends even that, for it is the science of how to reach this being, which is your essential nature.

It is an invaluable gift for mankind.

Yoga is defined as the unification of the many pairs of opposites, such as the unification of inbreath and outbreath, so also in one's blood and one's semen, the unification of the sun and the moon, or the individual soul with the supreme soul.

Yoga-bija (88–90ab)

BIRD'S-EYE VIEW OF THE HISTORY OF YOGA

oṃ saha nāv avatu saha nau bhunaktu
saha vīryaṃ karavāvahai
tejasvi nāvadhītam astu mā vidviṣāvahai
oṃ śāntiḥ śāntiḥ śāntiḥ

May we together be protected,
May we together be nourished.
May we work together with vigour.
May our study be illuminating.
May we be free from discord.
Oṃ peace, peace, peace!

BRAVERY

The history of Kundalini Yoga is undoubtedly connected to the emergence of Indian civilization and thought. Although the concept of Śakti (or, Energy) as the consort of Pure Unmanifested Being still lay in the distant future at the dawn of India's history, Indian thought was suffused by spiritual inspiration. This spiritual wonder about the world contained within it the seed of future discoveries about the numinous.

Indian thought has always been unique. Not only has there existed a deep belief that reality is permeated by the presence of the divine, but Indians as a whole tend to be philosophically inclined. Reality has never been taken as that which can be comprehended with a single answer – indeed, one answer has never been (and, in all likelihood, will never be) enough. The question concerning the nature of all seems more real than its answer. This philosophical endeavour was, and is, an expression of bravery.

Discovering that knowledge that is unknown

means to step in the darkness and to

face one's own unknowingness.

Doubt is the expression of not knowing what lies beyond one's comprehension. Accepting this doubt, and therefore your own vulnerability, is an act of true bravery, and the first step towards understanding the great unknown. In this way, early Vedic culture was truly exceptional in that it accommodated for (rather than punished) doubt. They allowed one to accept one's own vulnerability and so discover the greater truth. The *Nāsadīya Sūkta*, The Hymn of Creation, serves as proof for this unsurpassed honesty in dealing with one's own limitations. It honestly asks if even the creator himself can know the origin of all...

Many cultures throughout history have lacked the special openness and bravery that laid the foundation for India's philosophical richness. Perhaps it was India's deep underlying spirituality that allowed doubt to be turned into a potent force of evolution. After all, everyone doubts, but only those who feel carried through this world by the invisible hand of the good can turn their uncertainty into something truly meaningful. Those who feel that greater meaning lies beyond their comprehension, and those who surrender to the great unknown in the world, can find the bravery to face their doubt. In so doing, doubt turns from darkness into light. They make it a force of endeavour and growth. This bravery of heart and mind is the force which birthed the precious science that is Kundalini Yoga.

EARLY BEGINNING

From its foundation in 3300 BCE, the famous Indus Valley Civilization founded many major cities and, together with ancient Egypt and Mesopotamia, blossomed. The later Vedic texts refer to this time as a golden age. The Vedas referencing this ancient period were themselves sung between approximately 1600 to 500 BCE. We are fortunate in that these texts provide us with glimpses through time in which we can observe the thoughts and forms of worship of the people from this distant past.

The Vedas are religious texts said to have been carefully collected by sages, and contain essential information on mantras, rituals, forms of worship, and cosmology. The four main Vedas are: the *Ṛgveda*, the *Yajurveda*, the *Sāmaveda*, and the *Atharvaveda*. Each of these contain four further subcategories: the *Saṃhitās*, the *Āraṇyakas*, the *Brāhmaṇas*, and the *Upaniṣads*. The *Upaniṣads* are especially important to us as they discuss meditation, philosophy, and esoteric knowledge. The Vedas are in themselves a science, and their discussion constitutes an eternal journey. In essence, they express wonder for the vastness of the universe, how best to approach the deity in terms of worship and ritual, and how the individual can achieve final happiness in this world.

Here is the aforementioned *Nāsadīya Sūkta*, the Hymn of Creation, found in the *Ṛgveda*, the oldest Vedic text. It is said to have been composed in approximately 1500 BCE. It expresses a fundamental astonishment about existence, and talks of love, doubt, wonder, and surrender. Above all, however, it expresses honesty. This honesty is the openness which constitutes the very gate to deep understanding.

Then even nothingness was not, nor existence,
There was no air then, nor the heavens beyond it.
What covered it? Where was it? In whose keeping?
Was there then cosmic water, in depths unfathomed?

Then there was neither death nor immortality
nor was there then the torch of night and day.
The One breathed windlessly and self-sustaining.
There was that One then, and there was no other.

At first there was only darkness wrapped in darkness.
All this was only unillumined cosmic water.
That One which came to be, enclosed in nothing,
arose at last, born of the power of heat.

In the beginning desire descended on it –
that was the primal seed, born of the mind.
The sages who have searched their hearts with wisdom
know that which is, is kin to that which is not.

And they have stretched their cord across the void,
and know what was above, and what below.
Seminal powers made fertile mighty forces.
Below was strength, and over it was impulse.

But, after all, who knows, and who can say
Whence it all came, and how creation happened?
The Gods themselves are later than creation,
so who knows truly whence it has arisen?

Whence all creation had its origin,
the creator, whether he fashioned it or whether he did not,
the creator, who surveys it all from highest heaven,
he knows – or maybe even he does not know.

Nāsadīya Sūkta (10:129)

I would urge you to take a moment or two to reflect, let these words gently settle, and absorb their immense profundity.

ROOTS OF YOGA

'Yoga' literally means union, and is derived from the Sanskrit root *yuj*, which means to attach, join, or yoke. Often confused with our later understanding of yoga as mere union, the early use of the word refers to the rein between the war chariot and its horses – the so-called yoga-chariot believed to carry fallen warriors to heaven. This rein is the link between the warrior and goal the wagon aims to realise. This picture therefore emphasises the individual that seeks to move towards its higher destiny. This concept is exactly how we understand yoga today – the power that encourages the individual to unify with the greater goal.

The term 'yoga' first appears in hymn 5.81.1 of the *Ṛgveda* and refers to magical power. While no examination of yogic techniques can be found in these early Vedas, there did exist a strong ascetic tradition that used bodily practices and meditations, and evolved parallel to Buddhism and Jainism in approximately 600 BCE. There is an early reference to this strong ascetic culture (in approximately 1000 BCE) in hymn 10:136 of the *Ṛgveda*, in which a long-haired ascetic uses visionary meditation techniques. The first textual description of yogic techniques as we understand them today appears in the *Bṛhadāraṇyaka Upaniṣad* (from 900 BCE) and refers to *prāṇāyāma*:

> *Now there is this verse; 'The Gods observed the vow of that from which the sun rises and in which he sets. It is [followed] today, and it will be [followed] tomorrow.' The sun indeed rises from the vital force and also sets in it. What these [Gods] observed then, they observe to this day. Therefore a man should observe a single vow – do the functions of the prāṇa and apāna [in- and out-breath], lest the evil of death [fatigue] should overtake him. And if he observes it, he should seek to finish it. Through it he attains identity with this deity, or lives in the same world with it.*

Bṛhadāraṇyaka Upaniṣad (I:23)

THE PRE-CLASSICAL ERA

The Śramaṇas

These ascetics, known as Śramaṇas (meaning 'strivers'), developed in approximately 500 BCE around the site of modern day Allahabad. While they developed independently from Brahmanic traditions, it is certainly possible that they were influenced by Vedic thought. Their main concern was to develop meditation techniques (*dhyāna*) to escape the circle of death and rebirth so as to reach enlightenment (*nirvāṇa*) or liberation (*mokṣa*). Their techniques were designed to achieve a complete 'destruction of one's own being'. While these techniques were not themselves termed yoga, their aim of liberation through the complete mortification of one's own being planted the seed for later yogic austerities. Despite the rejection of the Vedic authorities, their ideas found their way back into the Vedas. Indeed, the 3rd century BCE *Mahābhārata* speaks of *dhyāna yoga* (yoga of meditation), which was derived from the Śramaṇa tradition.

Important practices of the Śramaṇas include:

1. Standing upright during life (until death) and never sitting down.
2. Fixing one's eyes up to heaven and never looking down.
3. Fixing one's hands on the chest and never again opening them.
4. Extending one's hands horizontally and never letting them drop.
5. Hanging one's head down on a tree over a fire with smoke entering one's mouth.
6. Placing a betel nut on the ground and standing with one's head on the nut and feet in the air.
8. Burying one's head and chest in the ground, feet in the air, and silently repeating the name of God.
9. Having both arms forcibly raised to the sky and never putting them down.
10. Stay forever in a sitting posture and never lay down or rise.
16. Daily being surrounded by a small circle of fire and smoke under the sun, with one's mind fixed on the deity.

These are a selection of the 18 ascetic devotions to Brahma. Many of them may appear terrifying to us and, if successfully practiced, lead to death. They build the foundation for yogic tapas, or austerity. Somewhat surprisingly, many of these techniques are still practiced today in their original form.

The Bhagavad Gītā

Roughly 100 years after the development of the Śramaṇas, the Bhagavad Gītā examined the ways of union, pondered the true nature of being and existence, and detailed the four main paths of yoga. These are:

Karma Yoga – the yoga of action.

Bhakti Yoga – the yoga of devotion.

Jñāna Yoga – the yoga of knowledge.

Rāja Yoga – the royal path (use of meditation and *prāṇāyāma*).

Being a classical dualistic text, its significance for the spirit of yoga is often overlooked, depriving many of its stunning beauty and drama. It is a jewel on the path and laid the ethical groundwork for the sage Patañjali. The Gītā possesses this special and priceless quality that we call heart. It is a must-read for every seeker.

I am the Oblation, the Sacrifice and the Worship;
I am the Fuel and the Chant, I am the Butter
offered to the fire, I am the Fire itself, and I am
the Act of offering.

I am the Goal, the Sustainer, the Lord, the
Witness, the Home, the Shelter, the Lover and
the Origin; I am Life and Death; I am the
Fountain and the Seed Imperishable.

Bhagavad Gītā, (9:16,18)

Yogācāra Buddhism

Two centuries prior to Patañjali's Yoga-*Sūtras*, Buddhist schools began their practice of meditation techniques, which they called 'yoga'. These schools were known as *Yogācāra*. The knowledge and textual corpus is said to have been more extensive than that of Patañjali's yoga. The *Yogācāra* ripened into Buddhist tantra and are the foundation for today's Buddhist tantric yoga..

THE CLASSICAL ERA

The Yoga-Sūtras of Patañjali (Pātañjala-Yoga-Śāstra)

Based on the theory of reality developed by the Sāṃkhya and Buddhist influences, yoga began its evolution; it was considered a theistic philosophy of self-realisation through mediation. Patañjali created an important work for yoga as we know it today – the Yoga-*Sūtras*. These *sūtras* (meaning 'thread') are a guideline through the path of rāja yoga (previously explored in the Bhagavad Gītā). These *sūtras* describe what yoga is, its path and practice, and the mystery of reality.

Patañjali refers to the yogic discipline *tapas* (literally meaning heat), as that power that can awaken *kriyāśakti* – the power of action. This *kriyāśakti* is the precondition for overcoming the causes of suffering (*kleśas*) and for reaching *samādhi*. *Tapas* refers to the aforementioned spirit of complete sacrifice as practiced by the Śramaṇas. This further evidences how Patañjali's yoga evolved as a refined branch from ascetic Śramaṇa traditions.

In *Sādhana-Pāda* (Chapter 2, Yoga-*Sūtras*) Patañjali explains eight successive stages of self-realisation as the eight limbs of yoga. Within this system, self-realisation is achieved by the gradual development of discriminative awareness, which distinguishes between the world and its eternal perceiver. As Patañjali's yoga emphasises the eight (*aṣṭāṅga*) limbs as stages of realisation, it is often considered to be Ashtanga Yoga. The tantras, which emerged approximately 500–800 years later, absorbed these teachings and further developed them into what we know today as Hatha Yoga (yoga of force).

The Upaniṣads

The *Upaniṣads* have long been considered to be part of a Vedic tradition – indeed, they are presented as forming part of the Vedas, or their end, as *Vedānta*. There are 108 *Upaniṣads* which build the canon *muktikā*, the collection of freedom. *Upaniṣad* is derived from the word *upadeśa*, meaning teacher, implying that the teaching within is alive, essential, and close to the teacher. Traditionally, this essence was experienced by sitting in small groups around a master, in the pleasant shadow of a tree, and philosophising about further aspects of reality.

The *Upaniṣads* all share an opposition to Vedic ritual and an openness to exploration. At their time of writing, they were highly alive, or active, scriptures which referred to the most contemporary practices of spirituality. The later *Śākta Upaniṣads* explored the worship of the female as well as the tantras.

The very first *Upaniṣad* to name yoga as we use it today was the *Kaṭhopaniṣad*, written in approximately 300 BCE. As with former Vedas, it uses the image of the chariot as a depiction of the person striving for liberation. The person resting in the chariot is the *ātman*, the self. The *buddhi*, or intellect, is the charioteer and the mind (*mānas*) is represented by the reins. The senses (*indriya*) are the horses and the sense object is the path they take. This picture emphasises the importance of controlling the mind (*mānas*) as a guiding tool. The *Kaṭhopaniṣad* would later introduce yoga as a way to tame the wild mind.

The *Upaniṣads* were composed over an extraordinarily long timespan (from the 10th century BCE to the 15th century CE). The *Yoga Upaniṣads*, concerned with the philosophy of yoga and its practice, were composed from the 3rd century BCE to the 11th century CE. The Yoga Upaniṣads concern themselves with the *sūtras* or explore *āsanas*, and discuss *prāṇāyāma*, Kundalini Yoga, and meditation.

> *Then by this constant practice the Parichaya state (the third state) is gained. Vāyu (or prāṇa) through arduous practice pierces along with Agni (fire) the Kuṇḍalinī and enters the suṣumnā uninterrupted. When one's Citta enters suṣumnā along with prāṇa, it reaches the high seat (of the head) by means of this prāṇa.*
>
> *Yoga-Tattva Upaniṣad (81–83)*

The Tantras (Āgamas)

The individual conscious being, as a contraction of universal awareness, consists of the entire universe in a microcosmic form.

Pratyabhijñā-Hrdaya, (4)

The tantras were lineages of spiritual teachings concerned with the worship of God for both spiritual and material reasons. They all share a high regard and appreciation for the female aspect of existence.

Mahāyāna Buddhism was an important processor for tantric thought, and the first tantric scriptures (which appeared from 500 CE) were unconventional and free from traditional spiritual approaches. The most important early work of non-dual tantra is widely regarded to be the *Śiva-Sūtra* (appearing from 900 CE), which was revealed to Vasugupta in a dream. It is a highly mystical work which examines the foundation of Śaiva tantra and non-dualistic thought. Tantric philosophy continued to evolve along a variety of strands and colours until the end of the Classical period in the 13th century CE.

The nine primary schools of tantra in India were:

Śaiva Siddhānta	The Orthodox Doctrine
Vāma	The Left
Yāmala	The Couple
Mantrapīṭha	The Throne of Mantras
Amṛteśvara	The Lord of Nectar
Trika	The Trinity
Kālīkula	The Family of Kālī
Kaubjikā	Goddess Kubjikās Tradition
Śrīvidya	The Goddess of Auspicious Wisdom

They have been listed here in order of their inclination to the goddess, the female aspect, with Śrīvidya (the Goddess of Wisdom) as the deity most closely bound to the mother. The tantric schools developed bodily techniques of purification, gestures of energy (*mudrās*), breath control (*prāṇāymas*), and the chakra system. All told, they could be said to have founded the techniques of Hatha Yoga long before they were termed as such. Furthermore, early in its history, tantra absorbed Patañjali's *aṣṭāṅga* yoga. Indeed, the early Sanskrit source, *Haṃsavilāsa*, describes Hatha Yoga as being a tantric amplification of Patañjali's *aṣṭāṅga* yoga.

Some Hatha Yoga teachings that were directly derived from tantric sources include:

- The primal Goddess Kuṇḍalinī
- The system of the six chakras
- 72,000 *nāḍis* and subtle physiology
- The three primary *nāḍis*
- The ten vital energies, or *prāṇa-vāyus*
- Activation of the subtle centres with *mantra* and *bīja*
- The mantras *haṃsa* and *so'haṃ*
- Ascension of consciousness through *prāṇāyāma*, *dhāraṇā* and *dhyana*

Meditate on kuṇḍalinīśakti moving upwards like lightning
through all the chakras one by one to the dvādaśānta.
Then at last, the glorious form of Bhairava dawns.

Vijñāna-Bhairava-Tantra (29)

Abhinava Gupta and Tantra

Abhinava Gupta was born to a family of musicians and Brahmins in roughly 950 BCE. He was a singular person who showed a great talent for spirituality and the arts. He decided to live as a *Brahmachari* from an early age, but to remain living with his family while he did so. However, instead of combining his duties with his position as a householder, he concentrated solely on being a teacher of the arts and master of contemporary spiritual traditions. Abhinava Gupta was extremely curious and was spiritually initiated into 15 spiritual lineages in India, including all of the major tantric linages that existed at the time. He achieved mastery in all these lineages and earned the title, Śrī Abhinava.

He contributed large volumes of knowledge to the art of music and aesthetics. He also turned his hand to poetry, gaining great renown for both his poems and analytical texts on the artform itself. All things considered, Abhinava Gupta was the most influential intellectual of his time, and his contributions changed the paths of arts and spirituality forever.

The tantric corpus of practice and belief at this time was as wide as it was scattered. Many different schools practiced and developed their own secret techniques and teachings, with no thought to systematisation for a broader understanding. Abhinava Gupta, who had been initiated into the secret teachings of all schools, began composing a mammoth work of 37 books, the *Tantrāloka* (Light on Tantra), in order to systematise and engage with the deeper meaning, and inherent beauty, of the soul of tantra. The *Tantrāloka* is often considered his most important work, despite its entirety constituting only a fraction of his contribution to spirituality. *Tantrāloka* compared and fused the rituals, meditation, and philosophy of 64 *Āgamas* (tantric traditions) into a single comprehensive piece. The invaluable teachings of this long-forgotten time can be understood thanks to this one work alone.

Tantrāloka was so voluminous that Abhinava Gupta decided to compile a text about its essence so as to allow lay people to also benefit from the gift of tantric thought. This comparatively small piece, named *Tantrasāra* (Essence of the Tantras), is an invaluable gift for understanding the tantric teachings of Trika.

Abhinava Gupta died in 1020 CE. It is said that his bodily form disappeared while reading his *Bhairavastava* to his devotees.

The entire universe is shining on the clear inner core of the Self. The multifarious forms shine on the surface of the mirror, but the mirror is not aware of them. On the other hand, supreme consciousness, by means of the continuous flow of its own delight of self-consciousness. reflects the universe.

Tantrasāra, (3)

THE POST-CLASSICAL ERA

Overview

From roughly 800 CE onwards, Muslim armies pushed eastwards and finally established the great Delhi Sultanate in 1206 CE. The Muslim rulers were merciless towards Hindu practices and thousands of monasteries were destroyed. Indeed, it is recorded that during the Timur invasion in 1398, the vast majority of Delhi's inhabitants were massacred and the few who survived were carried off as slaves. Tantra, which during the Classical Era was a widely spread and institutionalised practice, was pushed into the forests and rural areas, and the practitioners rapidly declined in number. Originating in the Kashmir Valley, tantra migrated south where its teachings were partly preserved. It is widely believed that the loss of institutional support weakened the philosophical basis of tantra and led to a shift in focus to Hatha Yoga as its practical application.

In 1300 CE, the south Indian tantra lineage of Kaubjikā practiced a technique in which the *kuṇḍalinī* energy was ascended through a path of six chakras along the spine – a technique found in the later Hatha Yoga texts. The bridge between Hatha Yoga and tantra was firmly established by the 10th-century master, Matsyendra. He founded the Kaula lineage of tantra and his student, Gorakṣa, is credited with having founded Hatha Yoga.

Matsyendra is one of the *navnāth*, the nine masters of the *nāth* lineage. While in many ways he can appear an unusual master, sometimes depicted as a fallen hero, entangled in ancient tantric self-indulgence, he is most often perceived as the bright master over illusion – Māyā Pati Dādā. If Gorakṣa is considered the father of Hatha Yoga, Matsyendra must be thought of as its grandfather (*dādā*).

The work of Gorakṣa, the *Gorakṣa-Śataka*, is the earliest scripture of Hatha Yoga and the basis for the *Yoga-Cūḍāmaṇi Upaniṣad*. Moreover, the *Haṭha-Yoga-Pradīpikā* and the *Gheraṇḍa-Saṃhitā* use and explore the teachings of the *Gorakṣa-Śataka* and were derived from Kaula Tantra.

Matsyendra and Gorakṣa

The following story is from the *Caturaśīti-Siddha-Pravṛitti* or *The Life Stories of the Eighty-Four Siddhas* by Abhaya Datta.

At some distance from the land of Kāmarūpa, a fisherman names Minapa lived on the shores of Ita Ocean. One day he sailed out to the sea and cast his nets into the waters. An enormous fish was caught in his net. The fish, being far stronger than the fisherman, dragged him into the sea and swallowed him whole. Miraculously, the blessed fisherman survived in the belly of the fish waiting for his destiny to come...

At this time, the Goddess Pārvatī asked Śiva to teach her how to achieve freedom in this dark age – *kaliyuga* on earth. Śiva warned her that this knowledge is too secret to be taught indiscriminately among the people, so he asked her to descend to the ocean floor where they would be free from prying ears. There, in the ocean depths, the fish (and the fisherman within) swam close by the god and goddess. When Śiva began teaching this knowledge of the way of Yoga, Pārvatī fell asleep, unable to listen to all the secrets.

After a while Śiva asked her, 'Are you still listening?' The fisherman, hidden in the belly of the fish replied, 'Yes, I am!', so Śiva resumed his instruction on Hatha Yoga. When Śiva finally finished, Pārvatī awoke and apologised for having fallen asleep, to which Śiva replied, 'If you haven't heard the teaching, then there will be no Hatha Yoga in the world! He paused for a moment and then asked, 'Who was it then who told me they were listening?'

Minapa emphatically replied, 'I was listening!' Śiva contentedly realised that he had taught a new disciple and that there would be Hatha Yoga in the world.

For twelve long years, the fisherman diligently practiced his *sādhanā* in the belly of the fish as instructed by the primal guru. Years later, the fish was caught by local fishermen and cut open. The imprisoned former fisherman and yogi emerged shining.

He became the "Lord of the fish", Matsyendra Nāth. He taught the world the secrets of *haṭha*, and gave the blessing of the primal teacher.

> *One has to descend to the bottom of one's inner sea, to listen to the secret voice of the primal guru residing there. Carried with power of persistence, one day, one will rise again from the darkness of the deep waters as a new master.*

Years later, on one of his many journeys, Matsyendra Nāth passed through the village of Chandragiri. A friendly householder, Suraj, invited the master into the home he shared with his wife, Sarasvatī. Once he had rested, and been served with plenty of food and drink, the time came for Matsyendra Nāth to continue on his journey. Before leaving, he asked Sarasvatī if he could do her a favour in return for their generous hospitality.

Sarasvatī burst into tears and told him about her unfulfilled wish to have a child. Matsyendra Nāth assured her that she could easily conceive a child with his blessing. He took some ashes, blessed them, and handed her the ashes saying, 'Swallow these and you will receive a child.' Without further instruction, he left the village and continued on his way.

Sarasvatī was confused and angry. Had the yogi just ridiculed her and made light of her suffering? 'I've got plenty of ashes around here, I don't need a yogi to give me any more', she thought. Disappointed, she threw the ashes into the pile of cow dung beside her house.

Twelve years later, Matsyendra Nāth found himself again passing through Chandragiri. He entered the village and went to Sarasvatī to ask her if the boy he had prayed for her to have was well. Sarasvatī was astonished and told him that was still without child. So Matsyendra asked, 'Then what did you do with the ashes I gave you. Didn't you swallow them?' Flushing with shame and embarrassment, Sarasvatī admitted to have thrown them into the cow dung. Matsyendra grew upset at this slight and told her to show him to this place immediately. At the pile he called out loudly, 'Where are you, my child?' From deep within the pile a voice was heard in reply, 'Here I am.' The dung was immediately cleared away to reveal a beautiful boy of twelve years sitting in quiet meditation.

Matsyendra said, 'You are the child born from the ash, that I had given to that women a long time ago. Because she failed to use this gift properly, she has no claim

on you anymore. Now you will become a yogi just as I am, your name will be Gorakṣa Nāth – the one who defends cows.' The two left the village and continued their pilgrimage together.

Gorakṣa Nāth founded the *Nātha Sampradāya* (Nāth lineage). Famed for its simplicity and clarity, it aimed to cast off the extraneous tantric ballast that clouded the essential teaching. *Kaivalya* (meaning solitude or detachment) was the ultimate and highest aim. He is the founder of today's Hatha Yoga.

Ash is the gift of fire, it is the residue of all that was once known. Fire has consumed all form. It is the pure father and the very soil of all thing. Source of all things, from there grows the spiritual power. To walk to the source one must transcend the mother of all form.

Amṛtasiddhi and Dattāreya-Yoga-Śāstra

The *Amṛtasiddhi* is an 11th-century tantric Buddhist text. It contains yogic techniques, such as the preservation of semen (*vajrolī mudrā*). While it does not specifically term its techniques *haṭha*, it is still considered to be the very first piece to detail the techniques of Hatha Yoga. The *Dattāreya-Yoga-Śāstra*, together with the *Gorakṣa-Śataka*, later drew from these tantric Buddhist practices. Together with the *Yoga-Sūtras of Patañjali* (*Pātañjala-Yoga-Śāstra*) they laid the foundation for modern-day Hatha Yoga.

Gorakṣa-Śataka

The aforementioned *Gorakṣa-Śataka* is a collection of a wide variety of techniques containing, among others, purification practices, *bandhas*, *kāranas*, *āsanas*, and *mudrās*, as well as meditation techniques using visualisation. These techniques are designed to awaken Kuṇḍalinī and make her rise. Therefore, it can be argued that the *Gorakṣa-Śataka* is the first comprehensive Hatha or Kundalini Yoga handbook – indeed, it depicts itself in this way. The author, Gorakṣa, did not stop with the creation of this book. Instead, he travelled far across India to collect tantric techniques and is also believed to have authored several other influential works about yoga.

The Great Goddess sleeps, with her face covering that door, the door by which the place of the Creator Brahma, unaffected by māyā is to be attained. Awakened by the yogic fire, produced from the strike of the mind and the vital air (concentration and breath), she moves upwards through the middle channel as a thread sized by a needle. Awakened by the yogic fire, she raises upwards through the middle channel in the form of the shining serpent, auspicious like a filament of a lotus.

Gorakṣa-Śataka (48–50)

Haṭha-Yoga-Pradīpikā

The *Haṭha-Yoga-Pradīpikā* was composed by Yogi Svātmārāma of the *Nātha Sampradāya* in the 15th century. The Nātha yogis were considered to be the heirs of Gorakṣa and his teachings. While their practices lacked substantial philosophical basis, they were rich in terms of their techniques and practical value. The *Pradīpikā* is said to be a collection of roughly 20 works previously written in the *Nātha Sampradāya*. Significant for the *Haṭha-Yoga-Pradīpikā* is its novel and comprehensive examination of the practice of *āsana*. The *Pradīpikā* is highly influential for all Hatha Yoga and remains the most commonly referred to text from the 15th century onwards.

Śiva-Saṃhitā

We should begin our discussion of the *Śiva-Saṃhitā* by first noting its beauty. While this may be a subjective view, and beauty is certainly in the eye of the beholder, I am confident that everybody who honestly reads the core text would agree with this view. It is full of both mercy and beauty. The *Śiva-Saṃhitā* is written in the classical tantric dialog form of Śiva and his consort Śakti. The Śiva-Saṃhitā, composed in the 15th century, is a work of the *Kaula* tradition and (correctly) depicts itself as a tantra. The *Śiva Saṃhitā* is a key text in modern yoga. Seldomly is a text so detailed in its philosophical views and practices. The text explains the yogic view of reality, the way of a yogi, and yogic techniques.

Gheraṇḍa-Saṃhitā

The 17th-century *Gheraṇḍa-Saṃhitā* portrays itself as having been derived from the tantras. In the text, the yogi Gheraṇḍa explains the techniques of self-realisation to his student Chanda Kapali. The *Gheraṇḍa-Saṃhitā* is both an accessible and comprehensive text or handbook, chiefly concerned with postural yoga and *mudrās*.

> *Sitting in siddhāsana, close the two ears with the two thumbs, the eyes with the index fingers, the nostrils with the middle fingers, the upper lip with the fore fingers, and the lower lip with the little fingers. Draw in the prāṇa-vāyu by kaki-mudrā, and join it with the apāna-vāyu; contemplating the six chakras in their order, let the wise one awaken the sleeping serpent-Goddess Kuṇḍalinī, by repeating the mantra hum, and haṃsa, and raising the Śakti [Force-kuṇḍalinī] with the jīva, place them at the thousand-petalled lotus. Being himself full of Śakti, being joined with the great Śiva, let him think of the various pleasures and enjoyments. Let him contemplate on the union of Śiva [spirit] and Śakti [Force or energy] in this world. Being himself all in bliss, let him realize that he is the Brahma. This yoni-mudrā is a great secret, difficult to be obtained even by the devas. By once obtaining perfection in its practice, one enters verily into samādhi.*
>
> *Gheraṇḍa-Saṃhitā (37–42), on 'yonimudrā'*

MODERN YOGA

Overview

Hatha Yoga and its techniques of raising Kuṇḍalinī continued to be disseminated in secret until the 19th century. Still, it should be noted that yoga no longer formed part of the public consciousness and the great yogis for which kings had built temples in the Classical Era were almost forgotten. While Bhakti Yoga was widely practiced, *haṭha* techniques and meditation were considered unusual practices adopted by ancient and superstitious people from a long-forgotten past. Yoga was revived mostly through Western interest. The rise of psychology and the swarms of ethnologists that travelled the world discovered yoga and keenly wondered what it might reveal about human nature and reality.

While this may be hard for us to believe, much of what Indian people understand about yoga today stems from the curiosity of these early-19th century Westerners. Especially important for the rediscovery of yoga was Sir John Woodroffe's *The Serpent Power* (1919). His work, and those of others, were at least as important for our knowledge of yoga as the yogis who felt inspired to start spreading the teachings of the initial ground-breaking pioneers.

Almost all of what we know about the practice of Hatha Yoga is down to one yogi and his effort to unveil a science that was long concealed – Tirumalai Krishnamacharya, the father of modern yoga.

Tirumalai Krishnamacharya

Krisnamacharya was born in 1888. He studied philosophy, Sanskrit, and Ayurveda, and was introduced to yoga by a Tibetan Hatha Yoga master named Rāmamohan Brahmacārī. He acquired degrees in all six *āstika* schools of Indian philosophy, namely: *Mīmāṃsā*, *Vedānta*, *Sāṃkhya*, *Yoga*, *Nyāya* and *Vaiśeṣika*. Krishnamacharya was the first yogi to publicly spread yoga for the welfare of humankind. He held public demonstrations in which he stopped his heartbeat, lifted heavy objects with his teeth, or stopped a moving car with his bare hands.

He was the founder of Vinyāsa Yoga as well as the synchronization of movement and breath. At the age of 16, a disembodied being (*Nāthamuni*, a *Nātha* yogi) appeared to him in a vision and taught him the *Yoga-Rahasya*, a long-forgotten text on Hatha Yoga which emphasises the importance for yoga in our time. Interestingly the *Yoga-Rahasya* also repeatedly stresses the importance of yoga for women. Since this visionary text was clearly the seed for modern Western yoga practice, this could explain (in part, at least) why so many women today are yoga practitioners. I should add, in case you are wondering, that to take help from disembodied beings is nothing unusual for yoga masters.

Many influential yoga teachers and founders of modern lineages studied with him

:

Indra Devi (1900–2002) – founded many studios around the world

B. K. S. Iyengar (1918–2014) – founder of Iyengar Yoga.

K. Pattabhi Jois (1915–2009) – founder of Ashtanga Yoga.

A. G. Mohan (* 1945) – famous practitioner and teacher.

More than men, women have the right and obligation to practice Yoga... Women need to maintain good health to bring forth healthy offsprings and need to be free from afflictions and diseases due to microbes, and women should not allow themselves to become ill and diseased.

Yoga-Rahasya (1:2)

Swami Lakshman Joo

Lakshman Joo was born in Srinagar in 1907. A mystic and great yogi, he was first initiated into the mysteries of tantra when he was just five years old. His spiritual teachers reported him to have a heart of gold, and that he would spontaneously immerse himself in deep meditation as a little boy. In later life he was simply called Lal Sahib (the Friend of God) by all his followers.

Swami Lakshman Joo was said to have a childlike playfulness, be genuinely kind and loving, to be humorous, and like a friend to all. He could enthral his students by talking with childish enthusiasm about the intricacies of tantric yoga and then suddenly, from one moment to the next, fall into a deep trance where he remained motionless, immersing himself into the one absolute for hours or days at a time.

The way of Trika tantra was almost forgotten until it was rediscovered by scholars such as Alexis Sanderson, Mark Dyczkowski, and Bettina Bäumer. Being a yogi at heart, Lakshman Joo could experience that which was written of in the scriptures. While certain tantric practices were already known, it was only through the fertile seed of Lakshman Joo's direct experience that they ripened and spread. His introduction to these secret practices kept Kundalini Yoga and Trika tantra alive – indeed, more so than it had ever been in the West. Anyone who speaks of tantra today, who can say they feel its mystic energy, can do so thanks to the transmission of this great master who opened our hearts to the Divine in all.

The whole universe is just a means to recognize lord Śiva.

Swami Lakshman Joo

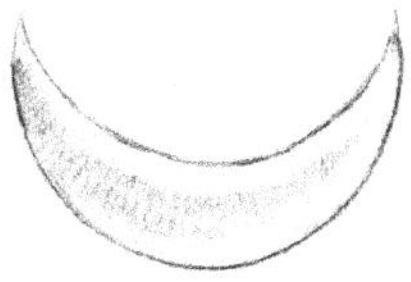

PHILOSOPHY OF YOGA

To understand Yoga you don't need a book, just look inside
- you are the book, just read your soul

My teacher Rainer Neyer

SPIRIT OF THE GĪTĀ

The Bhagavad Gītā, or the Song of the Blessed One, is a dualistic text which explores the relationship between the individual soul and the all-encompassing Absolute. This text is of the utmost importance for yoga as one cannot ascend in any of its branches without breathing the spirit of the Gītā and settling its message in one's heart. There is no early scripture that can match the Gītā's clarity or practicality. Not only is the text interested in the nature of this wondrous universe, it also explores how one should act, and how these actions can carve a way through life's difficulties.

The Battle Inside

Life demands choices; making no decisions means to fall prey to the choices of others. Life demands action, as inertia means to fall prey to the world's actions. Therefore, life demands that we clearly bring forth our innermost truth in the face of a continuous stream of outer and inner impressions. Somehow, it is the ever-raging inner battle that threatens to carry one away. The Gītā addresses this conflict as field in which one's heroic nature can be revealed. There is no hero without a dragon, no victory without the possibility of defeat, no eternal pleasure without pain. The Gītā is the torch which lights the four main paths of yoga to lead one through the war of life, to overcome its struggles, and finally reach peace.

Arjuna, son of the Pāṇḍava, the pure and loving soul full of virtue, is forced to defend his kingdom and throne against the Kauravas, his sinful and murderous cousins who are the sons of the blind King Dhṛtarāṣṭra. When the armies gather on the battlefield of life, Prince Arjuna asks his charioteer to bring him between the two armies to allow him to observe his opponents. Arjuna raises his gaze and sees his friends, teachers, uncles, and beloved childhood companions, all eager to fight and kill. Seeing this, Arjuna falls in despair. He casts aside his bow and cries, how can he ever kill those he loves? How can victory be gained through such misery? Any victory will be a loss, any loss a defeat.

> *And his heart melted with pity and sadly he spoke: O my Lord! When I see all these, my own people, thirsting for battle, my limbs fail me and my throat is parched, my body trembles and my hair stands on end. The bow Gandeeva slips from my hand, and my skin burns. I cannot keep quiet, for my mind is in tumult.*
>
> *Bhagavad Gītā (2:29–31)*

This is war, the war of life, where that which you love turns against you, and the individual, surrounded by injustice, is unable to justly act. The Gītā puts forth the most horrible situation of all – to kill some of whom you love lest everyone love be killed. This terrifying situation is the place in which yoga is put. The unfailing strength of yoga is proven through its power to even find an answer in this very edge of being. What is yoga worth if it cannot sustain the greatest suffering? Yoga is the way, and no darkness can dim its light.

THE FOUR MAIN PATHS OF YOGA

In the Bhagavad Gītā, Kṛṣṇa – the supreme soul, full of compassion – teaches four main paths (*mārgas*) of Yoga as a way to reach union with the divine.

Karma Yoga – The Path of Action

Even this book can essentially be considered a closer exploration of *Rāja Yoga*, yet Karma Yoga seems to be even more important in our modern age. Karma is the accomplished action and *Karma Yoga* is the art of acting. As Kṛṣṇa says, it is the path for those who have to act, for those engaged in life. All of us, with our families and jobs, are engaged in the turmoil of daily existence. *Karma Yoga* is the path that liberates us while being absorbed in action.

> *No man can attain freedom from activity by refraining from action; nor can he reach perfection by merely refusing to act. Therefore do your action perfectly, without care for the results, for he who does his duty without attachment attains the Supreme.*
>
> *Bhagavad Gītā (3:4 & 3:19)*

Life demands action. As even the maintenance of the body requires necessary actions, inactivity is impossible. All action creates fruit, which can either be bitter or sweet. This fruit is bondage to the one absorbed in it. How can one be free and still act? How can the action become an instrument of freedom and pass beyond the chains of cause and effect?

The Gītā tells us that, while one must act because action is superior to inaction, one must act in the spirit of renunciation. Indeed, it is not the action itself which creates bondage to its fruit, but the attachment to it. 'You have a right on your action, but not on your action's fruits', says Kṛṣṇa to Arjuna, meaning that one must act and surrender its fruit. The action is just like an arrow that one fires. One can draw the bow and aim the arrow with great concern, but how it flies is out of one's hands.

Further, the true self is ever unattached from action. In reality, you are never the doer as the forces of nature themselves are the ones who compel action. From this perspective, why would one attach to an action if it was never theirs in the first place?

> *Action is the product of the Qualities inherent in Nature. It is only the ignorant man who, misled by personal egotism, says: 'I am the doer'. The wise man knows that when objects act on the senses. It is merely the gunas*

[Qualities of nature] acting on the gunas, thus he stays unattached.

Bhagavad Gītā (3:28–29)

Since any action can be performed in surrendering its fruit, the main question that arises is not whether one should act, but what is the right action? To discover this, one must first renounce. Yoga of action starts in yoga of renunciation. One must renounce one's individual desires in order to glimpse the right path underneath distraction and illusion. Therefore, giving up graving and surrendering the highest good is the path to right action.

As fire is shrouded in smoke, as a mirror is covered by dust and a child by the womb, so is the universe enveloped in desire. Therefore, O Arjuna, first control your senses and then slay that difficult to conquer enemy called desire, for it is the destroyer of knowledge and of wisdom.

Bhagavad Gītā, (3:38 & 41)

Bhakti Yoga – The path of love

Everything starts in the heart, is beautiful when performed from the heart, and is ultimately meaningful when the heart is present. If there is no heart, what have we gained?

Bhakti is the path of transforming one's being through the heart. It is the exploration of the unfailing power of devotion. Whether you act, or strive for knowledge, whether you meditate or not. The heart transforms all your efforts, and turns them to gold.

Knowledge is better than action. Meditation is better than knowledge and the best of all is surrender which soon brings peace (...). He who is incapable of hatred towards any being, who is kind and compassionate, free from selfishness, without pride, equable in pleasure and in pain, and forgiving, Always contented, self-centered, self-controlled, resolute, with mind and reason dedicated to Me, such a devotee of Mine is My beloved.

Bhagavad Gītā (12:68–70)

Jñāna Yoga – The Path of Knowledge

Jñāna Yoga uses the knowledge about the ultimate reality as the path to its realisation. A correct, but limited, understanding is the sphere in which actual reality can expand. In this way, the philosophy of *advaitavedānta* understands *Jñāna Yoga* as that path in which the intellectual understanding of one's own nature allows consciousness to dive into the unmanifest ground beyond such a limited understanding.

This dissolution of one's own mind into the ultimate truth can be achieved through concentration on one of the four *mahā-vākyas*, the great expressions, such as *prajñānaṃ brahma* ('consciousness is Brahman').

It is worth noting that the tantric *śāktopāya* meditations, like those practiced in the Trika tradition, are not so different from *Jñāna Yoga*. While they may differ in the object of meditation, they share similarities in terms of the mode of realisation. In both traditions, a firm concentration on the truth allows one to be imbued by its essence.

Generally speaking, Jñāna Yoga is therefore also a path for studying and learning scripture. For this purpose, I have a quotation that can guide you through this path:

Don't mistake the finger for the moon.

Siddhārtha Gautama

Rāja Yoga – The Royal Path

Those who can reach the goal directly, by concentrating on and merging with, the goal should be considered royal. The direct path of meditation is *Rāja Yoga*. It is our path.

> *The man of yoga should practice meditation alone, mastering mind and body (...). Seated thus, his mind concentrated, its functions controlled and his senses governed, let him practice meditation for the purification of his lower nature. Let him hold body, head and neck erect, with posture steady and unmoving, gazing at the tip of his nose, not looking anywhere else.*
>
> *Bhagavad Gītā (6:10 & 12–13)*

Patañjali further expanded the secrets of *Rāja Yoga* in his *Yoga-Sūtras*. He defined *Rāja Yoga* as being of three parts: *dhāraṇā* (fixation), *dhyāna* (meditative absorption), and *samādhi* (return). These three aspects are also called Passive Yoga and are the core elements to practice. To reach this lofty goal of complete meditative absorption in the absolute, Patañjali prescribes the dedicated practice of the eight limbs of yoga, starting with the most important foundation of *yamas* and *niyamas*.

Approximately 1,500 years after the death of Patañjali, these eight limbs were further developed in the *Haṭha-Yoga-Pradīpikā*, which added a wide variety of *mudrās*, *prāṇāyāmas*, and *āsanas* to Patañjali's foundations. Svātmārāma, the author of the *Haṭha-Yoga-Pradīpikā*, never tires of informing us that the successful practice of Hatha Yoga leads to the development of *Rāja Yoga*. Svātmārāma seems to suggest that deep meditative absorption is the natural result of perfecting one's posture and breathing.

Therefore, *Rāja Yoga* is the foundation and goal of Hatha Yoga. Moreover, it could well be argued that Hatha Yoga itself finds its last stage of evolution in the tantric amplification of *haṭha* – Kundalini Yoga.

> *For those who wander in the darkness of conflicting creeds*

[and philosophies], unable to reach to the heights of rāja yoga [self-knowledge and cosmic consciousness] the merciful Yogi Svātmārāma has lit the torch of haṭha wisdom.

Haṭha-Yoga-Pradīpikā (1:3)

THE CLASSICAL WAY OF RĀJA YOGA

Modifying *citta* (the mind) also modifies *puruṣa* (the soul). This process is called the modification of consciousness, which entails attachment and bondage for the soul. This attachment leads to suffering, as all modifications contain objects which are inevitably subject to death and decay. These affections of one's mental condition are caused by the five causes of suffering – the *kleśas* (afflictions):

Avidyā –	Ignorance, not seeing things as they are
Asmitā –	Egoism, the sense of 'I'
Rāga –	Attachment
Dveṣa –	Aversion
Abhiniveśa –	Fear of death, which is clinging to life

When considering the five *māyās* in the upcoming chapters, we must be careful not to ignore the impression that the five causes of suffering seem to be the manifestation of the five cosmic limitations (*māyās*) on the individual level.

Puruṣa, the soul, is free and unchanging, and the purpose of yoga is to realise this true self as it simply is – free and unbound. Residing in this freedom is liberation. According to classical Patañjali yoga, this stage of freedom from entanglement is naturally reached upon the destruction of *avidyā*, the most fundamental of all *kleśas*. Patañjali continues to explain that discriminative awareness is the power by which *avidyā* can be overcome. Discriminative awareness is simply the realisation that the ever-free observer exists independently from any object of perception.

Ignorance can be eradicated by cultivating uninterrupted

*discrimination between awareness and the world (...).
When the limbs of yoga are practiced, impurities dwindle;
then, the light of understanding can shine forth,
illuminating the way to discriminative awareness.*

Yama	*restraints,*
Niyama	*commandments,*
Āsana	*posture,*
Prāṇāyāma	*breath regulation,*
Pratyāhāra	*retirement of the senses,*
Dhāraṇā	*concentration, fixation*
Dhyāna	*meditative absorption,*
Samādhi	*and integration.*

Pātañjala-Yoga-Śāstra (2:26–29)

Yoga is a gradual science in which the mind is incrementally brought to the truth. In this manner, discriminative awareness is not immediately achieved. Patañjali explains that the eight steps of yoga function as a ladder to help people gradually reach this power of awareness. The practice of the eight (*aṣṭāṅga*) steps serve to decrease the impurities that move the mind (*citta*), which in turn stops the modification of *buddhi* so that the pure light of the true self (*puruṣa*) can rest in its essence.

Prakṛti – the abundance of nature and *puruṣa* do not exist independently from another – both need the other to realise their inherent nature. Pure consciousness (*puruṣa*) needs the mirror of the world in order to understand its eternal freedom, which it could not do when resting in an unchanged state. *Prakṛti* instead needs the presence of consciousness in order to create a conscious perception of itself, and therefore to exist. Accordingly, both need the other to fulfil their purpose.

Patañjali describes this as such:

The world is the play of the guṇas – the universal energies of light, motion and mass. They take form as the elements and the senses. The purpose of the world is to provide us with experience and thus lead us to liberation (...). But the self is boundless. It is pure consciousness that illuminates the perceiving mind. In essence, the phenomenal world exists to reveal this truth (...). The true self is obscured by the world so that the reality of both may be discovered. Not seeing things as they are [Ignorance] is the cause of this phenomenon. When ignorance [Avidya] is destroyed, the self is liberated from its identification with the world. This liberation is enlightenment.

Pātañjala-Yoga-Śāstra, (2:18, 20 & 23–25)

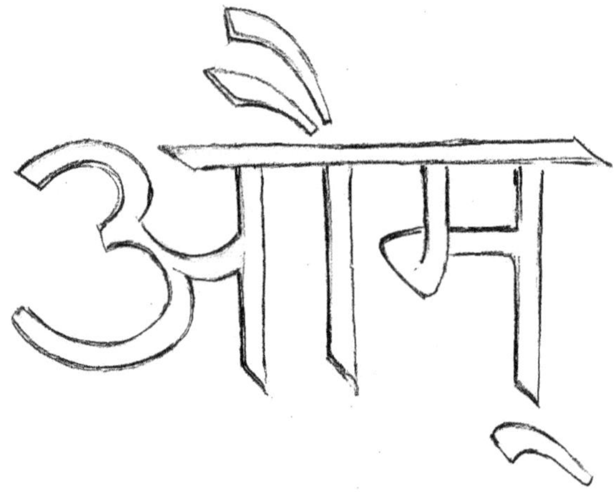

FOUNDATION OF HAṬHA & KUNDALINI YOGA

There is no yoga without a strong moral foundation. In reality, yoga is magical, *kuṇḍalinī* is the energy that brings all things into being, she is the framework of existence. As such, one cannot step into her ecstatic light when one's soul and path is unaligned with the highest good. The first step is intention. This is also the very first chapter of this book. Everything begins with one's intention. On the path of yoga, one must conduct and meditate on the eight limbs.

These limbs are the limbs of a body, the body of glory. The body of your true self. Whenever you act to form one of these limbs, you are making your true body act. Feel and love it.

Ahiṃsā – Non-Violence

This means to welcome the world exactly how it is. To harm is to impose one's own delusion on the world, to change the world into something other than what she already is in all her beauty, to diminish or cause her to disappear. The world will reveal herself to the yogi who is without violence. She will come and reveal her inherent truth. The yogi will be filled with her splendour and thus never be alone.

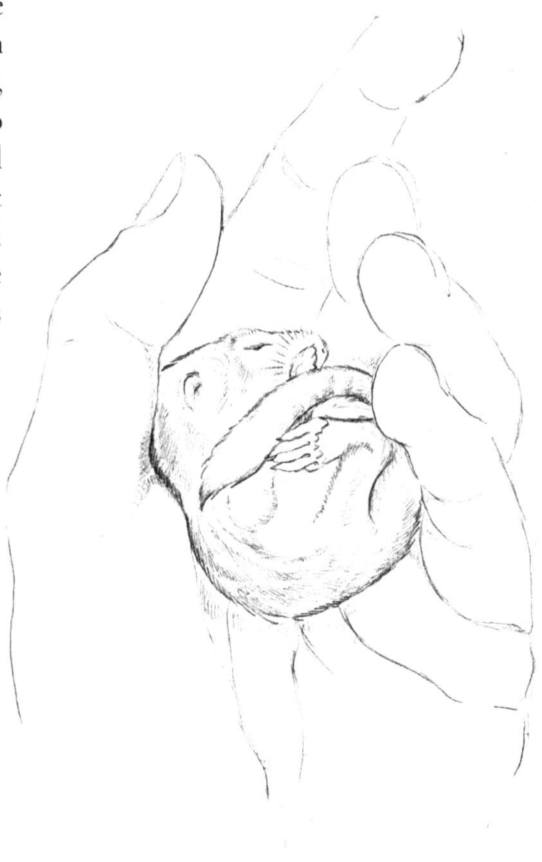

Satya – Truthfulness

The world is truth, her nature is her truth. When one is oriented to the truth, the world can be observed unclouded. Not to serve the truth means to be separated from the world. When a mind clouds the world, it dangerously traps both itself and all others. The one who is oriented to the truth will gain the strength to carry the whole world.

Asteya – Non-Stealing

Having no desire to steal means to rest in the true source of value. Having an inclination to steal means to desire an undeserved object of value. Following the desire distances oneself from the powers that are the source of all value. Once free from stealing, true value will appear.

Brahmacarya – Abstinence from Sensual Pleasures

Life is filled with thousands of voices which speak the languages of pleasure and pain. These two forces push the deluded through life. Hunting thousands of pleasures while constantly fleeing from pain will serve no purpose. Death is the only unavoidable goal of this path. However, relinquishing this aim once and for all will open the door to freedom. Once done, the goal instantly becomes crystal clear. Ever full of dignity one can walk without falling, smiling freely without fear, finally reaching the sun

Aparigraha – Non-Attachment

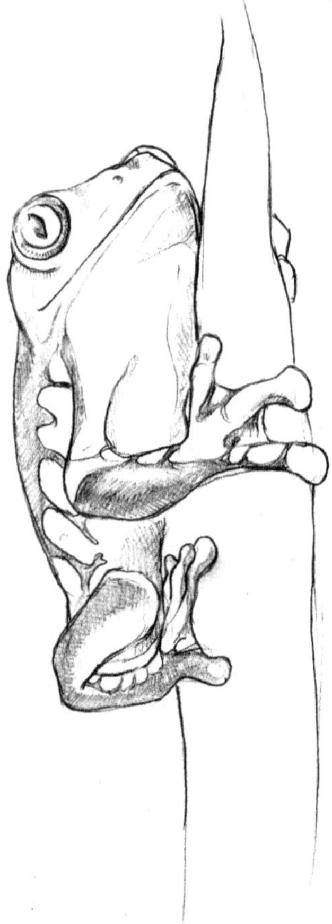

Who is unattached is free from any object of desire, and therefore possesses the highest object. Freedom is attained by meditating over the highest good – the unmanifested source in all that is one. Not to grasp is freedom. This freedom is heroic, and is true victory..

Śauca – Bodily Purification

As the body is your world, purity of one ensures purity of the other. When the Body is impure, then the world – which reaches you through your body – will die. When you honour your body, you worship the world. When you abuse the body, you abuse the world. The world is the goddess; freedom from the world results from worshiping her. Likewise, one must purify the body to be free from it.

Santoṣa – Contentment

There is no reason to be happy, yet there is every reason to be happy. You will die, all you have will be taken from you. Yet you were never born and nothing can ever be lost as you are eternal. Contentment is the art of living in eternity. Not living contentedly is to misunderstand who you truly are. Contentment is to accept your role in the world's play. Since the world is a marvellous theatre production, and death your greatest scene, contentment is the correct attitude for the audience.

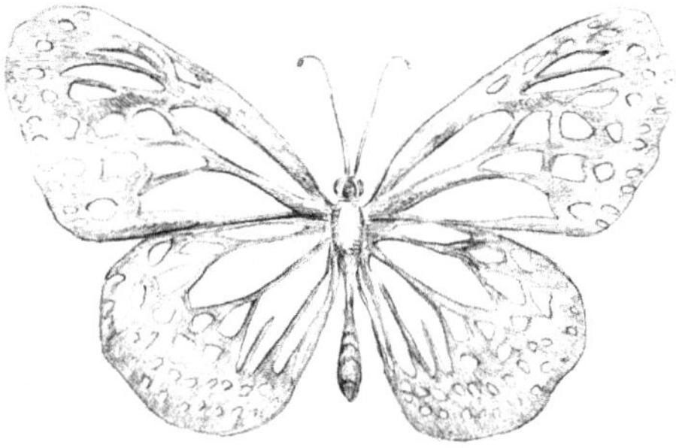

Tapas – Heat

Tapas is discipline, tapas is heat. Whoever acts passionately knows that all effort can flow with ease. Tapas therefore transcends forceful discipline in that it is a passion's fire. It is the heart placed into a goal. When you surrender to your mission from the depths of your heart, the heat will extend through all of your being, making the impossible possible, breaking all limits, and filling your life with wonder.

Svādhyāya – Self-Study

There is no path without knowledge. While all life is knowledge, it can be divided into that which is clear and that which is deluded. If your horses drink from the right bucket, they become calm and safely carry you to your goal. If they drink from the wrong bucket, they will become wild and your goal will be left unreached. Which bucket you place in front of them is up to you. Making them thirsty, however, will drive them to poisonous waters, as clearer waters are rare. It is the duty of every horseman to care for his horses.

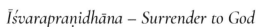

Īśvarapraṇidhāna – Surrender to God

Just like all plants grow towards the light, all action must follow a higher goal. Surrendering to God means to be filled with trust and dignity, and that all joy and suffering can be experienced as sacrifice. It means that everything is finally imbued with meaning. *Īśvarapraṇidhāna* is freedom in action. It alone is the final goal and all yoga is the way to its realisation.

These are the *yamas* and the *niyamas*, the foundations of yoga. Following just one of them with complete abandon will make you supremely happy and will make the goal easily achievable. Incorporating all of them will give you a complete radiance from achieving your heart's goal. Nothing that you can attain, can surpass this sense of happiness. It is full accomplishment.

Āsana, prāṇāyāma, pratyāhāra, dhāraṇā, dhyana, and *samādhi* will be explored more fully in later chapters.

THE TANTRIC REVOLUTION

As mentioned earlier, Patañjali expressed a dualistic view on the subject of reality. From his perspective, only one reality exists, yet the world and its phenomena are unreal. Discriminative awareness about the world and the self is key to understanding one's own nature.

Non-dualistic philosophies, such as Trika tantra, follow a different view. Experience, or even thought-modification (*vikalpa*) – which is essentially energy or *śakti* – can be used as a means of realisation. This tantric path describes itself as the 'easy new way', or *sukhopāya*. In this way, self-realisation can be achieved by the correct observation or understanding of the world of phenomena, as well as by insights into its underlying magic and spirit which is, in essence, the unlimited joy of one's own awareness.

> *'Cessation' of the mind was taught by previous masters [Patañjali] through the yoga method of renunciation [of the senses] and arduous practice. Here I will teach a cessation that is [comparatively] effortless.*
>
> *Svabodhodaya-mañjarī (12)*

As the play of reality is considered divine in every aspect, the rejection of mental activity (such as those described in the *Yoga-Sūtras*) would be very vain indeed. The way of *sukhopāya*, for example, includes such techniques as *bhāvanā*, which can be translated as the cultivation of awareness or simply creative contemplation. However, single terms cannot quite capture the majesty and complexity of *bhāvanā*. It is a kind of attitude towards the deity, it is wonder and imaginative power. It is an attitude so full of wonder that one's vision and imagination about this wondrous world fuse into a creative interplay between the meditator and the deity. *Bhāvanā* is, in essence, therefore a playful attitude of love and wonder. *Bhāvanā* can be practiced on any object of reality. An example of a *Bhāvanā* is the contemplation of pure thought (*śuddha vikalpa*), such as: 'Her body, that is the world, is of the pure nature of joyful awareness'.

Further examples of the new way include meditations that allow oneself to become completely absorbed in any sensory object. When the mind fuses with experience, but the experience naturally dissolves, so does the mind. The mind is then held in the threshold state after the experience has vanished. Through this process, the dissolution of one's thought constructs can occur which leads to the attainment of the realisation of one's inner nature. This way appreciates the emergence, sustenance, and natural dissolution of any object as a means of self-realisation. Accordingly, it differs greatly from Patañjali Yoga.

Knowing this, we should never forget that the path of purification and the development of discriminative awareness (between the object and the observer), as described by Patañjali, is a precondition for this higher path of practice. One will not be able to immerse oneself in meditations that include sensuality if the mind is full of attachment and desire. Letting go of any affection (*kleśa*) is a vital precondition for successful practice.

Keep an appetizing morsel – such as a sweet – on the tip
of your tongue; when the bliss of its flavour dies away,
kaivalya arises.

Svabodhodaya-mañjarī (42)

THE TANTRIC NATURE OF THE DIVINE

In any way one's own self is simply the all-pervasive bliss of freedom and the essence of consciousness. Absorption into that nature of one's own self is said to be the real bath of purification.

Vijñāna-Bhairava-Tantra (152)

In the beginning there is the heart. The heart is everything, the oneness of all, infinite potential, infinite emptiness, and full within itself. It is everything that is, or everything is within it. Since it is all, without being anything in particular, it is the essence of all. The essence of all must be consciousness, as it reveals all that is and, without it, nothing would be (revealed). This consciousness shines brightly at the very heart of all things. It is called *prakāśa*. The light of consciousness.

In this world, the highest aim to attained by a being is one's essential nature. That nature of all the existent entities is only prakāśa, as anything being non-prakāśa can't be established as the nature of something. That prakāśa is not divergent in nature. As there is no scope for any variety in prakāśa, anything divergent from it, other than the supreme consciousness cannot at all be part of the nature of prakāśa. Even time and space cannot create any variety in it, even their essential nature is prakāśa itself. This prakāśa, the self-luminous, enlightening existence, is the only one reality. It is in fact that which is consciousness (...). This shining of that light is not dependent on anything outside of itself. The state of being illuminated by another light should certainly, be called dependence, as the state of being illuminated depends on

others for its illumination. However, in the absence of any other light, there is only this single and autonomous light. It is precisely because of this independence that this light is not limited by time, space, or form.

Tantrasāra (Chapter 1)

The ultimate reality possesses the power of sovereignty (*svātantrya śakti*). Since it is solely self-dependent, it can express itself in five different forms without changing its inner nature. These five powers are an integral part of its reality. These five powers are:

Cit śakti	the power of consciousness
Ānanda śakti	the power of bliss
Icchā śakti	the power of will/desire
Jñāna śakti	the power of knowledge
Kriyā śakti	the power of action

These powers find their completion in *kriyā śakti* – the power of action. The ultimate reality manifests these five powers through the power of action in the form of the five divine acts. These five acts form the play, or dance, known as *līlā*, and are expressed in the figure of the dancing Śiva. Naṭarāja, the dancer, performs five gestures, each corresponding to one great act of this beautiful play. These five acts are:

Sṛsti	creation, emission
Sthiti	maintenance, preservation
Saṃhāra	dissolution, reabsorption
Tirodhana	concealment, forgetting, occlusion
Anugraha	revealing, remembering, grace

What exactly does this mean? Reality exists within the field of awareness. All things exist because they have entered the universal field of being. Simply put, without awareness, there would be no world. Even the ancient Sāṃkhya philosophers, the creators of the foundation of Patañjali Yoga, agree on this point. They hold that *prakṛti* needs *puruṣa* in order to be, as the physical reality cannot exist without the being that perceives it. The object of reality is therefore created within the field of perception. Within this school of thought, objective reality outside of any form of awareness is inexistent. The predominant Western view considers an object to exist independently from awareness, and would typically scorn the notion that awareness if required. A Western mindset would argue that the outside object must exist independently since independent individuals can confirm its existence. Countering this point, the tradition would reply that such independent individuals do not exist objectively, but are instead simply a mirror of a greater ultimate consciousness that individualises itself in order to perceive one object (contained within itself) from all its dimensions. Since there is no individual perceiver, all observations are but one single perception of the reality of the ultimate. In this way, there is no other self that could verify the objective reality of an object outside of you.

The ultimate awareness sustains creation with the force of consciousness. This means that the power of consciousness is the source of creation as all existence exists within awareness. The five acts are therefore five movements of awareness.

Sṛsti	Emission is the awareness movement towards an object of perception. A memory arises. Your gaze falls upon a flower. You recognise a friend walking down the street.
Sthiti	Preservation is the movement through the object of perception, its enjoyment and reality. You remember where you were last year. You are aware of this flower. You greet your friend.
Samhara	Reabsorption is when the object of awareness withdraws inside the field of perception. The memory fades. Your gaze moves away. Your friend passes on.
Tirodhana	Concealment is awareness's contraction into any object of perception.
Anugraha	Revealing is awareness's expansion into a greater range of self-revelation.

The ultimate reality is therefore within you – you are awareness, meaning that it is you who performs the five acts in a microcosmic form. The microcosm that you are is a reflection of the great macrocosm. All of your world is created, sustained, and reabsorbed within you. This is the secret. You are the source.

> *Then, due to continuous immersion into the fully expanded "I" — which is in essence the fusion of illumination and joy, and is the great potency of all mantras — one attains the state of being the lord of the innate circle of the goddesses of awareness, who are constantly engaged in the emanation and reabsorption of all things. All this is Śiva. May it be a blessing.*
>
> *Pratyabhijñā-Hrdaya, (20)*

THE TATTVAS

Tattva, or 'that-ness', is not an element but rather a category of reality. These categories include all qualities of being and perception that can be experienced by a conscious agent and, in so doing, they therefore incorporate the experience of the whole universe. The tantric master, Abhinava Gupta, provides the following definition:

> *A tattva is that which, by virtue of its realty, enables conscious agents to subsume the categories within it.*

Sāṃkhya

According to the ancient teachings of Sāṃkhya (500 BCE), there are 25 *tattvas*, or categories of reality, which encompass all experience. The first and most important is *puruṣa*, or the individual soul – also seen as the singular I-consciousness. This can be aptly demonstrated through experience as any object in our reality exists within the perception of the perceiver. The second *tattva* is nature, or *prakṛti*. *Prakṛti* is the source of any object able to be perceived, whether it be subtle like a thought or

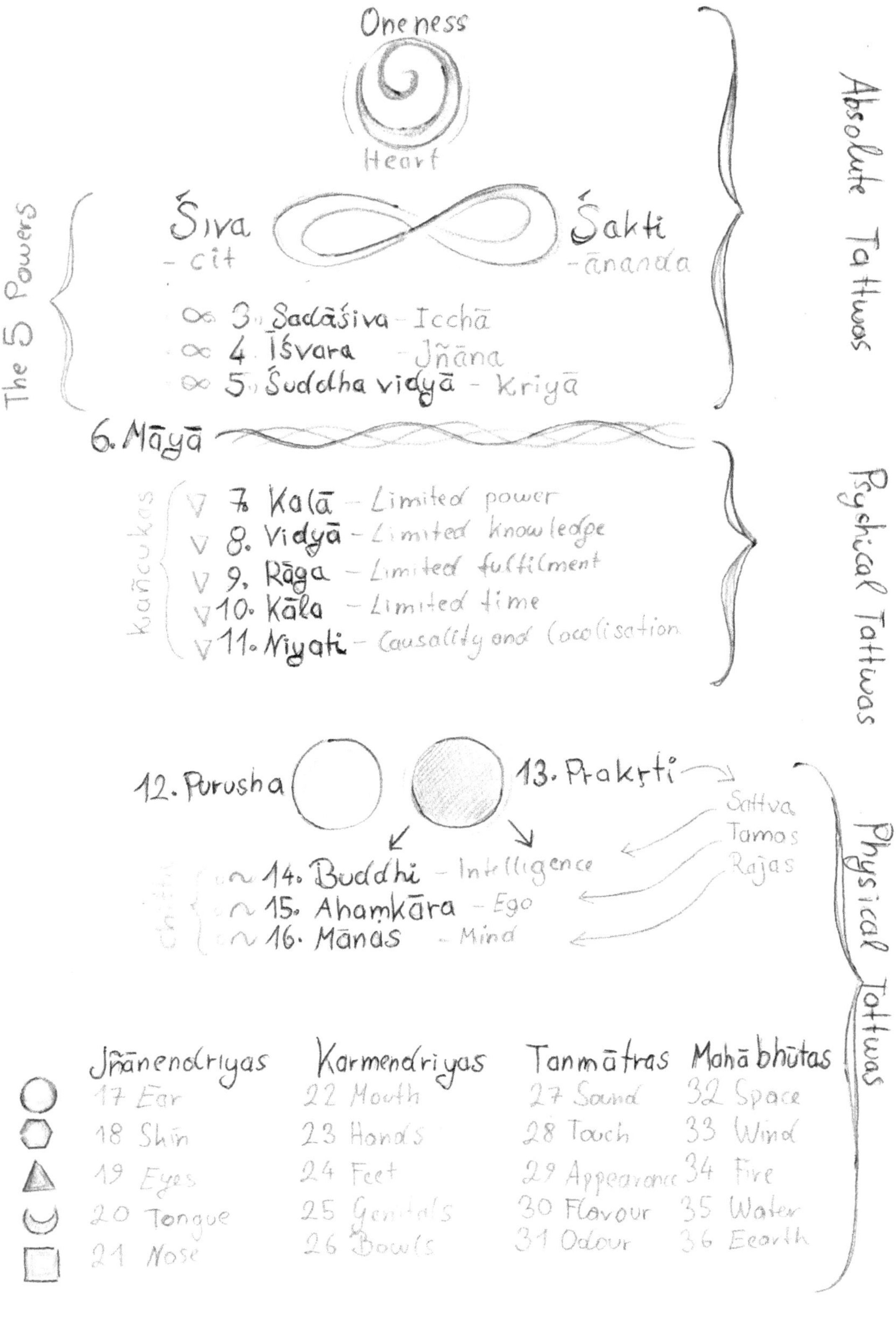
Oneness
Heart
Absolute Tattwas
The 5 Powers
Śiva
- cit
Śakti
- ānanda
3. Sadāśiva - Icchā
4. Īśvara - Jñāna
5. Śuddha vidyā - Kriyā
6. Māyā
Psychical Tattwas
kañcukas
7. Kalā - Limited power
8. Vidyā - Limited knowledge
9. Rāga - Limited fulfilment
10. Kāla - Limited time
11. Niyati - Causality and Localisation
12. Purusha
13. Prakṛti
Sattva
Tamas
Rajas
Physical Tattwas
14. Buddhi - Intelligence
15. Ahaṃkāra - Ego
16. Mānas - Mind
Jñānendriyas
17 Ear
18 Skin
19 Eyes
20 Tongue
21 Nose
Karmendriyas
22 Mouth
23 Hands
24 Feet
25 Genitals
26 Bowls
Tanmātras
27 Sound
28 Touch
29 Appearance
30 Flavour
31 Odour
Mahābhūtas
32 Space
33 Wind
34 Fire
35 Water
36 Eearth

crude (and material) like a table.

According to Sāṃkhya, the universe begins with nature (*prakṛti*) that exists in total equilibrium. This state of complete balance is known as *mūla prakŕti*, or the root nature. *Mūla prakŕti* contains three balanced components: *rajas*, *sattva*, and *tamas*, which are movement, lightness, and heaviness, respectively.

Purity [Sattva], Passion [Rajas] and Ignorance [Tamas] are the Qualities [Gunas] which the Law of nature brings forth. They fetter the free Spirit in all beings.

Bhagavad Gītā (14:5)

The Three Guṇas

These three qualities of nature are called the *guṇas*. Their existence is inferred through the Sāṃkhya doctrine that every material (natural) cause must carry within it the seed of its effect. Since all objects of perception are either pleasurable (light, or *sattva*), painful (dark, or *tamas*) or indifferent (moving, or *rajas*), the *guṇas* must exist in the cause of all objects before their manifestation. This final cause is *prakṛti*, and the three *guṇas* are its primary quality. Sāṃkhya scholars additionally explain that *puruṣa* (singular I-consciousness) disturbs the equilibrium between the three *guṇas*, meaning that all objects of reality are created through the interplay of the three *guṇas*. The first object then created is *buddhi*, the intellect, which concerns decision and discernment. *Buddhi* is dominated by *sattva*, and is light and transparent. This transparency is filled by the light of *puruṣa*, to which it is closest. Out of *buddhi* arises *ahaṃkāra*, the sense of ego. It is the primal agent of any desire because desire must be consumed by the ego. It is the ego that creates the mind, *mānas*, and its senses. At the culmination of the creation process, the five gross elements are manifested out of sound, touch, form, taste, and smell.

Perception and the Mind

A perception inside the self has a modification of *buddhi* as its primary cause. When the senses perceive an impression – let us use the perception of a table as an example – the mind (*mānas*) would recognise the table, *ahaṃkāra* would depict that experience as personal, and *buddhi* would understand what the table was – *buddhi*, by being completely transparent, would mirror the table and take its form. *Puruṣa*, also mirrored in *buddhi*, would fuse with this experience so as to form a conscious experience of the table. Any experience is therefore a modification of *buddhi* fused with the light of *puruṣa*.

Puruṣa is the soul, the *ātman*, the true self, the enjoyer. *Puruṣa* is unchanging, and all experience must take place as a modification of *buddhi* alone. In yoga, the modifications of *buddhi* and its subordinate mental organs (*ahaṃkāra* and *mānas*) are known as *citta*. *Citta* is the mental experience or field of the internal instrument (*antaḥkaraṇa*). In yoga, experience, as a modification of *citta*, is described as *cittavṛtti*. This is synonymous with the modification of *buddhi*, since *buddhi* is the highest agent of *citta*.

In classical Patañjali yoga, which derived the *tattvas* from Sāṃkhya, *puruṣa* is the highest element within the 25 *tattvas*. The tantrics included a further 11 which they claimed had been overlooked by Sāṃkhya. *Puruṣa* is seen here as a contracted form of a non-individual universal consciousness. It is worth exploring why the *tattvas* of Sāṃkhya were expanded, as such a path of enquiry would reveal deep insights into

The Tantric Tattvas

It is worth mentioning that adherents of Sāṃkhya teachings have tended to perceive *puruṣa*, the highest agent, as manifold. To them, *puruṣa* is an unchanging, shining consciousness that illuminates the internal organs and all sensory objects, thereby giving them the appearance of being self-conscious by projecting the light of consciousness upon them. Although adherents of Sāṃkhya understood *puruṣa* to be this very essence of perception, they still considered *puruṣa* to exist as a particular point of consciousness manifested as many distinct entities (the doctrine of *bheda* – difference). This is the idea of many souls, or entities, which is not dissimilar to the beliefs within Abrahamic religions. Sāṃkhya believes in the eternal existence of countless *puruṣas* (souls) that are the distinct individual conscious agents of all living things.

The philosophy of tantra, in contrast, rejects this view as being inconsistent. The enlightened master Kṣemarāja, in his commentary on the *Śivasūtras* – one of the first great tantric revelations – explains the tantric view of reality in this specific context:

> *Though Highest Śiva has an infinite number of other attributes, such as eternity, all-pervasiveness, formlessness, because of eternity they are also possible in others. We show the predominance of absolute freedom, which is not present in any other being. This characteristic is indicated as an abstract noun, Caitanya, the state of being conscious by excluding other attributes (just as an abstract noun excludes all other attributes). Therefore this caitanya or consciousness which is absolute freedom is ātma or self, rather than something else of varied nature, as assumed by the dualits, those who support the doctrine of bheda or difference among selves. Are these different selves conscious beings or non-conscious beings? If ātma, or varied nature, is assumed to be non-conscious, then it would be inconscient matter and thus not self. If it be considered to be of the very essence of consciousness, then*

there can be no valid reason for considering one ātman or self as different from another self. Difference in the case of consciousness cannot be established either by means of space or time or form, for if these are different from consciousness, then being deprived of the light of consciousness, they cannot appear at all and thus are unreal; if they appear, then they are consciousness itself for it is only consciousness that can appear. Thus it is not possible to attribute difference to consciousness (i.e. self) on the basis of difference in space, time and form. As it is now clear that selves are only consciousness and nothing else, then difference in the nature of the various selves cannot be established since consciousness is the only nature of all selves, therefore they are the same; nor can difference be maintained on account of their contact with limiting conditions, since they are not something outside consciousness as I will explain. Even though limiting conditions may exist before liberation, they ceases to exist after it. It is, therefore, impossible to maintain the theory of the plurality of self. If it be maintained that even in the state of liberation, there is a possibility of the residual traces of limiting conditions remaining behind, or one is even then far below the beginningless Śiva, (Anadi Siva) then those so-called liberated souls would still be in the state of transmigratory existence and not really liberated. As has been said, 'Consciousness is only one self'. This proves the invalidity of the theory of plurality of self.

Kṣemarāja in his commentary on the Śiva-Sūtras (1)

Simply put, Kṣemarāja states that, since all things exist within consciousness, nothing can exist outside of it. Even if something could, it would still be inexistent as it would remain unperceived, even by itself. The very nature of all is therefore consciousness. The self, as the ultimate perceiver, must therefore be consciousness as nothing is without the self. Since all possible experience, like that of many individual selves, differs only in the nature of experience (not in existence), there cannot be a plurality of the essential self. Furthermore, he suggests that multiple selves imply a difference between that which comprises one self and another. Were this to be the case, there must be a difference in the very nature of consciousness of these selves. However, as consciousness is the very ground and mirror of being, it must therefore be unchanging. This is also a core assumption of Sāṃkhya philosophy, which claims that the self is the *puruṣa* or formless consciousness, and that it is only differentiated from *prakṛti* precisely because of its unchanging nature. In this manner, the establishment of different multiple selves cannot be explained. Therefore, there must exist only one universal self:

Contemplate on consciousness in ones own body
is just as consciousness in another's body. Thus
giving up concern about ones own body, one
becomes all-pervasive in the course of time.

Vijñāna-Bhairava-Tantra (107)

The meaning and implication of this proposition is remarkably profound and can shake one's understanding of reality to the very core. This is what is meant by the New Age term, 'we are all one'. Often, the very people who quote this line hardly comprehend what they are actually trying to say. That we are 'one' does not mean that we will in future join as one in a greater sense, or that we should live for greater unity and harmony. It means much more than this. It means instead that, ultimately, there is only one being. There is only one self from which to experience all. Further to this, the one self is consciousness, the giver and source of all. Everything comes from this self and must eventually return to it. It is all that is, and all that ever will be. Whenever you see somebody, be aware that this person's consciousness is just like yours. It is you now, and it always was.

One should concentrate with an unwavering mind
on all existence, the body, and even the universe,
simultaneously as nothing but consciousness, then
the supreme consciousness arises.

Vijñāna-Bhairava-Tantra, (63)

In the tantric view, the world is born from *prakāśa*, the ultimate light, the greatest sound, the one heart. It is the total fusion of energy (*śakti*) with the light of consciousness (Śiva). The second and third *tattvas* are expressions of the power of consciousness (*cit śakti*) and the power of bliss (*ānandā śakti*) as the one ultimate reality. The tantric Sadāśiva is the expression of *icchā śakti*, the power of will. Īśvara is an expression of *jñāna śakti*, the power to know, and *śuddha vidyā* is the expression of the absolute power of action, *kriyā śakti*.

These last five *tattvas* describe the essence of the divine, and reaching any one of them would lead to complete liberation. *Śuddha vidyā* would be the power of Mantra. Mantra is regarded here as a conscious being, an independent and ultimately free divine consciousness, such as an angel in the Christian tradition. Īśvara refers to the level of the personal God, the level of complete balance between creation and its source. This level of being is described with the Sanskrit phrase '*aham idam aham*' ('I am this, this I am'). Sadāśiva as the next *tattva* is the formless deity inseparable from its creation. Śakti is the underlying potential found within this formless ground. It is the spiritual energy, *kuṇḍalinī*. The last element of reality is the void of pure consciousness that is the absolute unity of conscious will and its power of awareness.

> *In Śivatattwa there is predominance of citśakti. In Śaktitattva contains the predominance of ānandā śakti. At the stage of the predominance of will, there is Sadāśiva tattva, because will contains both knowing and doing in the state of equilibrium. Īśvaratattva has its place in the prominence of Jñāna śakti. In the state of prominence of the power of action there is Vidya tattva.*

Tantrasāra

Māyā, the force of individuation, conceals this universal energy through five layers of illusion (*kañcukas*), thereby increasing the density of its appearance. From these illusions spring the individual consciousness (*puruṣa*) and nature (*prakṛti*). From here the aforementioned chain of creation continues – *prakṛti* creates *buddhi* (intellect), from which comes *ahaṃkāra* (ego) and *mānas* (mind). The five elements and all sensory objects are thus birthed from these three.

These five *kañcukas* correspond to five limitations that serve to undermine the aforementioned five ultimate powers of the divine. These five *māyās* are:

Kalā	Limited agency, limited *kriyā śakti*
Vidyā	Limited knowledge, limited *jñāna śakti*
Rāga	Limitation in self experience, limited *icchā śakti*
Kāla	Limitation in time, limited *ānandā śakti*
Niyati	Limitation in space and causality, limited *cit śakti*

WHITE, RED AND BLACK TANTRA

Speaking of illusions, *māyā*, and ignorance, it is high time that we shed light on the dark side of tantra. It is commonly claimed that there exist three varieties of tantra – red, black, and white. While this distinction is purely notional, it does serve to explain the different streams of practice within tantra. Tantra as a tool for power is said to be black. Tantra as tool for pleasure is seen as red, and tantra as a tool for realisation is seen as white.

Intention is the force that dictates the morality of an action. If I slap my child because of unrelated anger, I am a bad person. If I slap my child to quickly reinforce the lesson that it should not cross the road while fast cars are approaching, I am a concerned parent. The intention behind any action is its soul, and determines whether its fruit will be sweet or bitter.

The same is true for tantra, which was initially a set of actions and rituals designed to awaken energy within nature. Tantra used the five elements, the power of mantra, and the many forms of the goddess to awaken the very framework of being, or the consciousness within all. This process is often referred to as being magical in nature. The popularity and power of modern-day yoga can be explained by its practitioners' deep belief that there is a magic in yoga. It is a dance around the elements, designed to awaken the beautiful body of the goddess with its mantras.

When people attend a class, they often feel a magical or spiritual transformation. The ritual that is the class carries a power that in itself far surpasses the individual abilities of the teacher. It is the ritual and magic of the class that is the soul of Hatha and Kundalini Yoga.

Since I am teaching tantric yoga here, I feel duty-bound to speak of the shadows at the roots of this tradition. One must understand that the power to create a space of energy was not always used to expand consciousness. The intention was, and perhaps will always be, what guides a process to its goal. In its initial stages, tantra was simply magic – rebellious, dark, and with many shades of grey. It was not until the great saints came from the mountains to assume control over tantra's terrifying magical techniques, and transform it into a tool for realisation, that it became suffused with spiritual endeavour. Tantra in itself was simply the science of the power of the great goddess – fierce, terrible, and full of light. She is both illusion in one form and the pathway to heaven in the other.

Tantra is well-known these days, and it seems perfectly likely that its fame will continue to spread. The reason behind performing tantric practices should be clearly delineated lest some find a spiritual justification for furthering their own desire for power and control – much like how spiritual and moral justification for unrestrained hedonism was found in the *Brahma-Yāmala.* There are many scriptures shrouded in darkness that stem from the early left-handed traditions. They are black magic to the core. Here I have cited the *Jayadratha-Yāmala* which, while largely unknown to the wider public, is hugely significant to the *Kālīkula* tradition. Having no clear discernment about intention risks the purity of the practice of tantric yoga. Once these problems arise, one must know how to face them. You must be sure to differentiate between the paths to freedom or bondage.

> *Next the Sādhana of the most terrible Goddess, called the terrible Ekatara who is bent on the destruction of Kulanagas. This most grim Kali, the supreme Ekatara, who is eager to devour all beings (...). He should go to a grim creation ground and there choose an area that is perfectly level, pale in colour pounded flat with a skull, and perfumed with black aloe paste (...). on it he should worship the Goddess with all substances that are offered by heroes, with human flesh, alcoholic liquor, and the like*

(...). thereafter the noble sadhaka can accomplish here
without doubt any of the common supernatural effects.
Subjection, causing dissension, expelling, killing,
paralyzing controlling rain clouds, the wind and lightning
and the rendering of malevolent seizing spirits
may be accomplished by reciting her spell.

Jayadratha Yamala (Kālīkula/Krama tradition)

This is something in which we must be clear. Know that our Kundalini Yoga emerged from the white and non-dualistic tradition of the Trika. Swami Lakshman Joo, the last Trika master who provided us with almost all of our understanding about tantra today, has consistently said that one must maintain constant awareness. Even tantrics like himself – who can glimpse the divine in any state of being, burst of anger, feeling of doubt, joy of orgasm, or any perception of miraculous reality – know that the strong yogi never forgets to discern. They always know which path leads to the light and which to suffering. As Swami Lakshman Joo teaches us:

Always maintain awareness.

KARMA AND REINCARNATION

It is vital for us to understand karma's relation to Indian thought. Karma means action. It is any action undertaken or experience felt. One may ask why one has specific experiences. Indian thinkers determined that every experience is the result of a cause, which itself has a cause of its own. The world should thus be viewed as a chain of deterministic events, where every cause leads to a result, and every result is the cause of the next.

The action that results in an effect is by itself morally neutral as it has itself been motivated by a cause. Accordingly, the action is reflexive and somehow unavoidable. Just as the *Gītā* tells us to refrain from inaction, it is the attachment to this action that binds the self to a certain result. Making the action your own, instead of simply experiencing it, causes ownership of the result and binds you to it and all its fruits.

Karma is therefore your experience of the fruits of the actions to which you are attached. Good Karma would be the self-experience of freedom untethered to any object of experience. Bad Karma, conversely, is the suffering that occurs when the self is attached to the object of experience and must then confront its transitory nature.

Karma is often understood in the *Vedānta* as the good or bad deeds reaped from the fruits of one's actions. These good or bad deeds are observed by God, the giver of Karma. Tantra (*āgamas*) understands Karma as the self-evident result of the chain of cause and effect. Karma is therefore not a judgment, but rather the just and willed self-experience of one's own consciousness.

Justice

Claiming karma to be the result of one's actions may cause people to question why some experience suffering while others do not. Some may also wonder that, if bad karma is the result of attachment, why does the self have a proclivity for attaching itself when it is inherently free and unbound? When we are all the same in our essence – free and pure – how can karma be just?

The great tantric Kṣemarāja explained that there is only one self. If this is the case, any action that brings about joy or suffering is never solely contained within the one who caused it. This is to say that, if you hurt somebody, you literally hurt yourself. No action can be done to anyone who is not you. No planet can be polluted by one greedy man who is not everyone else. No animal can be killed without itself being the murderer. There is only one self. Understanding this, Karma becomes visible as the self-experience of one eternal being rather than the net which catches lonely and lost souls. Furthermore, the question of justice ceases to be relevant. The world in this light is a place where joy and suffering all reside within one eternal and inseparably unified heart.

Awareness, independent and free is the cause of absolutely everything.

Pratyabhijñā-hṛdaya, (1)

At the height of tantra's influence in the 10th century, the world was understood as having no existence independent from consciousness. This amounts to saying that the world is created and maintained by consciousness itself. Since the world has many shades, and suffering and joy occur in all forms, it must be the specific form of contraction (modification) of consciousness that creates a specific form of experience. Consequently, this view proposes Karma as being the experience of reality that is dependent on a specific form of consciousness.

One may object that reality exists independently from observation, and therefore from consciousness. If this is a view you ascribe to, perhaps the following quotation and chapter may cause you to wonder:

Time doesn't exist, it appears.

Swāmī Lakshman Joo

The Dependency of Time

Any experience one can have is the perception of an object of experience. Without an object there can be no (objective) experience. Objects exists, whether mentally or materially due to their being temporally and spatially extended. Their extension in these dimensions creates their respective properties and being. Spatial existence is, in many respects, completely dependent on temporal existence. Patañjali says that every object exists in different forms in multiple sectors of time. By this he means that objective existence changes with time. Since every part of any object is in constant movement and a state of interaction with all other objects, expanding time as infinite would infinitely expand the object's properties through space along with their infinite movement. Any objective (particular) existence, or experience of it, is therefore dependent on time.

If an absolute (and independent) time were to exist, so would absolute objective existence (independent existence). Conversely, without an objective moment of time, there could be no objective existence. Yet this still begs the question, is time independent?

When we measure time, we usually do so by measuring the speed of its progress relative to another time moment. Moreover, if we want to measure time inside a single system, we calculate it using the speed of a physical process that is itself dependent on time. This means that time is measured by time itself. There is no reason to assume why time should have one certain speed and not another. Only its speed relative to another 'time frame' is clearly defined, not its absolute one. This raises the question of why one then experiences a certain reality completely dependent on time. If the speed of time that creates the world for any observer is not fixed in absolute terms, why do I experience this world and not another? Why am I me and not something else?

While we may certainly doubt the reality of our experience, what we cannot call into question is the observer. As Descartes said, 'cogito, ergo sum'. I think, therefore I am. Thinking is not the cause of being, but rather the experience of one's thought.

Experience proves the experiencer, who is the only independent ultimate proof for being. Extending this line of reasoning, we suggest that the experiencer is nothing more than consciousness, as only consciousness can establish an independent existence. It is thus the ultimate 'awareness-maker'.

We should now remember what we have said earlier: time has no independent existence from itself. Since it has a particular existence inside one's own limited reality – established by the observer (experiencer) – time must be dependent on an experiencer who is nothing more than consciousness alone. Time is that which brings forth all forms of objective existence. Furthermore, as time creates all objects, time being dependent on consciousness must leave objective existence to consciousness.

This leads us to the necessary recognition that all objective existence is dependent on consciousness alone. This is the ultimate law of karma.

Awareness (power of consciousness), free and independent

is the cause of the performance of everything.

Pratyabhijñā-hṛdaya (1)

In this context, reincarnation is the reappearance of the self in the world of objects as a result of its bondage to a certain object of experience. The quality of this reappearance depends upon the self's degree of awareness or attachment (degree of modification of consciousness).

It is reasonable, or perhaps even healthy, to be sceptical of the concept of reincarnation. I will here provide some insights that could alter the view of those who doubt.

The Impossibility of Non-Being

The self is a reality. Our experience of existence renders it a truth. The main question that bothers humanity is whether this existence will continue and, if so, how?

No experience is eternal. Just as every experience must have a beginning, so it must have an end. If experiences were to last forever, they would be unrecognisable as a context. As that which is endless cannot exist conceptually alone – because concept is that which is limited in extension of meaning – experience must therefore be transitory.

The cause of experience is also its object. The object of experience is subject to causality. Since a chain of causalities can only result in further causes rather than finality, the appearance of any object of experience (bound in causality) must be unlimited and without end.

While everybody knows this, how do they react to this? Will the self that is experiencing that object end?

The self is either unlimited and not subject to circumstance, or it is.

If the self, the knower, is not subject to circumstance and will continue through every change of experience, the question of the self being either infinite or finite would be answered. The self would then be eternal.

It would be more interesting, therefore, to assume that the self is subject to circumstance as part of a deterministic universe. If the self is subject to circumstances limited to body, birth, place, or time, the self would necessarily be extinguished at the moment of death as its causal circumstances would vanish.

That the self can exist in certain circumstances is proven by its self-experience. Circumstances are manifested in a deterministic world in relation to other circumstances. Their appearance in such a universe would depend on probability. The manifestation of any specific circumstance would then depend on a number of combinations of causal factors (particles, matter, energy, birth, etc.). Whether in an infinite or finite deterministic universe, the number of possible combinations depends solely on time as the only limiting factor for its appearance.

The experience of self is subject to time as it experiences itself within it. Should the circumstance of its being vanish, time (as an experience in the self) would do so as well. Since we are assuming that this universe is deterministic, it must be able to continue without the self. However, in the absence of a time-experiencing self, time would progress infinitely and instantly as there would be no self to observe its progress.

When the time progress infinitely, the probability for the manifestation of the circumstances that bring about self becomes absolute. After all, the chaotic manifestation of any circumstance depends on time. From the perspective of the self, the self would then be immediately manifested after its disappearance as the universe would formulate the required circumstances instantaneously.

The self would likely emerge from circumstances supplying the identical experiences in which it first vanished. This experience would continue to be subject to causality, as it always was.

Therefore, one can conclude that whether the self is independent or not, it cannot cease to be. Once it exists, it will always do so. Accordingly, non-being is impossible – a notion that is both a cage and a source of rich potential.

Realising this draws one away from seeking mundane pleasure, and instead guides one towards understanding experience and exploring the quality of being. The question that arises here is not *if* you are, but *how* you are. Not if you exist, but in which form you do so. Yoga offers us the right tools to improve this form and recreate our eternal being through reincarnation.

There was never a time when I was not, nor you, nor these princes were not; there will never be a time when we shall cease to be.
That which is not, can never be; that which is, can never cease to be. To the wise, these truths are self-evident.

Bhagavad Gītā (2:12 & 16)

KARMA, FREEDOM, AND TRAUMA IN YOGA

We have seen how karma is the individual's entanglement in the consequences of their actions. The very idea of karma involves two parallel, but separate, representations of the world. On the one hand, the world in itself is a deterministic place in which each action is the result of a chain of cause and effect. The world can thus be seen as a cage prohibiting any individual freedom or growth as any future event must be determined by past actions. This view is counterbalanced in Indian philosophy by the idea of the actual self, or the independent and ever free observer. Realizing this observer as the ground of being is understood to be the ultimate freedom.

Two birds, beautiful of wings, close companions, cling to

one common tree: of the two one eats the sweet fruit of the tree, the other eats not but watches his fellow.

Mundaka Upaniṣad (3.1.2)

Freedom

These two birds are the soul and the limited self. They represent the world of freedom from determinism and the world of being bound by it. In tantric philosophy, the path to freedom is not undertaken by specific actions, instead it is freedom itself. Freedom is achieved by its own free choice. Indeed, it could not be otherwise as any means would again bind the person to consequences rather than giving rise to freedom. This innate freedom as a basic property of consciousness is called *svātantrya śakti*, or sovereignty. It is that which overcomes causality. According to Swāmī Lakshman Joo, this insight is expressed in *Vijñāna-Bhairava-Tantra* (interpretive translation):

One should meditate on the central nāḍi (suṣumnā) as being slender like a lotus fibre. Then by means of that consciousness of suṣumnā, (suṣumnā itself is realised) the divine is revealed.

Vijñāna-Bhairava-Tantra (35)

Suṣumnā is the *nāḍi* of the observer, the observer is therefore realised by its own means.

As there is only bondage as long as we act within it, this can have profound consequences on how we can act in the world. Freedom cannot be achieved, or lost, through any action. Freedom and bondage are both realised simply by making them real. This also means that even the practice of yoga does not lead to freedom. Instead, it creates a clear (sattvic) space in which this truth can be realised. Once understood, freedom is instantaneous.

Trauma

The Western view of the self has been (and continues to be) strongly influenced by psychologists, such as Freud, who theorised that humans are amalgamations of past traumas which determine their future selves. People who ascribe to this theory often believe that they can only achieve a brighter future when their past is completely understood, and all trauma has been accepted and integrated. This Freudian determinism, however, can have a stagnating effect on the human psyche. Indeed, as traumas are embedded in a causal chain, merely understanding them does not necessarily mean that they would stop ceaselessly repeating themselves. The Western world suffers from this theory. Many people think cyclically of their traumas and run from therapist to therapist making themselves a victim of the past instead of simply taking their present into their own hands.

In the Freudian sense, trauma is said to be the consequence of experience. If so, would this not mean that a specific experience would always lead to the same form of traumatisation? We know that this is not the case. It is not the bare experience, but how it is understood that creates the trauma. It seems that it is the meaning of the experience, not its appearance, that creates its quality. When a man loses his family and his job, he can either sink into misery and alcoholism, or work to better himself. Which future he creates is not dependent on his trauma, but rather on his choice of how to give this experience meaning.

Therefore, trauma as we understand it does not actually exist in yoga. Being a yogi means to make every moment new and to take responsibility for it. Accepting the determinism that underlines the belief in the reality of trauma would mean accepting slavery to the past. Yoga instead believes in final freedom.

In yoga, when a trauma actually appears it is instead considered an expression of one's inner beliefs rather than as the consequence of experiences. In this way, past traumas are seen as something drawn forth by one's being to justify the meanings that already exist in the heart. The being is free in its very core, but it chooses to take shape – and justifies doing so – by holding onto its past.

Again, the question is not what you have been, but what you desire to be now. Trauma is self-created. It is created by meaning.

The Vijñāna-Bhairava-Tantra tells us that there is a sound in your heart without beginning or end. This is to say that your heart is beyond causality; it is a free place that has never had a beginning and will never have an end. It is beyond bondage. It is from here that you can create new meaning and find freedom.

Therefore, look deep into your heart and choose freedom.

By concentrating on the lotus of the heart, there arises a state of sorrowless joy, which is infused with inner light. Such a state anchors the mind in a state of freedom.

Yoga-sūtra-bhāṣya (1 : 36)

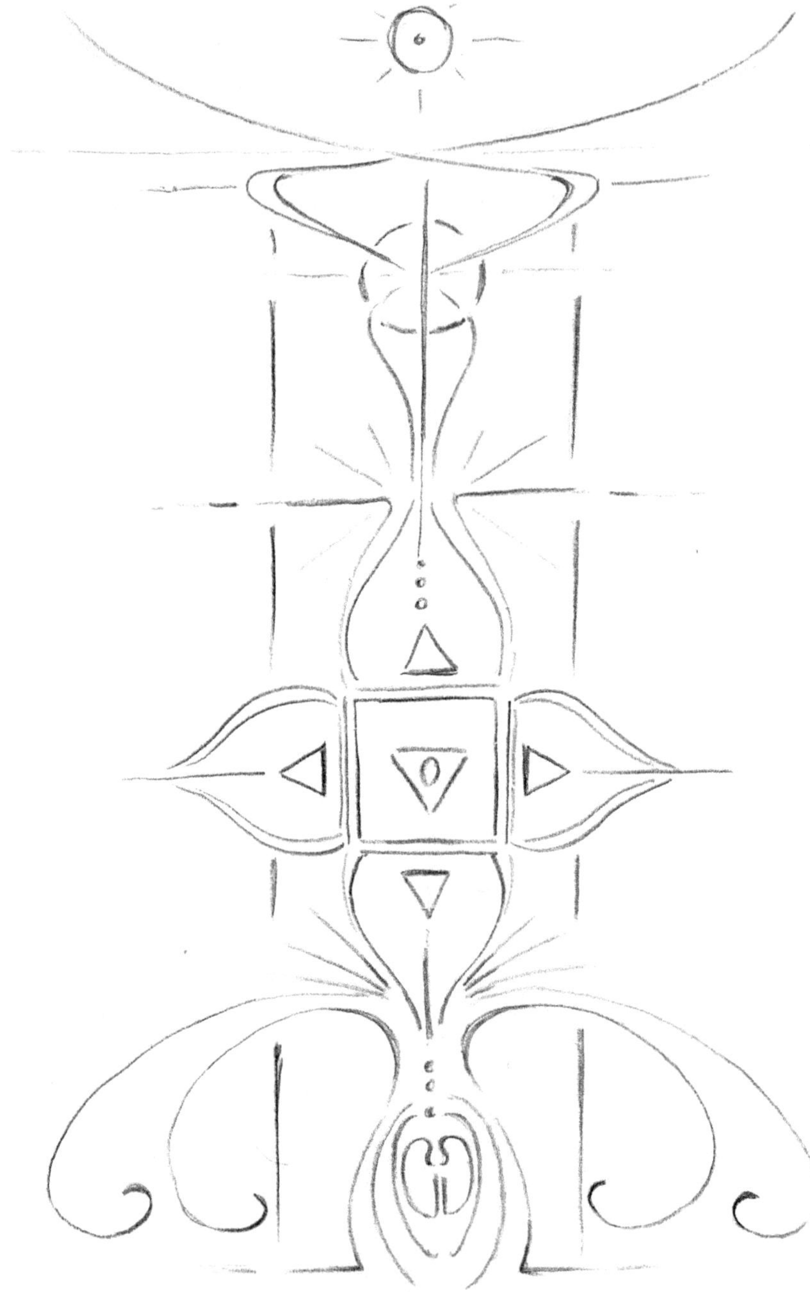

HAṬHA AND KUṆḌALINĪ-YOGA

Prāṇā goes out on the exhalation; the Apāna enters on the inhalation, and they form a coiled spring of mantric energy by the power of her will. That Great Goddess Kuṇḍalinī extends and lengthens by that power. She is the highest place of pilgrimage, both transcendent and immanent. Pursuing Her until one abides within Her in the sacrificial rite consisting of supreme delight, one who is penetrated and permeated by that Goddess attains supreme Bhairava.

Vijñāna-Bhairava-Tantra, (154)

AIM OF HATHA YOGA

You may be asking yourself: why do we keep talking about Hatha Yoga? Did I buy the wrong book? Don't worry, you are right where you need to be! Hatha Yoga, like all yoga, strives for liberation and union. The power of *kuṇḍalinī* is depicted as the key for liberation. This is primarily due to it being the driving force of awakening that can transform the limited experience into a universal one. The aim of Hatha Yoga is therefore the rise of *kuṇḍalinī*.

Hatha Yoga is Kundalini Yoga. Any attempt to conceal this truth by creating brands of yoga would be a gross mistake, and nothing more than the will to capitalise on a timeless tradition for one's own limited desires.

As one opens the door with a key, so the yogi should open the gate to liberation with the Kuṇḍalinī. The great Goddess Kuṇḍalinī sleeps, closing with her head the opening through which one can ascend to the crown of the head, to that place where there is neither pain nor suffering. Kuṇḍalinī sleeps above the kanda [where the nāḍis converge]. She gives liberation to the yogi and bondage to the fool. He who knows Kuṇḍalinī knows yoga. Kuṇḍalinī, it is said, is coiled like a serpent. He who can induce her to move upward is liberated. There is no doubt about it.

Haṭha-Yoga-Pradīpikā (3:105)

KUṆḌALINĪ

She is gross.
She is subtle.
She is the inwardly moving energy of consciousness.
She is Mahāmāyā who is the form of consciousness.

Manthāna Bhairava-Tantram (9:27)

Kuṇḍalinī (*kuṇḍalī śakti* – the coiled power) was discovered by the tantrics, and was first mentioned in the Trika tradition in the *Siddha-Yogeśvarī-Mata*-Tantra in the early 7th century. Here she is identified on a cosmic level as the source of a triad of *śaktis*, or powers. These are the power of consciousness (*anuttara śakti*), the power of will (*icchāśakti*) and the power of awakening (*unmeṣa śakti*).

In this system, it is Kuṇḍalinī that is said to be the womb of the universe and from her arise the triad of Śaktis and from them arise all sounds within human speech.

Siddha-Yogeśvarī-Mata

The later tantras identify Kuṇḍalinī as the goddess that sleeps in the form of the syllable AIM as the principle of the individual soul. The *Kubjikā-Mata-Tantra* states that 'all letters are fused together and have merged into the principle of the individual soul'. She is the energy of the soul. In her uncoiled form she is all the syllables (sounds, energies) and is thus the goddess of speech. All *bījas* are her body, all mantras are her prayer. Since all emerged from *nāda*, the primal sound, she is the source of all the universe and everything that is manifested (*prakṛti*). She guides the way to one's inner nature because she is that very nature, and in doing so she liberates from illusion. There are so many words for she who cannot be grasped by one's own mind. She is beautiful and unlimited and therefore terrible for the limited, she is 'mind beyond mind (*manonmanī*) whose form is light'.

Somehow all of these descriptions point to one single graspable picture of what she is. She is the vitality of being. She is vitality because she is breath, experience, and the brilliance of the soul. She is being because she is the mother of matter (*prakṛti*), the source of all forms.

In modern Hatha Yoga, she is understood to rest in the lotus of four petals after her work of creation has been completed. Sleeping in *mūlādhāra*, she blocks the mouth of *suṣumnā* with her head, which is to say that she conceals the path to one's self. She is said to be surrounded by the aspects of the 'seen', and is thus the master of all that has been brought into sight. She can be awakened and made to move through yogic effort. Following this, she enters the opening of *suṣumnā* and that which previously was form becomes formless, that which was seen becomes the seer, and that which was dispersed becomes the centre. She will then gracefully return back to the source of the unlimited formless from which she emerged.

According to A.C. Mohan, uncoiling Kuṇḍalinī is always a process of involution – the controlling of the creative force back to its source, or the exchange of form with consciousness. The bliss of the movement of Kuṇḍalinī is the realisation that the way to greater consciousness of being leads inwards, that being is found within oneself (the experiencer) and not outside (the experience).

For this reason the *Manthāna-Bhairava-Tantram* repeatedly calls her the inwardly moving energy of consciousness. Kuṇḍalinī uncoils from her entanglement with the world, from her external creative work, and turns back, 'straight like a stick', somehow reabsorbing her own creation, finding the way back into the self, the seer, consciousness, absolute bliss. One must try to understand the movement of Kuṇḍalinī as one's withdrawal into the central axis. Uncoiling into this centre, the true self is touched.

Prāṇāyāma, *pratyāhāra*, and *dhāraṇā* – which form an integral part of Patañjali Yoga – are all techniques used to reverse the flow of perception to a single point, or to withdraw this flow back into oneself.

Prāṇāyāma	Favours the space between the breaths, in which the breath can find the one-pointed standstill and reverse.
Pratyāhāra	Withdrawing externality in exchange for internality.
Dhāraṇā	The control from the chaotic flow of thought to a single point of power.

The creator pierced us with outward facing apertures, therefore one looks out, not to the inner self. A rare wise man, turning the gaze around, looked inward to the self, and tasted immortality.

Kaṭha Upaniṣad (4:1)

Similarly, Kuṇḍalinī is understood as the *prāṇa* that flows in *suṣumnā* (*udāna prāṇa*). *Suṣumnā* is the *nāḍi* of non-moving awareness in which one is neither subjected to introversion nor extroversion. *Suṣumnā* is therefore the *nāḍi* of one-pointedness or central alignment. It has also been described as the *nāḍi* that is like a line without dimension. These descriptions are attempts to describe Kuṇḍalinī as the state of consciousness beyond uncentered and chaotic movement.

When a yogi can centre Kuṇḍalinī, the unsurpassed magic of reality is unveiled and the yogi is thereafter called *jīvan-mukti* (liberated soul). When one has reached this state, the ongoing process of creation can be observed within one's own consciousness: the process of involution through centring and evolution through expansion, as an unending flow back and forth, becomes manifest. From destruction to creation, and creation to destruction, from limited self to unbound self, back and forth. This is known as *krama-mudrā*, and is the experience of the Absolute in action. It is the experience of the living goddess. It is the highest bliss for the Kuṇḍalinī Yogi. This is the state of being truly liberated in self-experience and action.

KUṆḌALINĪ IN TRIKA TANTRA

Swami Laksman Joo provided us with deep insights into the many forms in which Kuṇḍalinī is experienced. We will here explore some of her forms that will shed light on her underlying nature.

Parā Kuṇḍalinī

Kuṇḍalinī is said to initially exist in the form of the supreme, all-encompassing, and universal Parā Kuṇḍalinī. She is the triad of Śaktis. While she cannot be experienced by a yogi in life, it is said that this becomes possible after death.

Cit Kuṇḍalinī

Kuṇḍalinī can appear in the form of *cit* (consciousness). *Cit* Kuṇḍalinī is pure and free from attachments. She usually ends in the state of *krama-mudra* and rests there as bliss (*ānanda*). She rises from *mūlādhāra* directly to the centre of the eyebrows (*bhrumadhya*) and from there diffuses into space (*brahmrandhra* or *dvādaśānta*), upon which one's whole being is filled by her. She is the highest Kuṇḍalinī that can be experienced individually and therefore will not be more deeply discussed in this book.

Prāṇa Kuṇḍalinī

Prāṇa Kuṇḍalinī is the phenomenon experienced when the yogi has attachments other than spiritual liberation. When these attachments are absent, Kuṇḍalinī appears in the form of *cit*.

The awakening of Prāṇa Kuṇḍalinī is simple and can occur in a variety of forms. Typically, the yogi centres their mind on one point – perhaps by concentrating on a pure thought, through *śāmbhavī mudrā*, the use of a mantra, or with *prāṇāyāma* and *mūlabandha*. The yogi then experiences a tingling sensation like that of ants crawling around the *mūlādhāra* area. This sensation intensifies, and then the goddess moves like lightening around the *suṣumnā*. The yogi must then fearlessly move her with grace and great strength so as to allow her to enter the mouth of *suṣumnā* and unleash the power of consciousness.

What follows is then out of the yogi's conscious control as the ordinary mind becomes the witness (rather than the agent) of the underlying energetic structures and desires that constitute the yogi's existence. Depending on the yogi's specific form of attachments, Kuṇḍalinī will either withdraw or rise to a specific point. Lakshman Joo describes this process thusly:

After Kuṇḍalinī is awakened in the *mūlādhāra*, she will cause it to move with great force; the yogi will hear the wheel turn with a distinctive sound. This wheel will then forcefully rotate up to the *nābhi chakra* (Navel chakra). It will then move to the heart's centre, before continuing to the pit of the throat. Subsequently, all of these chakras will vigorously rotate. The goddess will move to the *bhrumadhya* between the eyebrows and then, as long as the yogi is unattached, she will pierce the *sahasrāra* and the process of *Cit* Kuṇḍalinī will begin. Kuṇḍalinī can withdraw at any of these stages, leaving the yogi to resume their ordinary course of life. If the *sahasrāra* is not pierced, Kuṇḍalinī can awaken the eight great yogic powers: *animā, laghimā, mahimā, garimā, īśitvam, vaśitvam, prākāmyam, kāmāvasayitvam-vyāpti*. The use of these powers deprive yogis of their spirituality and can leave them feeling trapped. During the piercing or penetration (*vedha*) of *prāṇa Kuṇḍalinī*, the following experiences can occur:

Mantra vedha	When the yogi has the attachment and desire to achieve the supreme "I" that expresses itself in the Mantra *aham*, Kuṇḍalinī will then rise in great bliss and ecstasy.
Nāda vedha	When the yogi has the attachment and desire to uplift people for the benefit of humankind, Kuṇḍalinī will rise as the blissful force of *nāda*, the eternal sound.
Bindu vedha	When the yogi has the attachment to comfort and joy, Kuṇḍalinī will rise as semen and fill his body with indescribable sexual joy.
Śākta vedha	When the yogi has the attachment to never-ending strength free from fatigue or failure, Kuṇḍalinī will rise as Śakti and transform the yogi into the embodiment of energy.

Bhujaṅga veda	When the yogi has the attachment to Kuṇḍalinī being a serpent or another form, Kuṇḍalinī will rise in this form and the yogi will feel God's presence.
Brahmā vedha	When the yogi has the attachment to initiating only a few and keeping the mysteries secret, Kuṇḍalinī will rise in the sound of a humming bee and an intense bliss will follow.

You cannot control the way in which Kuṇḍalinī penetrates you. It depends on your deep-seated desires.

What Does All of This Mean?

Kuṇḍalinī is the source of all – both of the world and what is beyond. In her essence, she is the splendid power of your own soul, life and existence. In her limited form she sleeps at the root in the form of *kriyāśakti* – the power of action, therefore she will be awakened by austerity (tapas). When successfully awakened by the yogi, she will gradually or suddenly pierce the yogi with her bliss and manifest herself as the deepest desires lying hidden in the yogi's heart. Dreams will become true, life will be lived, because life must be lived. She will ask you: if you don't live your life, your dreams, your heart's desire, who will live it for you? She will be glorious and fierce. Her blessing is a graceful possession by the power of the ultimate. Loving surrender is the answer. To the fool she will be bondage, to the yogi liberation.

THE FORGOTTEN SECRET OF KUNDALINI YOGA

Uncoiling not Rising

In modern Hatha Yoga, Kuṇḍalinī sleeps in *mūlādhāra* from where she rises once awakened. This is consistent with the notion that Kuṇḍalinī is that force that surpasses one's individual existence and expands beyond. She rises insofar as she expands the limited being into the unlimited. However, Kuṇḍalinī is not only an upward movement. If the purpose of being is only to strive upward, we should leave behind whatever we are. And yet deep within us we know that what we are is what we have to embrace, in order to fully understand the purpose of life. Life is beautiful in all its suffering, and spirituality is not the science of leaving life behind, but the quest of how to infuse material mundanity with the divine. Know that we are secretly a sacred temple of the rhythm of life. That temple is not here simply to crumble and decay, but to worship and be worshipped.

The ancient tantric sciences share the same vision. Kuṇḍalinī is not initially awakened in *mūlādhāra* to be brought up to dissolve in the absolute, but instead is first awakened in the supreme state as Ūrdhva Kuṇḍalinī, then in the material existence as Ādhāra Kuṇḍalinī. Finally, these two powers of being – of which one is the blissful transcendental and the other is the passionate and loving – must meet another in the heart's centre. The upper is balanced by the lower, and the lower is balanced by the upper.

Suṣumṇā is the channel in which both must meet. It is the inner self, in which the yogi has to withdraw in order to guard the two eternal forces in the heart. Ūrdhva Kuṇḍalinī is like *iḍā* and the nectar dropping moon, while Ādhāra Kuṇḍalinī is like the desirous force of *piṅgala*. Their combination brings forth the third Kuṇḍalinī – she is the real one. She goes nowhere, neither rises nor falls, but resides in the heart as the one place of being and shines in the world. Truly, what else do we all wish for other than to shine from the heart in blissful love for this world, fully imbued with passion and insight.

The newer science of Hatha Yoga has unfortunately forgotten these three Kuṇḍalinīs, while excursively talking about *iḍā* and *piṅgala*, and their agents *prāṇa* and *apāna*, who awaken the one rising Kuṇḍalinī. This would be no great loss if they had not forgotten that Kuṇḍalinī secretly strives for the heart and that her real place of rest is not the crown, but in one's innermost being. The purpose of life is to live it fully, it is to unfold the secrets of the heart.

Kundalini Yoga

Kundalini Yoga is that which uses Kuṇḍalinī as a means for realisation. She is the power that secretly resides in the heart, as an eternal flame. Breath is one way and mantra is another, but both are typically applied in conjunction so as to awaken one's inner energy. The mantra is pulled by means of breath through the body and held at one place in *kumbhaka* (breath retention). The tantras teach us that Ūrdhva Kuṇḍalinī is awakened when the knot of Rudra at *ājñā cakra* is pierced. This can be achieved when Rudras *bīja* is uttered and pulled upwards until its nasal sound can finally pierce *rudra granthi*. Ūrdhva Kuṇḍalinī is the blessing of the absolute, the ecstasy of unlimited being.

> *And the expansion and contraction of energy (in the first*

instance) means cultivating and attending the modes of flowing out and coming to rest in the upper abode of Kuṇḍalinī (Ūrdhva Kuṇḍalinī). This abode is gradually reached through the piercing of the (centre) between the eyebrows by the subtle prāṇa śakti which intensifies gradually through vibration (of the anusvāra of the mantra) in the nasal cavity.

Kṣemarāja in his commentary the Pratyabhijñā-hrdaya (18)

Ādhāra Kuṇḍalinī, in contrast, can be awakened when *apāna* is pressurised upwards with *mūlabandha.* Once done, *Vāgbhava* (Brahmā's mantra), the very seed of the goddess, can pierce the base of *brahma granthi.* Various sexual practices in the ancient and secret Kaula lineages were used to make her move. She has the taste of super sexual joy, and she is passionate and fiery upon her awakening. The yogi, remaining both humble and powerful, must silently rest in the cavity of the heart, venerating these forces of existence.

One should focus on the Goddess of the word, who is Parā, vibrating radiantly in the form of the bīja, awakening the joy of awareness, having shattered brahmagranthi

Vāmakeśvarī mata, visuddhi-magga (4:23d-24c)

These techniques cannot be taught on the page, but must be learnt in an intimate student–teacher relationship. There is of course one exception: the teacher within you can reveal them. Kundalini Yoga is easy, if the yogi allows himself to fall in love with the energy, she is close by.

With one's sense faculties dissolved in the space of the heart – in the innermost recess of the lotus – with one's attention on nothing else: O blessed lady, one will obtain blessedness.

Vijñāna-Bhairava-Tantra (49)

KUNDALINI YOGA AS TAUGHT BY YOGI BHAJAN

Bhajan's yoga is strong and arousing, and emphasises the generation of *prāṇa* through *kapālabhāti*, *bhastrikā* and dynamic exercises. It should be noted that his yoga lacks a broad and substantial connection to Kundalini Yoga's traditional sources. Some say that he actually invented his system rather than being initiated into any tantric lineage, as he claimed. It has been proven almost beyond doubt that the majority of Bhajan's yoga came from two sources. The Yogi Svāmi Dev Mūrti and a more famous yogi called Dhīrendra Brahmacārī, a *haṭha* yogi in whose ashram Bhajan gave classes before he went in the U.S.. While this alone would not automatically invalidate his yoga's status as a revelation in itself, his credibility was further damaged as allegations of severe abuse were brought forward in 2019.

We should not overlook the positives, and it must be mentioned that his yoga served to build a beautiful community in which the will to strengthen one's basis for improving both oneself and the world is practiced. Sometimes it seems more important to have good students than good teachers. Yogi Bhajan was a predator, but his students had a fervent desire to build a better community, which they succeeded to do. Furthermore, the contribution of his yoga to the public awareness of the science of Kuṇḍalinī is remarkable. The yoga of Bhajan can be considered a series of energising Hatha Yoga techniques, which remove energy blockages and generate *prāṇa* for the purpose of expansion and spiritual experience.

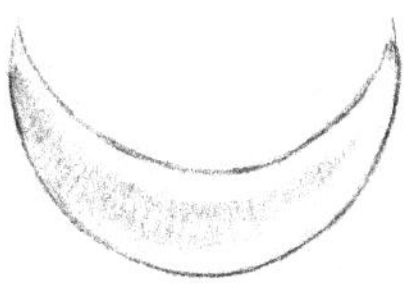

ROOTS OF KUNDALINI YOGA

In this way, in accord with the proper method, the self-born Lord fashioned Rudra's energy whose form begins with 'Na' and ends with 'Pha' from the letters born from his own limbs. Thus the Goddess who consists of all the letters (sounds), and who is marked by all the auspicious signs, greatly powerful, came forth and stood before Bhairava. The Goddess Mālinī (Kubjikā) said, 'Who are you?' He replied: 'I am the God'. She then asked 'How have I come here?' The God replied: 'How come you do not know me? O Goddess, who has fashioned you? O beloved, in order to play the game of creation, I have generated you'. The Goddess, somewhat piqued, replied: 'Well then who has generated you? Bhairava, say something!' O fair lady, I am the aggregate of letters, the self-born Lord of the universe. I have generated you from the seed-syllables born from my limbs. Thus you are the row of heroes who is said to be Rudra's energy'. Enraged by this reply Mālinī responds: 'If I have been generated by the letters born from your body, take your own letters back here and now!' Then handing back to Bhairava the garland of letters whose form consists of the principles of existence, she resumed her prior body made of the seed-syllable AIM, and she who is the Kuṇḍalinī of Nectar fell asleep (in a coiled form). Then the Lord of the Gods was confused: 'Where have all the letters gone?' Greatly astonished, he understood instantly that: 'they are all fused together and have merged into the principle of the individual soul (jīva). O great indeed is the Goddess's power!' Thus thought the lord of the universe.

Kubjikāmata-Tantra (1:71cd–80ab)

THE KAUBJIKĀ TRADITION

As mentioned earlier, Śakti is defined as the principle of energy that is the power of the ultimate God. Kuṇḍalinī, the goddess, is an expression of this Śakti as the creative force that brings all into being. As per the *Siddhayogeśvarīmata*-tantra, she is cosmically identified as the source of a triad of Śaktis, or powers, namely consciousness (*anuttara śakti*), will (*icchā śakti*), and awakening (*unmeṣa śakti*). Further to this, Kuṇḍalinī is the power of ecstasy that lies hidden in the world, waiting to be discovered through the abject surrender to its inherent divine nature. In this context, Kundalini Yoga is the science that uses the power of Kuṇḍalinī for the realisation of one's divine being.

Kundalini Yoga uses numerous techniques to awaken Kuṇḍalinī so as to facilitate this realisation of one's nature. Discovering Kuṇḍalinī as a principal force was the groundwork required for placing her in the framework of energy work and yogic techniques. The most important tantric school that developed modern day Kundalini Yoga's foundations is the Kaubjikā tradition. Many tantric schools concerned themselves with ritual, philosophy, meditation, and contemplation (such as the Trika). However, the Kaubjikā tradition differed from other schools by developing intricate visualisations, the system of the six chakras, *bījas*, and providing an in depth explanation of the vision of the hunchbacked goddess in elaborate detail. It is from this tradition, more so than any other, that our Kundalini Yoga emerged.

The Kaubjikā flourished in the Kashmir Valley between the 9th and 13th centuries. Its teachings were so highly secret and guarded that they were still practised and kept alive – unseen from the Hindu population – even during the Muslim invasion (when most tantric schools were destroyed). In the 20th century, some scholars traveling to these valleys discovered tantric practitioners and were allowed to translate some of their holy scriptures for reasons of preservation.

Kuṇḍalinī in the Kaubjikā

Kuṇḍalinī, as mentioned previously, is understood as a force operating on a cosmic level. The Kaubjikā tradition was interested in both Kuṇḍalinī's ultimate and coiled form. As such, she is seed, and to worship her is to make her remember. Tantra is compassionate, it is the science of a vulnerable and lovable being journeying into the light it so deeply longs for. The Kaubjikā were deeply imbued with this energy. Their compassion made them turn to the human being and worship this limited form as an expression of the ultimate and highest goddess in seed form. This coiled goddess, who is you, who is Kubjikā, is bent or hunchbacked. The awakening of Kuṇḍalinī is the unleashing of one's innate divine potential, the uncoiling of inner greatness. In the *Kubjikāmata-tantra*, Śiva addresses the goddess as he would any of us and explains to her what she is. Before you read these verses, remember that he is talking to any one of us who is still seeking:

Śrī Kubjikā asks:

> *How O God, is my name Tvaritā (the fast one) explained? Why is my name Khañjinī (the spatial one) used? How is the Kubjā (the bent one) defined? In what manner is the series of her (my) mandalas (form of sound body)? Śrī Bhairava answered: Well O Goddess very difficult to approach. How is it possible that you, O Parvati, are not familiar with that? Since you have arrived here from there, why then is it, that you do not know your own name? Because you move about with the swiftness of that part of time which is just like a hundredth part of a hair point which is split again thousandfold, therefore you are called Tvaritā, annihilating all injuries (regenerating the universe in the course of time). Khañjinī is proclaimed for you, many times, again and again, because the universe is situated within you and because you (she) are within the universe, therefore she is called Khañjikā, moving subtly*

in subtle matter. ('Kha'- all pervasiveness). The name Khañjikā is thus proclaimed to you. Hear now about Kubjinī. Certainly, this name is suitable given. You, O Lady of Kula, you are the One. In the gross, the subtle and the supreme reality, in the manifested and the unmanifested, as well as in the pure. All that is pervaded by the Goddess.

She is you! How is it possible that you do not know that? Just anyone with a tall body moves about in a small house and just as he enters it with his body bent (Kubjā), so is this great lady...

Kubjikāmata-Tantra (16:15–23)

Contemplating these verses can help one understand Kuṇḍalinī. She, Kubjikā, is bent because she is too tall for the house! Kuṇḍalinī is the force that must sleep because she surpasses your individual experience; she cannot fit inside your house! Your body, your mind, your being, all of these are too small to house the great lady who, being so tall, must bend so that she can accompany you. We can also thank the Kaubjikā tradition for the system of the six chakras, which codify the mystical ways in which the great goddess must ascend through the self in order to unfold her unlimited potential. In its inception, Kuṇḍalinī was simply seen as the universal power of the divine made manifest, creating the world through her body of sound. Now, Kuṇḍalinī is you, and you are about to realise yourself as being so much larger than the house you have become accustomed to be trapped in. Kundalini Yoga is therefore not only a science of how to awaken Kuṇḍalinī, but how to again unfold her and make her rise to the sky, for she is taller and larger than all. Understanding Kubjikā tradition is the key to understanding Kundalini Yoga. Expand yourself! Elevate yourself!

The Manthana-Bhairava-Tantra

Important texts of the Kaubjikā tradition (among a myriad of others) would include the *Śrīmatottara*, the *Kubjikāmata-Tantra*, and the *Manthana-Bhairava-Tantra*. The *Kubjikāmata-Tantra* is hard to come by as a comprehensive volume to meditate upon (only fragments of some chapters are available in English). Broadly speaking, the *Kubjikāmata-Tantra* simply elaborates upon the *Kumārikā-Khaṇḍa* – a part of the *Manthana-Bhairava-Tantra* – in more detail. Moreover, the *Śrīmatottara* sheds new light on the mystical aspects of the *Manthana-Bhairava-Tantra*. Therefore, immersing oneself in the *Manthana-Bhairava-Tantra* is perhaps sufficient. Thanks to the great scholar and tantric initiate, Mark Dyczkowski, the extremely voluminous *Manthana-Bhairava-Tantra* has been available in the English language since 2009. He dedicated over 20 years to his translation. He himself does not speak, advertise, or teach any of the content of this holy tantra. He has explained that it was the goddess who willed him to translate it for all seekers.

The *Manthana-Bhairava-Tantra* is comprised of approximately 21,000 verses. It consists of three main sections: the *Kumārikākhanda*, the myth of the virgin Goddess Kubjikā; the *Yogakā-Khaṇḍa*, and the *Siddhakā-Khaṇḍa*.

The beginning of the *Kumārikā-Khaṇḍa* is similar to that of a female heroine story. We discover the goddess as the young princess Kubjikā. She does not know who she is and so asks the God Bhairava about her nature. She then travels to the holy sites of India, finding herself in the process and finally marries Bhairava. It is a mythological story of the individual soul that forms part of a universal principle. This soul wants to achieve independence and therefore decides to separate from its source. In so doing, the soul falls asleep in a contracted (coiled) form and subsequently finds its own liberated self by travelling the sacred places that are both outside but secretly within. Finally, she makes her home in the holy city of the moon.

The highest God, Bhairava, then asks for her tutelage. At first she refuses, but after he proclaims his eternal friendship for her and begs her on bended knees to teach him the bountifulness of existence, she initiates him in the knowledge of Kaula (family), Kundalini Yoga. It is a story rich with beauty and importance.

And just as you were previously my wife, I was previously your lover. Just as, in the bliss at the conclusion of passion, swayed by our love we make love again, similarly may you again became another embodied being and I became a mortal embodied being. It is because of our transformation that the world of transmigratory existence has come into being and is thus full of passion (...).

O auspicious one, I am your disciple and you my mother. Help me! The previous collection of teachings was acquired from us in this way and fully learnt. Therefore, look upon me with love in order to grace me.

Manthana-Bhairava-Tantram (5:8–10 & 13–14)

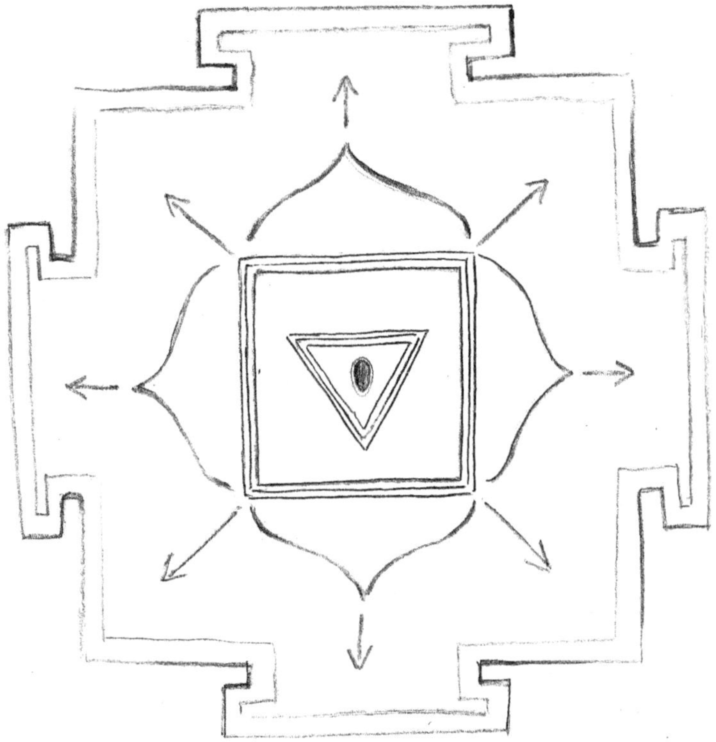

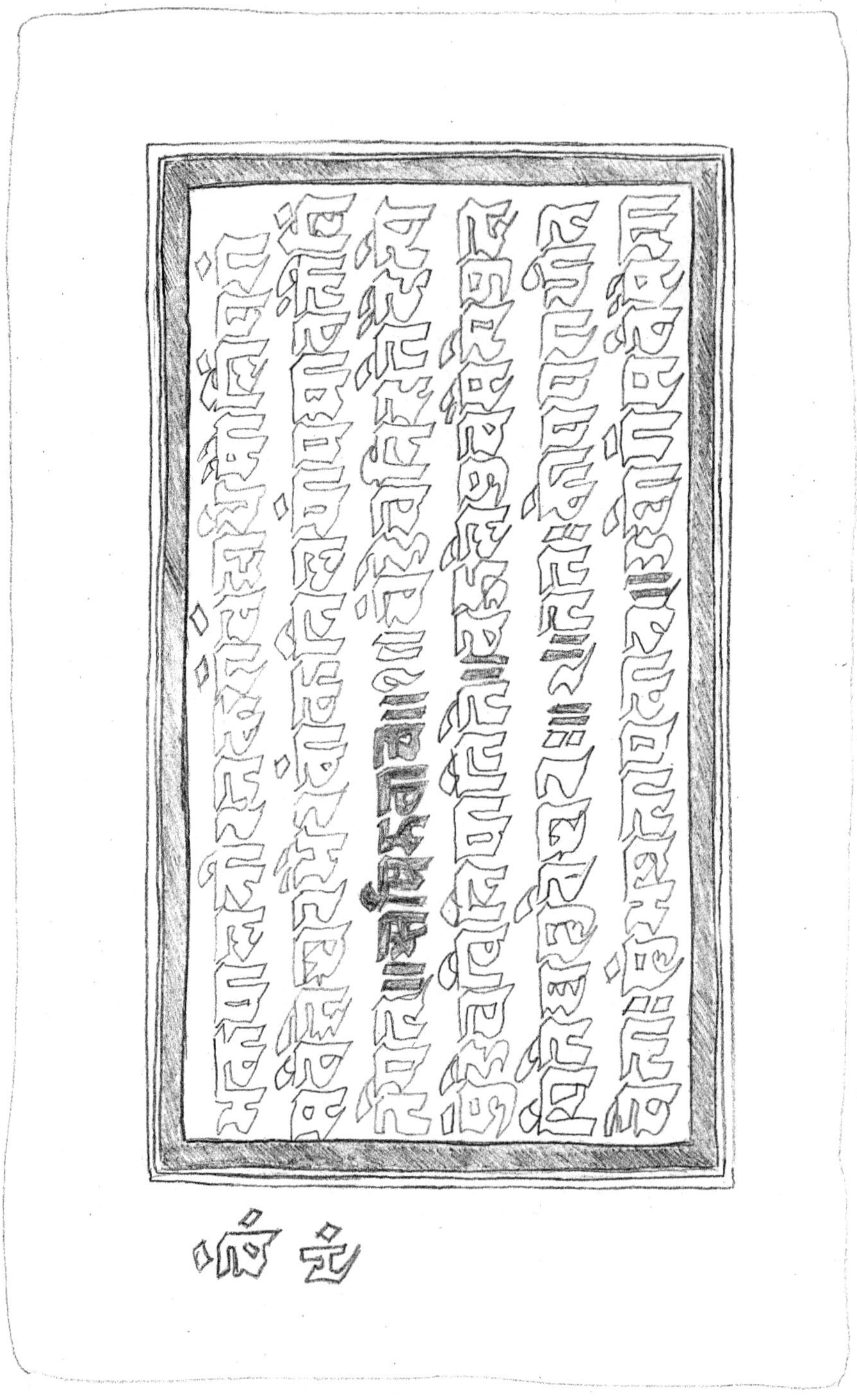

THE IMPORTANCE OF KNOWLEDGE

Truth resides within all the scriptures like the scent in a flower, the oil in a sesame seed, the soul in the body or nectar in water.

Tantrāloka (35:30–34)

THE KNOWLEDGE

We are lucky in that we have one another. We humans do not live alone, nor do we typically wish to. We move in cities and communities, we like to talk to and have each other, we love our friends and family, and abandonment can sometimes mean death for us. This is partly because we depend on our communities' guidance and knowledge – which is to a large extent unconscious, and is encoded in our behaviour and assumptions about the world. Alone we would struggle to even make fire; we would wander cold and naked through the forest, not knowing which berry to eat and which to avoid. The same is true for spiritual knowledge. How many have walked before us, tripped over stones, eaten the wrong berries, and died on our behalf, all so that we today can know what keeps us safe from harm and what leads us to it. This collective knowledge of how to live is immensely precious and surpasses the individual insight one can accumulate in one's short and dependent existence. Spiritual knowledge is meant to elevate the person to a state of realisation in which this knowledge is embodied. Once done, its necessity falls away as the picture of its ultimate experience transcends what mere words can express. Up until this point, knowledge is of crucial importance in saving us from regressing into an unconscious animal existence.

THE SCRIPTURE

Scriptures are expressions of this collective knowledge accumulated over thousands of years to stabilise our being for the betterment of all. Their spirit elevates and strengthens one's base for action. Scriptures supply the practitioner with a reference of practice and orientation in action. Without orientation, everything seems possible, yet nothing is ultimately achieved.

Furthermore, being aware of your roots sheds light on where you are, thus allowing you to go where you want to. As such, not knowing the source of yoga would make it hard for you to attain its goal.

INITIATION IN THE GOLDEN CHAIN

The Golden Chain is the initial mantra. It is the valuation of all the beings that came before you to provide you with the precious knowledge which now serves to elevate you. It is the chain of masters, where ultimately stands the greatest master of all – the highest reality out of which all true knowledge pours forth like golden rain.

Every yoga class – regardless of tradition or school – starts with a mantra or common ritual which is the humble surrender to this chain of knowledge. When you chant this mantra, be aware that you are honouring all of those souls, as well as the highest spirit, who worked tirelessly to elevate you into bliss.

In reality, there exists no initiation into spiritual consciousness. What does exist, however, is the knowledge that allows you to realise the consciousness that you have forgotten. Knowledge both conditions and hinders the mind in reaching the highest state. And yet, knowledge is also the means to remove limitations and allow one to return to the truth. This is because knowledge is a modification of mind and, insofar as it is energy or Śakti, it can contain more or less of the seed of truth.

In the ancient right-handed schools, a formal initiation was always a precondition for successful practice. In this way, however, there is no magical initiation as the all-pervading truth would never reject anyone from being initiated into its bliss. Only one's own limitations hinder one from standing in the light. As such, everyone must find the strength to initiate themselves into the path of yoga. If this strength cannot be found, no one can initiate you.

Even the master Abhinava Gupta, who was himself initiated into all the main tantric lineages of his time, agrees with this point. He explained that one's own inner spiritual calling, manifested in a spiritual awakening (*śaktipāta*), is one's initiation into the lineage and practice. The goddess of consciousness herself (who is you and who is all) will embrace you with her light.

> *The supreme reality is everywhere; it is omniform and self-manifesting. The forms of determinate knowledge are not capable of either lending any support to it or refuting it. Right reasoning (sattarka) spontaneously arises in a person keenly touched by Śakti. It is said that this kind of person is initiated by the Goddesses.*
>
> *Tantra-Sāra (4)*

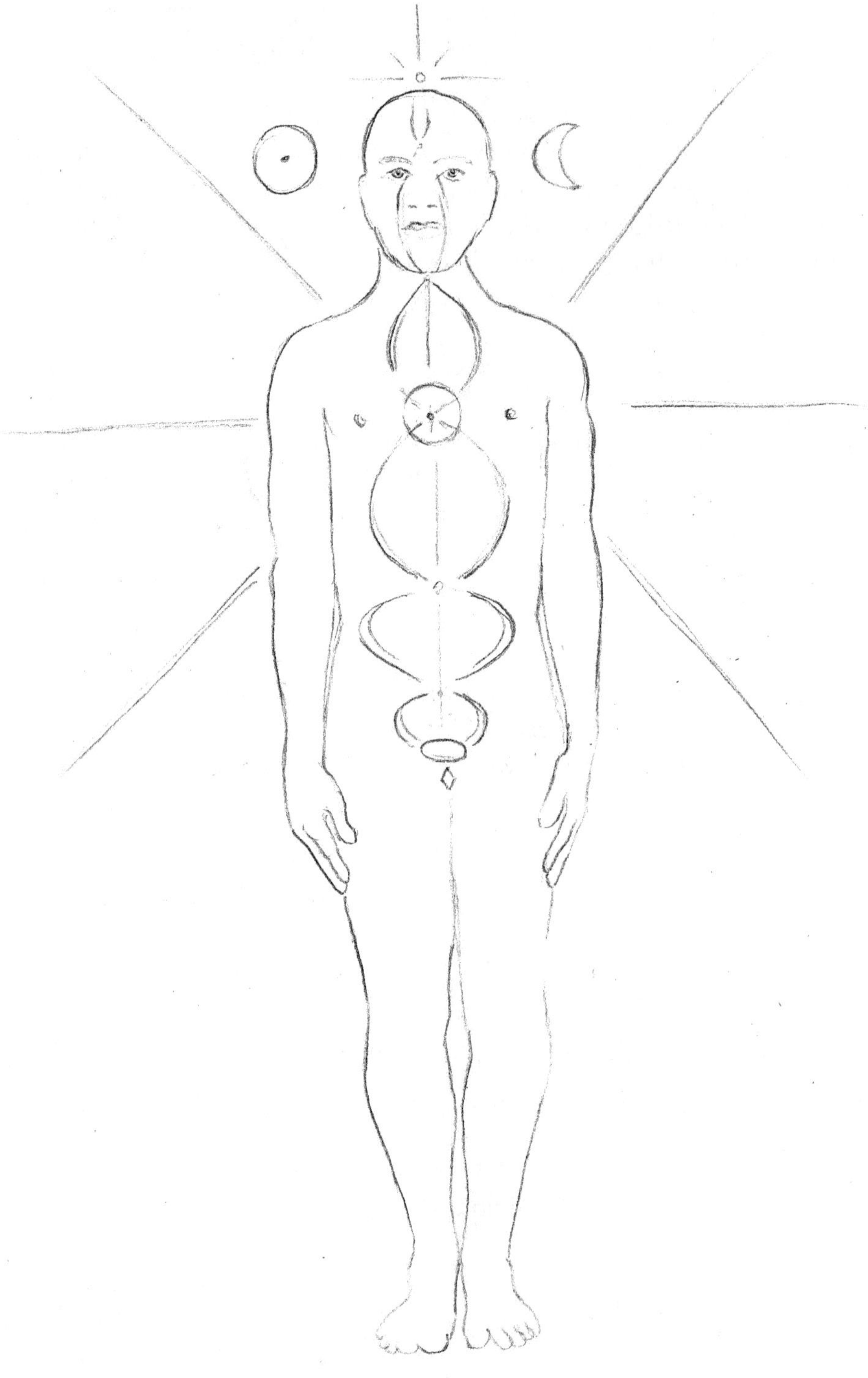

A GENERAL YOGIC ANATOMY

THE NĀḌIS

A *nāḍi* is a channel of *prāṇa* (life force), an energy channel. The *Śiva Saṃhitā* mentions that there are roughly 350,000 energy channels in the body (other scriptures put this number at about 72,000). While an obvious difference exists between these numbers, they share an incomprehensible vastness. This serves to tell us that we cannot comprehend the number of channels through which life is distributed in our body, just as most bodily functions are not consciously understood or even witnessed. The *nāḍis* are those psychic channels that transport *prāṇa*, the carrier of experience. All expressions and experiences of being flow through the *nāḍis*. If they are blocked, or polluted by experience, new states of energy cannot rise or manifest.

When the nāḍis are impure, breath cannot penetrate into the suṣumnā. Then the yogi achieves nothing, nor can he reach a state of deep concentration.

Haṭha-Yoga-Pradīpikā (2:4)

The *nāḍis* emerge from the lower part of the body. According to the *Śiva Saṃhitā*, they emerge from the *mūlādhāra* chakra, as with the three primary nāḍis. However, there is both a general consensus and scriptural authority to assume that there is a *pranic* centre between the navel and the genitals from which the *nāḍis* distribute energy through the body – which also corresponds with north Asian traditions. This centre, closely related to *svādhiṣṭhāna*, is called the *kanda*. It is said to have the shape of a golden egg and is the centre of all bodily energy.

Above the genital organ and below the navel is kanda of the shape of a bird's egg. There arise (from it) nāḍis seventy-two thousand in number (...). This chakra of the nāḍis should ever be known by the yogis. The three nāḍis iḍā, piṅgalā and suṣumnā are said to carry prāṇa always and have as their devatas, moon, sun and fire.

.

Dhyānabindu Upaniṣad (50–55)

The *Śiva Saṃhitā* (2:13) teaches us that while fourteen of these *nāḍis* are important, only three are key for yoga. Moreover, of these three, only one is especially significant. These three *nāḍis* are the *iḍā* (nourishment, sacrificial drink), the *piṅgalā* (reddish), and the *suṣumnā* (graceful).

Iḍā is the flow of the moon, transmitting the unconscious state of sleep, dream, vision, and introversion. *Piṅgalā* is the flow of the sun, transmitting wakefulness, conscious thought, action, and extroversion. *Iḍā* is also *citta* (spirit), the field in which everything mental is manifested. *Piṅgalā* is also *prāṇa*, which moves all things to life. These two states of being are viewed as two rivers, with a third existing between them – a state that is neither conscious nor unconscious. This is the state of meditative awareness, *suṣumnā*, which consists of three layers that reflect the threefold nature of the materialised universe. Its innermost layer, *sattva*, is called *citrini nāḍi*, which is said to be the gateway to heaven and the world beyond.

Furthermore, *suṣumnā* is the pranic *nāḍi* that reflects the detached and unmoving

	Meaning	Light	Location	Prāṇa	Aspect
Suṣumnā	*Graceful*	*Fire*	*Centre*	*Udāna*	*Knower*
Piṅgalā	*Reddish*	*Sun*	*Right*	*Prāṇa*	*Knowing*
Iḍā	*Refreshing*	*Moon*	*Left*	*Apāna*	*Known*

nature of consciousness, similar to how meditative awareness is the mental state of the disengaged knower. In the *Upaniṣads*, the *nāḍis* are likened to channels filled with oil. The oil absorbs the flavour of each action committed by the individual self. The *suṣumnā* carries that oil which cannot be flavoured, the oil that – much like the true self – is unmoving in nature and eternally stable. *Suṣumnā* is therefore the carrier of the energy of the self, the knower. This ever-liberated self resides in heaven, above our limited existence. This seems to be why the *Chāndogya Upaniṣad* considers *suṣumnā* as the pathway the soul should ascend at death to reach a stainless and eternal existence.

> *But when he thus departs from this body, then he proceeds upwards through those very rays, [if he is a knower] he surely goes up meditating on Oṃ or [if he is not a knower, does not got up]. As long as it takes for the mind to travel, in that short time, he goes to the sun. That indeed is the door to the world of Brahman, an entrance for the knowers and a shutting out for the ignorant.*
>
> *There is this verse about it: A hundred and one are the nāḍis of the heart; one of them leads up to the crown of the head. Passing upwards through that suṣumnā, one attains immortality, while the other nāḍis serve for departing in various other directions.*
>
> *Chāndogya Upaniṣad (8:6:5–6)*

THE PRĀṆAS

The *prāṇas* are the phenomena that occur on the level of *prāṇāmaya kośa* (the layer of *prāṇa*). *Prāṇa* is that which resides in the body as vital breath and what creates the organising intelligence in living beings that distinguishes it from dead matter. The *Taittirīya Upaniṣhad* depicts *prāṇa* as the body's soul. It describes it as filling the body and giving it life.

Prāṇa acts as the carrier of experience within consciousness and, importantly, was the first form to emerge from the formless. It thus provides life with substantiality. In this context 'OṂ' is called the *praṇava*, the sound that projects *prāṇa* into emptiness, meaning that it is *prāṇa* that emerges from the void. It is the first form of being.

The bodily *prāṇas* explored here are the forces moved during *prāṇāyāma*, or breath exercises. We should note that *prāṇa* moves differently depending on which body part it governs, and can be influenced by food, exercise, and breath. In my opinion, as no health benefits can be gained, it would be somewhat irrelevant for a yoga teacher to delve too deeply into the bodily influence of the five *prāṇas*. Instead, it would benefit us far more to simply practice *prāṇāyāma*, to experience its magic, and draw strength from one's own practice.

Name	Movement	Distribution	Governs
Prāṇa	*Inward*	*Heart*	*Liver, lungs, heart, circulation system*
Apāna	*Outward*	*Pelvis*	*Reproduction, large intestine, genitals, organs of excretion*
Samāna	*Central, circular*	*Stomach*	*Energizing, digestion, immunity, skin, agility*
Udāna	*Upward*	*Head, limbs*	*Consciousness, head, arms, hands, feet, brain, endocrine system*
Vyāna	*Pervasive*	*Everywhere*	*Circulatory, lymphatic system, immune system.*

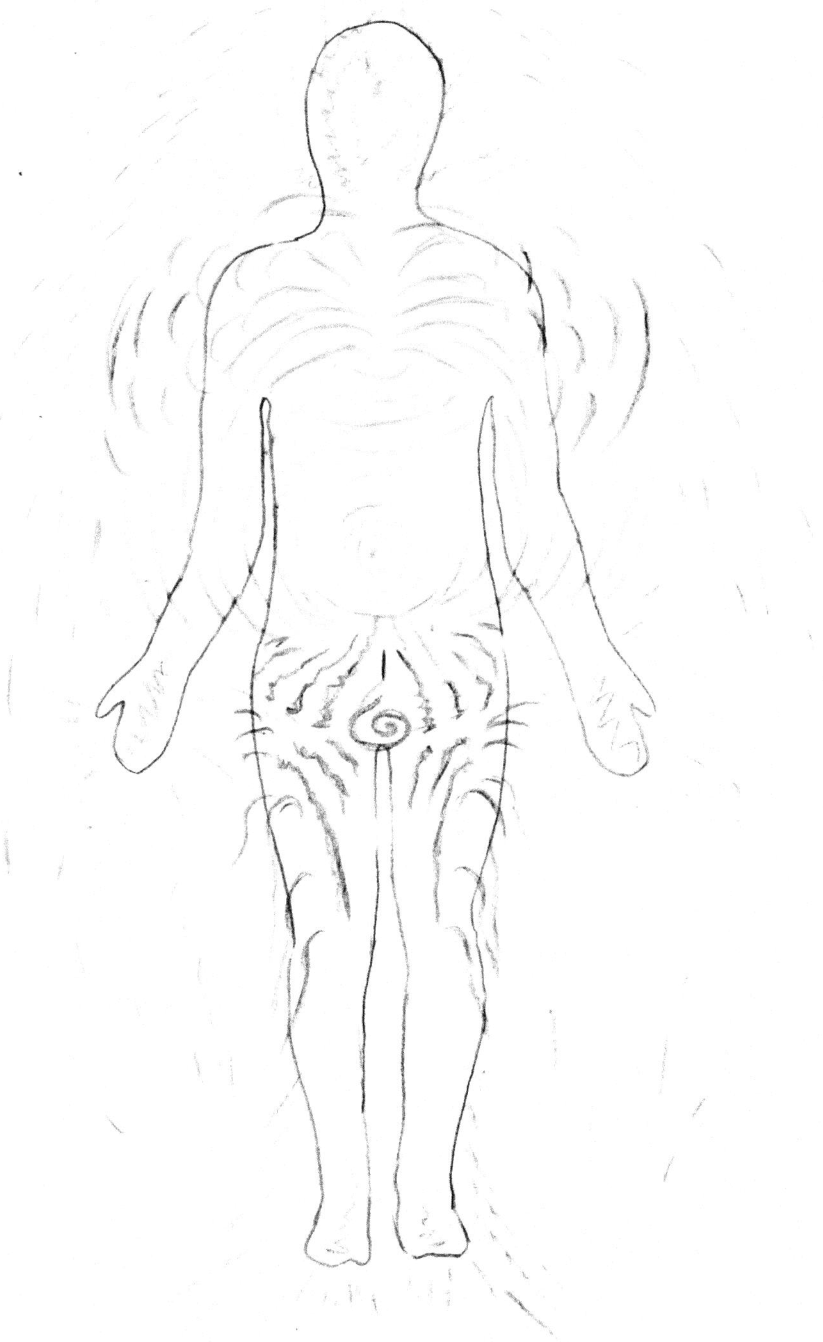

Modern description

The body is governed by 10 *vāyus* (winds), though only 5 are important for us. These are: *prāṇa, apāna, samāna, udāna,* and *vyāna*. The correct balance of the *prāṇas* ensures vitality, while imbalance leads to ill health.

> *Prāṇa, apāna, samāna, udāna, vyāna, naga, kurma, krikara, devadatta, and dhananjaya, these are the ten principal names, described by me in this scripture; they perform all functions, incited thereto by their own actions. Again, out of these ten, the first five are the leading ones; even among these, the prāṇa and apāna are the highest agents, in my opinion. The seat of the prāṇa is the heart; of the apāna, the anus; of the samāna, the region above the navel; of the udāna, the throat; while the vyāna moves all over the body... He who in this way knows the microcosm of the body, being absolved from all sins, reaches the highest state.*
>
> *Śiva Saṃhitā (2:4–9)*

Tantric Understanding

Initially, the *prāṇas* were not only understood as energy residing in different parts of the body, but were more often considered to be five stages of energy along a path of realisation.

In this light, *prāṇa* and *apāna* (governing inhalation and exhalation) are seen as agents of the two primary forces, *iḍā* and *piṅgalā*. *Samāna* is considered the one-pointed energy of stillness that arises when both forces are balanced. *Udāna* is understood to be the agent of Kuṇḍalinī that arises during one's resting *samāna*. *Vyāna* is considered to be the state of all-pervasive consciousness that is the final abode of Kuṇḍalinī.

This perspective appears invaluable for the practice of *prāṇāyāma*, or for spiritual

Name	Movement	Consciousness
Prāṇa	*Outward*	*Energy of external perception*
Apāna	*Inward*	*Energy of internal perception*
Samāna	*Central, singular*	*Energy of one-pointed silence*
Udāna	*Upward*	*Energy of meditative absorption in bliss*
Vyāna	*Pervasive*	*Energy of formless samādhi*

experience. The practicing yogi can focus on the ascending stages of *prāṇa* or consciousness to which their balance automatically leads. Embracing this view would help one understand the *prāṇas* as a successive chain of steps to ecstasy which one walks by simply practicing their balance.

Our modern view on the *prāṇas* and the directional flow of the two primary agents (*prāṇa* and *apāna*) is taken from their anatomical movements – for instance, *apāna* would be outward flowing just like the excretion that it governs. In this more refined view, however, *pranic* movements are related to their cognitive functions. This explains why tantrics like Abhinava Gupta taught an inverted understanding of the flow of *prāṇa* and *apāna*. Here, *prāṇa* is the force that creates the outer experience, so it is outflowing (or, exhalation), whereas *apāna* is the force that internalises experience, so it is inflowing or inhalation.

> *Then due to exhaling (prāṇa), awareness flows through the sense faculties and rests on an external object. Then filling himself with the 'moon', that is inhalation (apāna) bringing with it the object, he sees himself in all things and thus becomes free from any desire for another. Next due to*

the emergence of this equalising energy (samāna) in the centre, one experiences repose in the unity. Then the fire of the breath up-rises (udāna Kuṇḍalinī) he absorbs the operations of the perceiver, the perceived and the process of perception. When the fire absorbing subsides and the pervasive (vyāna) vital energy emerges, then one vibrates free of all limitation.

Tantra-Sāra (5)

THE KOŚAS

Introduction

The *kośas* are layers, or sheaths, of your being created by *māyā*, the force of illusion. These layers are, in one sense, constituents of your being, such as body and mind. In another sense, they are a layer of consciousness in which one can be bound, such as in unmoving matter, feeling, or thought.

Accordingly, the *kośas* comprise perceivable reality, as everything considered real is made out of these layers or bodies. Consciousness can either be trapped within certain layers of illusion or pass through to higher experiences.

Anamaya Kośa

This refers to the body that is made and sustained from food (*ana*). It is simply the physical body. *Anamaya kośa* is also the layer of one's consciousness which is limited to the dimension of that which is made of food. Every being that identifies itself with its body, or which bodily exists without self-consciousness (minerals, plants, etc.), has their self-awareness limited through the sheath that is *anamaya kośa*.

From that Brahman, which is the Self, was produced space. From space emerged air. From air was born fire. From fire was created water. From water sprang up earth. From earth were born the herbs. From the herbs was

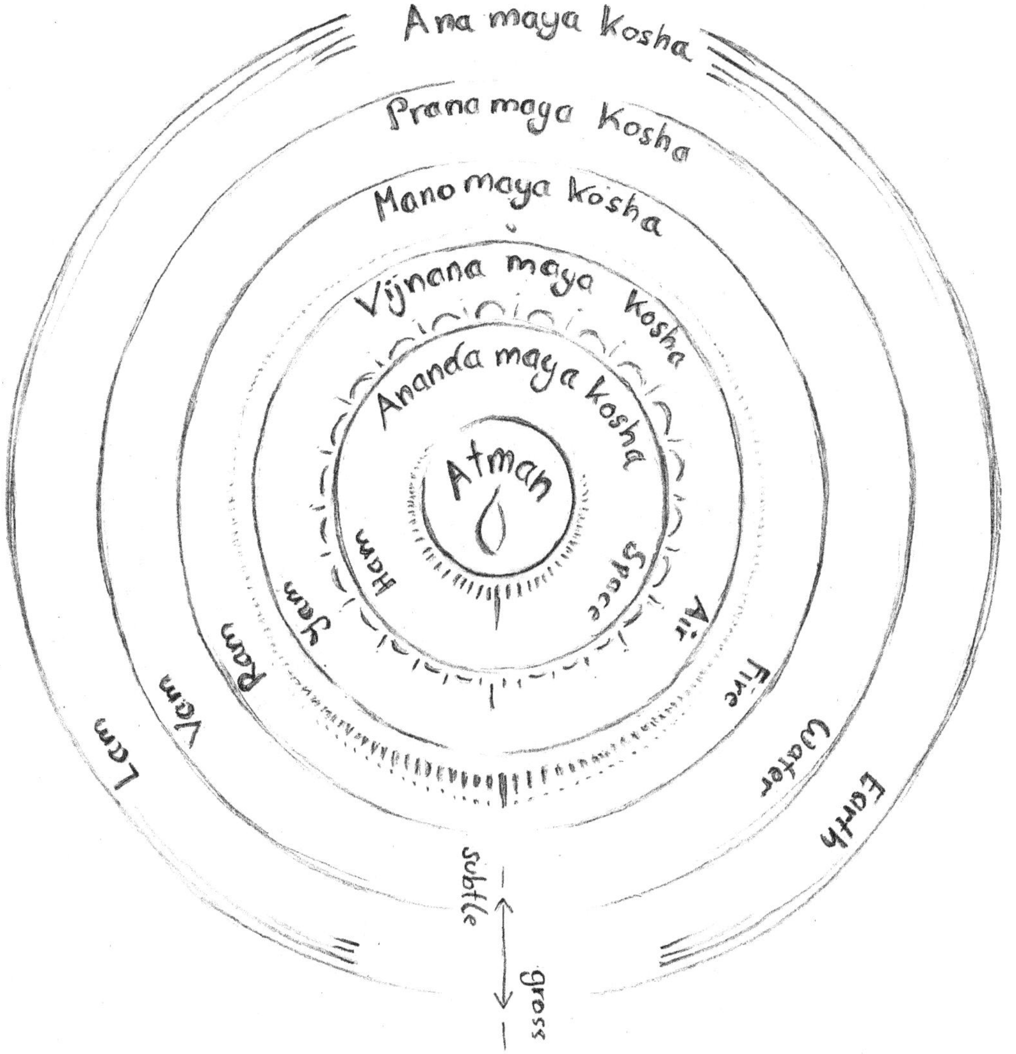
Ana maya kosha
Prana maya kosha
Mano maya kosha
Vijnana maya kosha
Ananda maya kosha
Atman
Ham
Yam
Ram
Vam
Lam
Space
Air
Fire
Water
Earth
subtle
gross

produced food. From food was born man. That man, such as he is, is a product of the essence of food.

Taittirīya Upaniṣhad

Prāṇāmaya Kośa

This relates to the body comprised of *prāṇa*. It is also that self which is limited to the experience of being *prāṇa*. *Prāṇāmaya kośa* is the dimension of life, and one's sense of being alive is perceived by feeling. This self is happy, ecstatic, unhappy, or miserable – it is comprised of emotions. It is the attachment to feeling and contains within it the craving for pleasure and avoidance of pain.

As compared with this self made of the essence of food, as said before, there is another inner self which is made of air (vāyu). By that is this one filled up. This self is also of the human form. Its human form takes after the human form of that earlier one, (anamaya kosha).

Taittirīya Upaniṣhad

Manomaya Kośa

The body made from mind and the layer of illusion that includes all mind. Within that which is mind exists all pictures one may project on reality or on oneself. Inside the sheath of *manomaya kośa* only the idea of what is real in the form of a mental construct of reality exists. This perception is formed by the impressions collected by *mānas*, the sensual mind. *Ahaṃkāra*, the ego, is fully developed at this stage of illusion. The self creates its own perception of the world and assigns all experience of mind as being itself, the 'I'.

One is not subjected to fear at any time if one knows the bliss that is Brahman, which cannot be reached by words (conditioned by the mind), as they fall back and fail to reach him. Of the preceding (vital) one, this mental one is verily the embodied self.

Taittirīya Upaniṣhad

Vijñānamaya Kośa

This is the body comprised of knowledge. It is the layer of illusion in which one is limited by one's knowledge about the nature of reality. This knowledge is not generated by the mind, but instead concerns the purpose of being and nature of existence, and lays the foundations for belief and ideology. It is the belief with which one faces the world and, through its form, imbues it with both colour and meaning. These beliefs form the vision of the world that one subconsciously aims to experience. It is the very heart of the life that one lives. Belief is something carried in the heart; it is indisputable. Evil people cannot be persuaded to compassion, just as good people cannot be reasoned into evil. In this way, one's own understanding of the true meaning of existence is limited by the illusional layer of knowledge – *vijñānamaya kośa*

> *... Of him (vijñānamaya kośa) faith is verily the head; righteousness is the right side; truth is the left side; concentration is the self (trunk); [the principle, called] mahat, is the stabilising tail.*

Taittirīya Upaniṣhad

Ānandamaya Kośa

The layer of illusion relating to bliss. It is this layer of being that limits one in the degree that one feels the bliss of *ātman*. It can be seen as the degree of enlightenment one carries in the heart. Either you see, or you do not. Either you know, or you do not.

> *As compared with this cognitive body, there is another internal self-constituted by bliss. By that one is this one filled up. This one, has a human shape. It is humanly*

shaped in accordance with the human shape of the earlier one. Of him joy is the head, enjoyment is the right side, hilarity is the left side; bliss is the self. Brahman is the tail that stabilises.

Taittirīya Upaniṣhad

Ātman

When freed from its bondage, it becomes the *parāmātman* (the soul of the world) that is nothing other than Brahman.

The soul, the essence of one's being, the self, the enjoyer, the observer, the true being, the indestructible, the unchanging, the unborn, the undying, the eternal, the self-illuminating, is as a light within a vessel.

It is then neither steadiness nor depth, neither light nor darkness, neither describable nor distinguishable. Sat (true-being) alone remains. One should think of ātman as being within the body, like a light in a vessel. Ātman is of the dimensions of a thumb, it is a light without smoke and without form, is shining within (the body) and is undifferentiated and immutable.

Yogakuṇḍalini Upaniṣad (3)

THE CHAKRAS

HISTORY

Chakra, or *cakra*, means wheel or circle. Interestingly, the Greek *kulkos* and even the English 'cycle' derive from this word. The chakra appears in early scriptures, such as the Vedic *Ṛgveda*. A closer inspection reveals that the word chakra was not at this time used to refer to a psychic energy centre, but instead denoted a wheel or power centre. In the 1st century BCE, early *Upaniṣads* speak of subtle yogic anatomy, such as the *nāḍis*. Similarly, the *Dhyānabindu Upaniṣad* of the 3rd century CE mentions the techniques of Kundalini Yoga, the rise of energy (Śakti), and the positions of the lower chakras. With the further development of tantric yoga from the 8th century CE onwards, the chakras faced closer inspection. The Upaniṣads composed in this time, such as the *Yoga-Kuṇḍalini Upaniṣad*, emphasise the importance of the chakras for Kundalini Yoga.

The path of yoga, as laid out by the *Gīta* or the later *Yoga-Sūtras*, is a road which leads to purification, surrender, and further enlightenment. The chakras were outside of yoga's early paths, and are a purely tantric teaching. Only in the later schools of Hatha Yoga and tantra is Kuṇḍalinī considered to be the key to enlightenment (*Haṭha-Yoga-Pradīpikā*, 3:105–110), and proper knowledge of the chakras is a precondition for her rise.

> *From the blowing of vāyu and agni (mūlabandha), the Kuṇḍalinī pierces open the brahmagranthi and then Viṣṇugranthi. Then it pierces rudragranthi [the three knots] after that, all the six lotuses are passed. Then Śakti is happy with Śiva in Sahasrāra Kamala (thousand lotuses chakra). This should be known as the highest state of being and it alone is the giver of final beatitude.*
>
> *Yoga-Kuṇḍalini Upaniṣad (85–86)*

CHAKRAS AS A TOOL FOR MEDITATION

A common modern misconception of the chakras is that they were not exclusively seen as a map of the subtle inner anatomy, but were also used as meditation tools. From their outset, yogis would use visualisation techniques in which they would place a turning wheel that resembled a particular deity on the body. These deities, or wheels, were placed on different parts of the body so as to invoke the deity's power in this specific area. While certain deities or energies were prescribed for certain areas, they were not used for descriptive purposes.

TRADITIONAL TOOLS

The common ground for the reality of the chakras is their vertical alignment along the axis of inner experience (or *suṣumnā*) – various different systems were created to place certain energies inside this axis. The Kaubjikā tradition routinely taught two very different systems, thereby alluding to the fact that the chakras should be employed for meditation rather than to describe a fixed energetic reality. Depending on the aim of the system one works with, a different number of chakras – and different tools therein – are chosen.

Most systems agree on seeing chakras as an expression of a level of spiritual awareness, and Kuṇḍalinī as a tool to transcend it. In this context, the chakra is a *granthi*, a psychic knot or blockage, that must be overcome. The tradition names three primary knots located in the body which represent three basic attachments. Of course, there are many other attachments besides these three, each with corresponding centres, energies, and elements. In fact, the very definition of a chakra is a knot which can be pierced by Kuṇḍalinī. The following tools used in different parts of the body represent forms of limitations (knots) that can be overcome (transcended).

> *Being aroused by the contact of agni with mānas and prana, she takes the form of a needle and pierces up through suṣumnā. The yogi should open with great effort this door which is shut. Then he will pierce the door to salvation by means of Kuṇḍalinī.*

Dhyānabindu Upaniṣad (5:66)

Tools of chakra mediation

A common technique taught to me by my master is *bhūta śuddhi*, the cleansing of the five elements. Five chakras – each expressing one of the five elements within one's being – are placed in the body. Once the five elements are invoked, Kuṇḍalinī can rise. The five elements represent the limitations posed by each element. When the element is invoked by means of the mantra, the energy is pierced by the power of awareness and mantra (*mantraśakti*), allowing the element to be transcended and its power granted.

Students often find it confusing to differentiate between that which limits and that which elevates. The five elements are limitations, and yet they are invoked so as to be transcended. This is because the goddess, manifested as the five elements, is understood to simultaneously be both limitation and freedom, just as *māyā* is both the goddess of illusion and the mother of all things. Whether she is bondage or liberation does not depend on the element in which she appears, but on the degree of awareness with which the particular element is faced. When the lowest of all elements (earth) is not invoked by the power of awareness, she is bondage and hell. If it is instead invoked by the powers of mantra, *prāṇa*, or awareness, it can be transcended and provide a source of great strength.

Remember, while everything may appear as a demon, it must be embraced with full awareness so it can become nothing but a power of your own infinite consciousness.

Through prakṛti you'll rise. It is prakṛti through which you will fall.

Swami Lakshman Joo

Cause Deities

Another important approach is to install the six or seven cause deities inside the body. These deities were the highest gods worshiped in India throughout different periods in history. Indians considered them to be representations of spiritual evolution. As such, to install them in a successive order in the body and transcend them one after the other (from lowest to highest) is a symbolic but powerful journey through one's own inner spiritual evolution.

Bhairava/Maheśvara	highest left-handed fierce Śiva
Sadāśiva	Tantric Śiva
Īśvara	Formless God
Rudra	Destroyer God
Viṣṇu	Pervading God
Brahmā	Creator God

The Six Realms

These are six levels of attachment considered to have created the whole world of affection and bondage. These are be placed within the body and transcended one by one until freedom is attained.

God Realm	Attachment to one's own greatness and pleasure
Titan Realm	Attachment to one's own superiority
Human Realm	Attachment to one's own knowledge
Animal Realm	Attachment to one's own stupidity
Hungry Ghost Realm	Attachment to one's own need
Demon Realm	Attachment to one's own hatred

The Vowels

Sound in India is holy. The whole universe was said to have been created by the primal sound, Oṃ, from which all other sounds emerged – viewed as pre-manifested aspects of the universe. Every sound is both a god and goddess, and together they are understood as Kuṇḍalinī. When the sounds are placed in the body and transcended, the energy of the whole universe is transcended or pierced. Even in our modern system the chakras refer to sound. The number of petals on the lotuses make 50 (4+6+10+12+16+2), corresponding to all 50 vowels of the Sanskrit alphabet which make the sound (vibration) of all.

SYSTEMS

One of the earliest systems of the chakras emerged in the 6th century BCE from the *Kālottara-Tantra*. This was a conservative system of five centres which placed the lowest (*mūlādhāra*) in the heart, with each subsequent centre rising steadily upwards. The *Kālottara*-Tantra imagined Kuṇḍalinī rising through the five elements upwards from the heart. Many other systems emerged that favoured energies in different positions. Our now-famous system was first mentioned in the *Kubjikāmata-Tantra* of the Kaubjikā tradition as one of the two major systems taught. This system would later reappear in the *Śiva Saṃhitā* and in the *Ṣaṭ-Cakra-Nirūpaṇa* (translated into English at the beginning of the 20th century) and find its way into the new age movement. Far from being a traditional text, the *Ṣaṭ-Cakra-Nirūpaṇa* was a treatise written by the 16th century scholar, Svāmī Purnananda. He merged everything he had heard and read about the chakras into one assortment of cause deities, animals, and symbols. The text is descriptive and contains no guidelines for meditation.

The table below notes chakra systems with fewer than 9 centres. The *Kaula-Jñāna-Nirṇaya* and the musicological text *Saṅgīta-Ratnākara* favour up to 11 centres, and the *Vijñāna-Bhairava-Tantra* mentions 12.

CHAKRAS AND THEIR REALITY

This said, it should be noted that there is also a reality to the chakras independent from the projection with which one may work during meditation. Just as the *nāḍis* are said to be situated throughout certain areas of the body, subtle inner experience is also assigned to different body parts. *Suṣumnā*, as the vertical axis of the body, is the playground of inner experience. If you were to observe yourself in your daily life, you may recognise that all of your meaningful inner experiences can be perceived along the verticality of *suṣumnā*. Your love is not in your elbow, but in your heart. Your sexual arousal is not in your ear, but in the centre of your pelvis. Your fear is in your belly, as is your strength. When you have a great idea or burst of insight, you may feel a momentary flash of light over your head. This vertical orientation of your psychic inner experience – common to us all – is the natural reason for chakras being placed along this very axis.

The ancient tantrics knew this, and accordingly placed energies and their deities in these sensitive areas of self-experience. The reasoning behind this is that, if a meaningful energy is placed in this area of self, then that energy must become the self.

The very first understanding of the chakras as meaningful centres came from Taoism, and is still taught today in the form of the lower, middle, and higher dantien (*tan t'ien* – Sea of Qi). This dantien existed – and continues to do so – in the exact same form today in traditional tantra. The lower dantien is called *kanda*, and is described as being in the same position and having the same attributes. It can be found three fingers under the navel, egg-like in its shape, and of a golden colour. The middle and higher dantien correspond to what is in yoga *anāhata* and *ājñā*, respectively. This division of the energy that is below, central, and above, is the most fundamental and undeniable discoverable reality of the chakras. The ancient tantrics used a meditation technique by which Kuṇḍalinī was imagined to be present in three parts of the body: the *kanda*, the heart, and the head. Kuṇḍalinī was to be awakened in these three centres so as to move her to the heart and merge her with the soul – the centre of being.

THE GREAT IMPORTANCE OF THE CHAKRAS

Nowadays, the chakras are typically seen as seats of our emotional well-being and supernatural-powers. Crystals, colours, singing bowls, and massages are said to help awaken the hidden energy within these centres and lead us back to harmony. While all of these methods can work, the most important treasure hidden in these teachings has thus far been absent.

The greatest gift is that the chakra represents an energy or experience that can be localised in the body. In this way, the energy has its own space in which it can be found. These specific places are gateways through which the yogi can gain entrance to or access a certain power. The Śiva Saṃhitā (3:73) mentions that prolonged meditation (e.g., dhāraṇā for two hours) on the location of a chakra allows the practitioner to overcome the residing element's limitation. For instance, fire is overcome by meditation over maṇipūra or air is overcome by meditation in anāhata. Successive dhāraṇā on all centres allows one to 'drink the nectar of immortality'. These techniques are just a fraction of the myriad pathways to awaken and overcome powers through their location in the body. Without their locations, access to these internal landscapes would be challenging to the point of impossible. Kuṇḍalinī can also be awakened by prolonged concentration on mūlādhāra or breathing exercises that emphasise the contraction of the perineum.

The knowledge to localise experience in our bodies is a great gift given to us by the old sages. The body must be a mirror of the universe, so all deities and worldly experiences must therefore reside within it. The body is a vast landscape, filled with temples, oceans, mountains, and sages. One can traverse this landscape using the power of awareness. The knowledge of the chakras encourages us to look deep inside as all of the world's wonders lie sleeping, ready to be awakened.

> *In this human body, Mount Meru (the spine) is surrounded by seven islands; there are rivers, seas, mountains, fields, and lords of the fields too. There are in it seers and sages; all the stars and planets as well. There are sacred pilgrimages, shrines; and presiding deities of the shrines. The sun and moon, agents of creation and destruction, also move in it. Ether, air, water and earth are also there.*
>
> *Śiva Saṃhitā (3:1–3)*

MODERN UNDERSTANDING OF THE KAUBJIKĀ SYSTEM

When the *Ṣaṭ-Cakra-Nirūpaṇa* was first translated into English in 1912, the idea of psychic centres within the body resonated strongly with readers and practitioners alike. The Theosophical Society, led by the occultist Madame Blavatsky in Chennai, was greatly interested in the idea and merged the concept with human anatomy. In their opinion, chakras must have anatomical counterparts which could be understood as such fixed psychical organs as glands. Later, the magician and occultist Aleister Crowley wrote about Kundalini Yoga and the chakras, and quickly became a hero of the new age movement. Carl Jung, the pioneering Swiss psychologist, spent three months travelling throughout India where he had a vision after visiting a temple of Kali. He was so entranced by the spiritual power within India that he offered lectures about Kundalini Yoga in 1932. From these highly-celebrated lectures was born his famous book, *The Psychology of Kundalini Yoga*. Jung proposed many ideas that later merged with the new age movement and provided us with our understanding of the chakras as an expression of an individual spiritual evolution, which is to say a progressive movement through psychological layers into higher levels of self-awareness and understanding.

A lot of what modern Indian people know about the chakras is in large parts influenced through this Western interpretation. Most Indian yogis follow the teachings of Woodroffe and Jung. Indeed, even the Bihar School of Yoga uses this interpretation.

While some may reject these Jungian ideas as a distortion of the original tradition, others could argue that every human being is blessed by intuitive insight and every era needs its own language to understand hidden truths. The chakra system is certainly multi-dimensional and many interpretations can point to the truth. As such, this Jungian understanding is in large parts still a revelation that can deepen our understating of ourselves and the path towards expansion of consiousness. The new age understanding of the chakras that I will present in the following chapters is largely influenced by this great thinker and visionary.

Let us discover these ideas together.

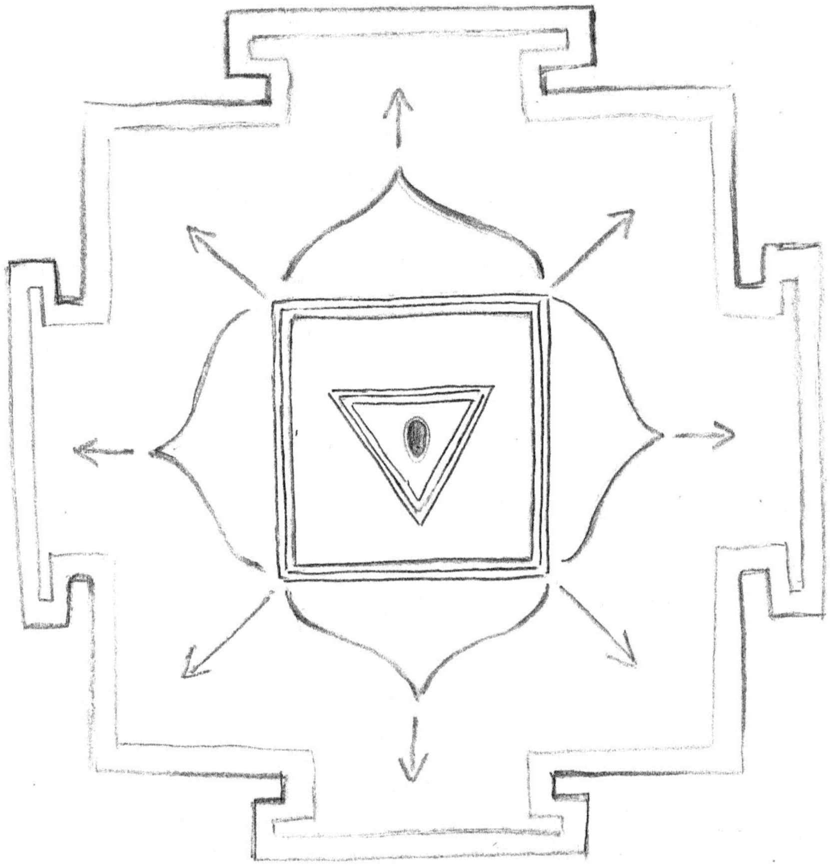

MŪLĀDHĀRA

Now we come to the adhara lotus. It is attached to the mouth of the suṣumnā and is placed below the genitals and above the anus. It has four petals of crimson hue. Its head (mouth) hangs downwards. On its petals are the four syllables from Va to Sa, of the shining colour of gold. In this lotus is the square region of earth, surrounded by eight shining spears. It is of a shining yellow colour and beautiful like lightning, as is also the bīja of dhāra (Laṃ) which is within.

Ṣaṭ-Cakra-Nirūpaṇa

SEAT OF THE BEGINNING

This centre is considered to be the base of existence. It is an expression of the manifestation, and limitations, of being itself. It is the seat of the sleep of both human consciousness and Kuṇḍalinī. In this way it can be viewed as the seat of unconsciousness, or non-consciousness.

Just as matter is the ultimate unconscious, *mūlādhāra* must therefore be the seat of matter itself, the seat of all physical and bodily existence. For this reason, *mūlādhāra* is said to be the expression of *anamaya kośa*. *Mūlādhāra* is the early development of life. From the viewpoint of both evolution as a whole and the life of a single human, it is the early stage of life. The power of *mūlādhāra* governs human needs and controls its actions from birth onwards.

The energy of *mūlādhāra* creates those needs which secure a direct building of the human body and its base for existence. These include the requirements for territory or a home, for warmth and comfort, for food and nourishment, and for predictability (which is to say security).

One could easily overlook *mūlādhāra's* tremendous importance for yoga if viewed from this perspective alone. *Mūlādhāra* is also the seat of *apāna*, *prāṇa*, and *mūlabandha*, which play vital roles in awakening and guiding Kuṇḍalinī. The purity of *mūlādhāra*, and the control of its energies, is therefore essential to the rise of consciousness due to its inseparable dependency on the strength and purity of this centre

CHARACTERISTICS

Balanced	Strong, well-built body. Good blood circulation and sleep patterns. Easy and healthy excretion. Simple-minded, linear thinking, avoidance of non-constructive thoughts. Avoidance of unnecessary actions. Acceptance of existence and its limitations, as well as suffering. Feelings of security. Great power.
Unbalanced	Obesity, signs of bodily pollution. Difficulties in excreting healthily, and establishing bodily rhythms of eating, working, and sleeping. Unrestful sleep and lethargy. Unnecessary actions and movements. Panic. Strong fear of death. Bodily weakness.
Meaning	Root, support
Mantra	*Oṃ pṛthvī namaḥ*
Element *bīja*	Laṃ, earth
Age	0–7 Years
Anatomy	The lower end of suṣumnā. For women – at the cervix, the inner end of the vagina. For men – half-way between the anus and genitals at the perineum.
Symbolism	A lotus of four pedals, a yellow square

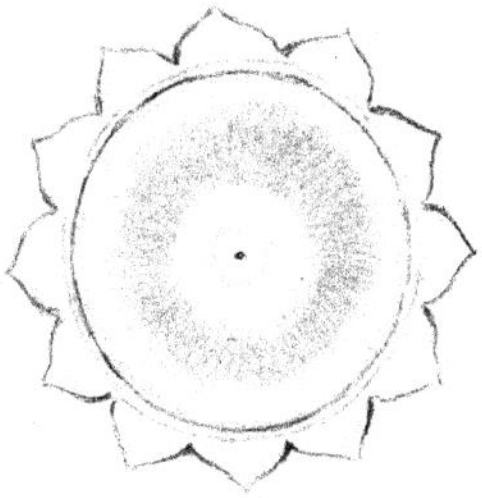

SVĀDHIṢṬHĀNA

There is another lotus placed inside the suṣumnā at the root of the genitals, of a beautiful vermilion colour. On its six petals are the syllables Ba, Bha, Ma, Ya, Ra, La with the bindu superposed, of the shining colour of lightening

Ṣaṭ-Cakra-Nirūpaṇa

SEAT OF DESIRE

Svādhiṣṭhāna, meaning one's own seat, is where one can identify with feeling. A person is essentially comprised of the feelings they attach to. When deeply considered, a feeling is that which qualifies your state of being. As such, *svādhiṣṭhāna* is the seat of the quality of being. These qualities, whether good or bad, create in their entirety 'a flavour' of self-experience. The self becomes good, bad, afraid, secure, joyful, great, or inferior. Consequently, *svādhiṣṭhāna* is known as the seat of the self, as the self becomes perceivable though its qualities of feeling.

Prāṇa, the universal carrier of experience, serves to transmit quality. Being the seat of this quality, *svādhiṣṭhāna* must therefore be the seat of *prāṇa*. It thus follows that *svādhiṣṭhāna* is the seat of *prāṇāmaya kośa*. The *Taittirīya Upaniṣhad* (II–2–1) states that *prāṇāmaya kośa* is the soul (which is filled) of the physical body. In this sense, *prāṇa* governs the body in much the same way as the force of vitality gives dead matter life. It is not the existence of the physical which depends on *prāṇa* as such, but health, vitality, and actuality.

Furthermore, the nature of *prāṇa* is movement, growth, and decay. Procreation is an expression of this creativity that is held in balance with death. For every death there must be one birth in order to retain life's balance. The nature of life, therefore, pushes the self (bound in *svādhiṣṭhāna*) into procreation, sexual desire, bondage, and death. This bondage – expressed in desires – colours the world according to its quality. The world is seen through the lens of its feelings rather than its objective appearance. This phenomenon of not seeing the world for what it is is called ignorance. *Svādhiṣṭhāna* is therefore the seat of primary ignorance or illusion.

CHARACTERISTICS

Balanced	Vitality, actuality, effective immunity. Sexual potency. Charismatic and energetic. Balanced emotions, the ability to let go and adapt. Resistance to resistance.
Unbalanced	Weak immune system, sickness of body, confusion, sexual perversions. Strong emotional affections. Weakness of emotional strength, dependency. Irresponsibility, no resistance to hostile environments. Exhaustion.
Meaning	One's own seat
Mantra	*Oṃ samudrai namaḥ*
Element *bīja*	Vaṃ, water (*āpas*)
Age	7–14 Years
Anatomy	Located in the central axis of the pelvis. The Bihar School of Yoga depicts its temple or location (*kṣētraṁ*) as being four fingers in width below the navel. Some say it is the pubic bone.
Symbolism	A lotus of six petals, a thin silver moon

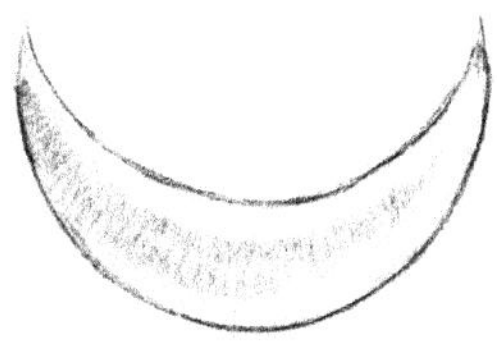

MAṆIPŪRA

The chakra in the sphere of the navel is called maṇipūraka (house of gems), since the body is pierced through by vāyu (prāṇa) like gems by a string. The jīva urged to actions by its past virtuous and sinful karmas whirls around in this great chakra of twelve spokes, as long as it does not grasp the truth.

Dhyānabindhu Upaniṣad (48–50)

SEAT OF POWER

Maṇipūra, meaning house of crystal, is thought to be the centre of self-empowerment. It is the force that rises from the sea of desire, sorrow, and blind affections that exists in the lower centres. The old adage states that knowledge is power. This is true, insofar as power is the force that enables action, but action is fruitless without the proper knowledge of its performance. This is why 'know-how' is essentially the power to do. As *maṇipūra* is understood as the knowledge of action, it must be related to *mānas*, the sensual mind. Indeed, *maṇipūra* is considered the seat of *manomaya kośa* – the layer of mind.

The actions of the self may be driven by desires, but they are directed by goals and visions. As the mind, *maṇipūra* generates these self-same goals and visions that anticipate results or states of being. Being able to clearly visualise an aim implies an awareness of the strength needed to withstand the desires that appear as obstacles to achievement. The directed mind is, by its very nature, self-controlled and disciplined as, without this quality, no goal would be attainable. This also serves to explain *maṇipūra's* elevating nature. *Maṇipūra*, being control and discipline, is therefore the foundation for the type of sustained personality impossible to achieve when one is driven by pleasure or the absence of pain. Yoga requires a strong *maṇipūra* and yogic schools, such as Kundalini, greatly emphasise this.

Maṇipūra is the storehouse of visions of self. Visions of being a doctor, a revolutionary, a successful businessman, or an unsuccessful father, exist in contrast to what they are not. For instance, a good revolutionary cannot simultaneously be a good police officer. This shows that, whatever vision the self attaches to, it will find itself in conflict with something else. Every 'yes' on the level of *maṇipūra* becomes a 'no' to something else. The sensual mind is dividing, separating, and judging. It will both achieve and fail. Its power depends on its success and its failure results in its death. The self is therefore bound in its past decisions and karmas. It is a slave to itself.

CHARACTERISTICS

Balanced	Willpower, concentration, clear vision of one's position and future. Action oriented thinking, ease in decision making and action. Activity and health. Full control over one's body. Full understanding of ones bodily and emotional needs. Healthy skin, easy digestion, strong metabolism, balanced weight.
Unbalanced	Weakness of will, mind, and focus. Difficulty in establishing a personality, inclination to drug abuse. Laziness of mind and action. Nervous disposition. Unclear thoughts and irrational actions. Unstable metabolism, underweight. Aggression. Digestive pain and problems. Inflammatory diseases. Skin problems.
Meaning	House of crystal
Mantra	*Oṃ agni namaḥ*
Element *Bīja*	Raṃ, fire (*agni*)
Age:	14–21 Years
Anatomy	Situated in the central axis behind the navel. The Bihar School depicts its location at the navel.

Symbolism: A lotus of 10 petals, a downward pointing triangle that is radiant like the rising sun.

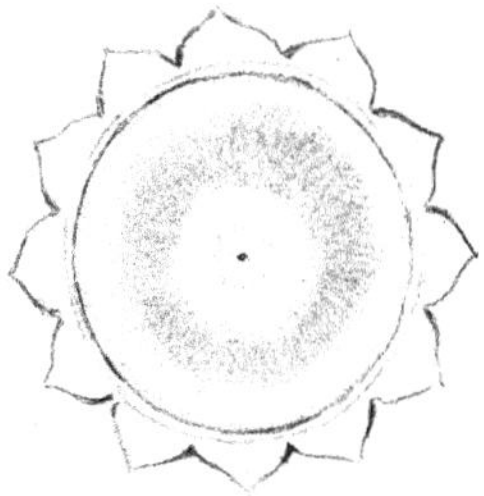

ॐ

ANĀHATA

When one listens to sound in the heart, that is just like a rushing river, without beginning or end, this one will take a bath in that sound that is one with God (śabda-brahmaṇi) and will enter the highest state.

Vijñāna-Bhairava-Tantra (38)

THE PLACE IN THE MIDDLE

Anāhata, meaning unstruck or unbeaten, refers to that which exists without a cause – just like the sound of one hand clapping. While the energy of *maṇipūra* is radiant due to its achievement, *anāhata* in contrast, exists simply because it has always done so. Existence manifests itself first as a point (*bindu*) and then as *nāda* (primary sound). *Anāhata* is that place in which *nāda* can be perceived as *nāda anāhata* (the sound of the heart). This sound has neither beginning nor end. It is a mirror of the divine. This sound is Oṃ, the *unstruck* sound that is the inner mantra of the heart.

This *nāda anāhata*, or Oṃ, is *Śabda-brahman*, the divine in sonic form. Brahman, the divine, is the actual nature of *ātman*, the individual soul. Due to this oneness of *ātman* and Brahman, *ātman* itself resides in the heart and burns there as a smokeless eternal flame. She, the flame, is called *akhaṇḍa jyoti* and burns without beginning or end. She has four rays of light and is the true self.

That which has no end cannot be defeated. It cannot be taken away or generated. It simply exists unconditionally. This is the source of unconditional love that shines onto the world regardless of who steps into her light. This unconditional energy is the source of beauty that radiates from the world and lives in all beings. *Anāhata* is governed by air and its nature is expansion. Due to this expansion, it is in constant contact with the world and shares in common with all things the unstruck sound in their hearts. This intimate connection with the world reveals the innermost nature of all things to those who open their hearts. Suffering is thus seen as suffering and joy as joy, and natural compassion is birthed as the heart mirrors all of the pain and joy that it shares with the world. The beauty of this is that the individual being cannot be ignorant of the world's suffering as it is also one's own pain. A deep desire to end suffering, both for oneself and for all, naturally arises.

Anāhata is also the seat of *vijñānamaya kōśa*, the body formed of knowledge. This knowledge is distinct from the kind generated by *mānas* and experience. *Vijñāna* (meaning consciousness or discernment) refers to the knowledge that results from a state of awareness. It is the sum of all true knowledge one possesses about reality itself. *Vijñāna* as consciousness is no more than the assumptions one proposes about the nature of reality (e.g., that the world is a place to give love or acquire wealth). In terms of personality, this knowledge crystallises as moral guidelines or religious convictions. It is here where all deep structures of belief lie and where certain convictions about the nature of the divine and reality guide one's own path. Consequently, *anāhata* is considered the place in which the individual forms an intimate picture of the divine.

Furthermore, if *anāhata* is where the deepest convictions and beliefs reside, it must also house destiny seeing as one's deepest beliefs must come true. It is said that there is a beautiful garden in *anāhata*. At its centre is a lake, in the middle of which is a mystical island. The *kalpataru*, the wish fulfilling tree, is on that island. It is this tree that grows the fruits of one's deepest wishes for one's enjoyment and suffering. That which is in one's heart is destined to become true. Be wary of which wishes you carry there.

CHARACTERISTICS

Balanced	Joy, openness, clear and open speech, high creativity, knowledge of the deeper meaning of reality, appreciation for the beauty of living and dying. Compassion. Willingness to trust. Strong breathing, long life and vitality into old age.
Unbalanced	Cruelty, nihilism, totalitarian tendencies, arrogance, small-mindedness, difficulty to open to new possibilities. Doubt in others. Shallow or irregular breathing. Short lifespan. Heart complications.

Meaning	The unstruck, unbeaten
Mantra	*Oṃ vāyu namaḥ, oṃ*
Element *bīja*	Yaṃ, air
Age	21–28 Years
Anatomy	In the middle of the central vertical axis (*suṣumnā*). In the centre of the chest. The Bihar school depicts its *kṣētraṁ* in front of the body on the ribcage.
Symbolism	A lotus of 12 petals, two interlaced triangles, a flame without smoke.

VIŚUDDHA

He who always contemplates it, is truly the lord of the yogis, and deserves to be called wise; by the meditation of this viśuddha lotus, the yogi at once understands the four Vedas with their mysteries (...). Even if, by chance, the mind of the yogi is absorbed in this place, then he becomes unconscious of the external world, and enjoys certainly the inner world.

Śiva Saṃhitā (5:92–93)

THE CROWN OF THE WORLD

Viśuddha, meaning purity, is the place where one may rest when the being has been transformed by the power of the heart. Just as the light of the soul that shines from the heart is superior to this world and is the gateway to what lies above, *viśuddha* itself is a state of elevated existence that surpasses human mundanity. To understand purity, one must first understand its opposite. Impure is that which is accompanied by what it is not. Similarly, an impure action is one accompanied by an intention that contradicts (or perverts) either the goal or the essential nature of the agent performing it. Since the presence of a contradictory force in an action will hinder its positive outcome, the impurity itself can be considered a hindrance. When impurity and hindrance are so inextricably linked, purity must therefore mean an absence of that which hinders. Understanding this, the nature of *viśuddha* as that energy that can unfold itself in the absence of any hindrance becomes clear.

Viśuddha is governed by the fifth element in which the powers of the other four are included. In this way, living through the energy of *viśuddha* means to possess power over the elements, and therefore power over the world in its entirety. *Maṇipūra*, in contrast, signifies the power over the material aspect of the world that is incorporated in the spirit of fire. *Viśuddha* does not master the material world alone. It masters both fire and the mind governed by it. As such, *viśuddha* has mastery over the mind and, consequently, over the self. Once the self is mastered, no obstacle can stand in its way. The only enemy worth fighting is one's self. Once done, the last hindrance to freedom is surpassed and the way to the sky is open.

The consciousness of *viśuddha* allows for that which was previously poisonous to be transformed into a nourishing nectar. Hindrances become opportunities. The sheer power of wisdom enables one to transform what is bad into a new beginning and a greater power. This transformative power of wisdom – something that is typically alien to the ordinary mind – further explains the superior nature of *viśuddha*. Śiva is sometimes called Nīlakaṇṭha the Blue Throated One, which refers to his capacity to swallow the greatest poison and transform it into personal wisdom.

Viśuddha is the seat of one's own vibration which one sends out into the world. The development of *viśuddha* allows this vibration to become an expression of one's mastery over existence. Physically, this vibration refers to one's voice and the tone at which it is emitted. The more purified the ether, and the greater *viśuddha's* presence, the clearer the voice. A person with a present *viśuddha* says what they mean and does what they say. There is complete synchronicity between thought, word, and deed. This is the source of integrity.

Imagine the life that you would truly want to live. One where doubt and fear are instead replaced by knowledge and freedom from your own shackles, and where you can act and live freely from the bottom of your heart in integrity and strength. This is purity, this is *viśuddha*.

CHARACTERISTICS

Active	Character, strength, integrity, intelligence, responsibility, and coherence of thought, speech, and action. Honesty and heartfulness. Well-established in life. Stable metabolism, stable mind, silent mind.
Meaning	Purity
Mantra:	*Oṃ ākāśai namaḥ*

Element *Bīja*:	Haṃ, space
Age:	28–35 Years
Anatomy:	In the central vertical axis behind the pit of the throat .The Bihar School depicts its location on top of the throat pit.
Symbolism:	A golden, or grey, lotus of 16 petals, a silvery disk, a white elephant.

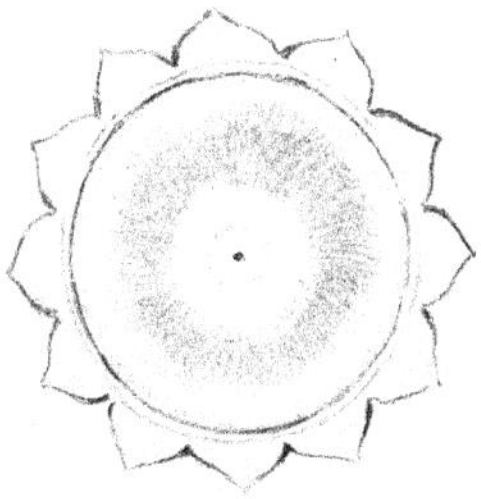

ĀJÑĀ

The lotus named ājñā is like the beautifully white moon. On its two petals are the syllables Ha and Kṣa, which are also white and enhance its beauty. It shines with the glory of meditation.

Ṣaṭ-Cakra-Nirūpaṇa

THE ENDLESS MYSTERY

Ājñā is not only the command, but also its place. The place of unity where one's own will and that of the world become one. When one's will and the world find mutual balance, knowledge of one's own path becomes clearly visible. This awareness on how to live and act is the way of the divine and, in a sense, the divine's commandment. It is divine will within all. *Ājñā* is a state of great trance from which the supreme void – the cause of all existence – as the source of all can be seen. From this void one can see that surpasses all, because it is the edge to that which expands beyond the limited self. It is also a trance, because it is a joyful dance between the form and formless, between what is and what is not.

Ājñā is described as Vārāṇasī or Benares, the city between India's two holy rivers. These rivers are light and dark, and flow down from the holy mountains. This metaphor describes *iḍā* and *piṅgalā* as the two rivers which flow down from *suṣumnā*, the one mountain. *Ājñā*, being in between, is thus the space free from the influences of *iḍā* (*citta*) and *piṅgalā* (*prāṇa*). Since *iḍā* and *piṅgalā* represent the two forces between which the world and all its elements comes into creation, *ājñā* must be the place superior to the world created by two contrary forces. In this sense, it is the place of the end of duality and its birth.

Since the self can only exist in contrast to what it is not, *ājñā* must also be the end of self as it is the end of duality. Indeed, *rudragranthi* – the last attachment to self – is located between the eyebrows in front of *ājñā*. This place is called *bhrūmadhya*. Through piercing this space, one can open the pathway to oneness with the universal that can only be experienced in the absence of the self.

The world has two paths – one which flows downward and one which flows upward. One is *iḍā*, the nourishing moon which seeks to manifest, and the other is the sun that strives for subtlety. *Ājñā* is both of these forces, creation and extinction, because it is the ultimate creative force and not merely the end of creation of the individual. It is the ultimate explosion of everything out of one singular and dimensionless point (*bindu*). This explosion of all is the trancelike ecstasy of *ājñā*, the super sexual joy experienced in prolonged meditation over *ājñā*. Concurrently, *ājñā* is the final oneness of both rivers in conjunction with each other and their final resting point – the reaching of one's own inner way.

CHARACTERISTICS

Active	Joy, knowing the unknown, perceiving the mystery, clairvoyance, ecstasy, indifference to all. Spontaneous meditation.
Meaning	The command
Mantra	*Oṃ, Oṃ mahālakṣmī namaḥ*
Element *bīja*	Energy (Haṃ/Kṣaṃ)
Age	35–42 Years
Anatomy	Behind the eyebrows in the centre of the scull/pituitary gland. Also called *bruhmadya*.
Symbolism	A white lotus of two petals, a grey disk, a black *liṅga*.

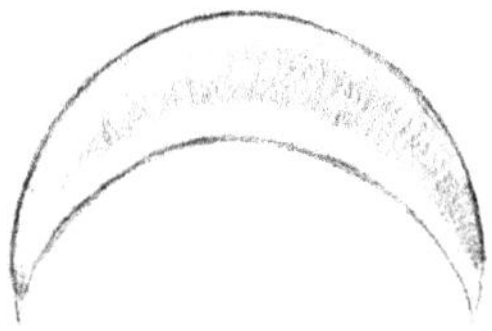

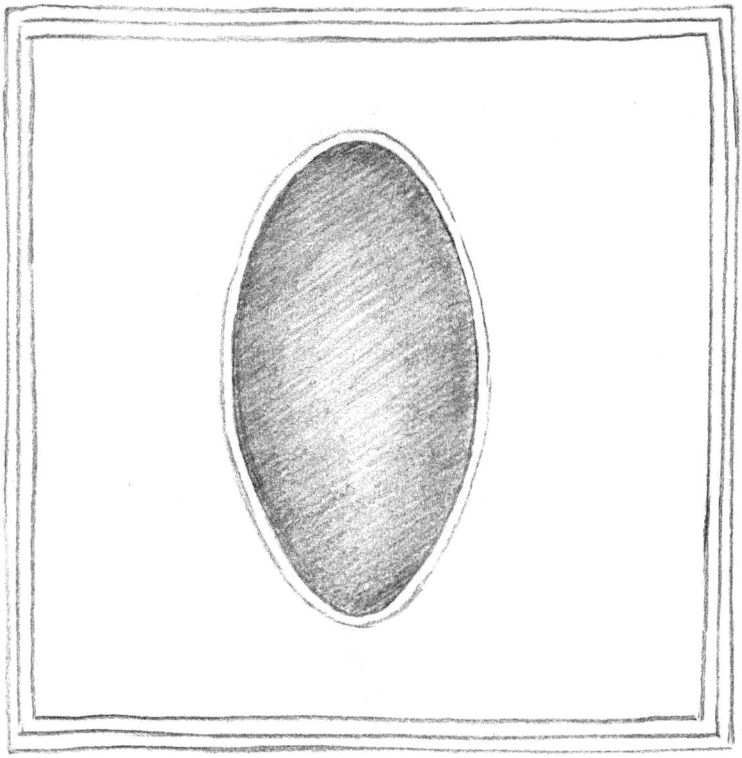

SAHASRĀRA

Within her is the everlasting place called the abode of Śiva which is time and space less, which is free from māyā (illusion), attainable only by Yogis, and known by the name of Nityananda (always in bliss). It is replete with every form of bliss and is pure knowledge itself. Some call it the Brahman; others call it the haṃsa. Wise describe it as the abode of Viṣṇu, and righteous men speak of it as the ineffable place of knowledge of the ātma, or the place of liberation.

Ṣaṭ-Cakra-Nirūpaṇa

THE PLACE OF LIBERATION

Just as every beginning has an end, every journey has a destiny. *Sahasrāra* signifies the end of all craving for fulfilment. It is depicted as a state of fullness and oneness with the ultimate goal. Patañjali says:

Concentration locks consciousness on a single object. This is called dhāraṇā. When absorpted, the entire perceptual flow is aligned with that object. This is dhyāna. When only the essential nature of the object shines forth, as if formless, samādhi has arisen.

Yoga-Sūtras (3:1–3)

The capacity for controlling the mind for the sake of meditation is known as the power of *viśuddha*. However, the alignment (or oneness) with the object of meditation can instead be assigned to *ājñā*, as it is precisely that oneness that dissolves the limited self, allowing for greater expansion. According to Patañjali, *samādhi* is the mystical stage that follows this complete alignment with the object of meditation. This is the last of the yoga's eight limbs, and so signifies the highest stage of yogic evolution. *Sahasrāra* also refers to this highest spiritual state. Through its contemplation, one can see that the opening of *sahasrāra* is nothing else than gaining entry into the state of *samādhi*.

In yogic philosophy, the spatial and temporal world stems from the emptiness that creates all forms by means of *māyā* (illusion, or *śakti*). This energy (*śakti*) sleeps in *mūlādhāra* and, once awakened, reverts to the source from which she came. *Sahasrāra*, being outside of time and space (and is therefore emptiness), is the state which is the original source of being. As such, Śakti finds her resting place in *sahasrāra*, as the place of final marriage between energy and its greatest expansion, namely consciousness.

Sahasrāra can also be understood as the complementary and opposite energy to *mūlādhāra*. *Mūlādhāra* expresses one's nature as matter. One of the clearest qualities of matter is its temporal and spatial limitation. *Mūlādhāra* also signifies one's life as being born and with form. *Sahasrāra*, as its opposite, must therefore be that which is timeless and without space, that which is without both limitations and form. Therefore *sahasrāra* must be death and the unborn state, the state of transcendence.

CHARACTERISTICS

Active	Silence
Meaning	Thousandfold
Mantra	*Oṃ śrī ma, Oṃ mahāsarasvatī namaḥ*
Element *bīja*	*Śrī, Oṃ* consciousness/void
Age:	42–48 Years
Anatomy	Over the top of the head.
Symbolism	A lotus of 1,000 petals, a radiant white *liṅga*.

INTERACTIONS BETWEEN THE CHAKRAS

In this body, Mount Meru is surrounded by seven islands; there are rivers, seas, mountains, fields; and lords of the fields too. There are seers and sages; all the stars and planets as well. There are sacred pilgrimages, shrines; and presiding deities of the shrines. The sun and moon, agents of creation and destruction, also move in it. Ether, air, water and earth are also there. All the beings that exist in the three worlds are also to be found in the body; surrounding Meru they are engaged in their respective functions.

Śiva Saṃhitā (2:1–4)

PROGRESSIVE INTERACTION

The energy of the chakras is hierarchical. This means that the higher centres incorporate and dominate the lower. However, this also means that the higher centres draw their power from the lower. There is a successive chain of dependence from high to low. *Mūlādhāra*, for example, provides the basis for *svādhiṣṭhāna*, just as a well-built and healthy physical body lays the foundations for vitality and movement. There can be no constructive desire in life when basic physical security is not ensured. Similarly, *svādhiṣṭhāna* is the base of *maṇipūra*, as the development of ideas and goals depends on the underlying creative enthusiasm. Were this to be absent, all goals would seem vain, and building up a personality to achieve these goals would appear useless. Furthermore, *maṇipūra's* strength forms the base of love.

The transformative power of the heart is the base for purity, which in turn is the base for absorption into the one power. *Dhyāna* is the base of *samādhi*.

PARĀ AND APARĀ

As mentioned earlier, the yogic perspective views the world as having been caused by a manifestation of divine forces comprised of unchangeable and eternal principles. The process of manifestation brings these principles into being, which consequently deprives them of their eternal nature, but which leaves the underlying principle visible.

For example, Śiva and Śakti are understood as the two causes of the visible universe. They are consciousness and its energy which, through their unity, exploded all things into being. As a manifestation of their cooperation, men and women came into existence, thereby expressing the fundamental duality required to create existence. This duality is mirrored in the sun and moon, life and death.

That which is unmanifested and the very self of all beings is called *parā*, whereas that which is manifested is called *aparā*. These two can be understood as pure and supreme *parā*, and the impure and transient *aparā*. *Parā* is the will to exist (*icchā śakti*), and in this way the self. *Aparā* is the manifest world and with it the power of self-expression and action (*kriyā śakti*).

Similarly, the lower chakras are called *aparā* because they correspond to the consciousness captured in the limited, but enabling action and existence. The higher chakras are called *parā* because they correspond to the consciousness that aims for self-awareness and liberation. In between these two resides the heart, the seat of *vijñānamaya kośa* and the power of knowledge (*jñāna śakti*), the place where right insight into the nature of life can take place.

Since *parā* gives birth to *aparā*, the higher chakras give birth to the ones below. The higher and the lower are a mirror of another. The pure and impure form one eternal being. They are one and the same.

THE MIRROR

Mūlādhāra, the basis for life in limitation, must be the manifestation of that which forms the basis for being. *Mūlādhāra* is therefore considered to be the lower *sahasrāra* (the seat of formless and limitless existence). As such, *mūlādhāra* is birth and *sahasrāra* is death. Their relationship is as intimate as it is obvious.

Svādhiṣṭhāna is the seat of the desire to create, and the attachment to joy and pleasure. Its pure form must therefore be eternal creation and limitless joy. These qualities apply to *ājñā*, the central point at which the two rivers meet and the place of universal creation.

Maṇipūra is the will to dominate, the desire to have power over the world, and the wish to elevate oneself to a place of victory or completion. *Viśuddha*, in contrast, is power over the world by means of power over the self. It is the domination of ignorance, and the fullness, completion, strength, and serenity of one's own being.

Anāhata resides in between the two triangles. One face of this great chakra looks down into limitation, while the other gazes up towards freedom. *Anāhata* is the power of true knowledge (*jñāna śakti*) that can discriminate between what is liberation and what is darkness. The gateway between the higher and the lower. Everyone must pass through this door if they want to enjoy the fruits which are free from sorrow.

THE TRANSFORMATION

The purpose of *haṭha* and Kundalini Yoga is to activate and purify the energies of the lower chakras in order to transform them into their higher forms. The sages taught us that freedom from mind and body can be attained by their purification, thus allowing the qualities of the higher chakras to shine through. Almost all exercises in the lower stages of Hatha Yoga work with this principle.

Āsana focuses predominantly on the purification of the body so as to achieve freedom from it. *Prāṇāyāma* purifies the *prāṇa* so one can be free from sickness and enjoy the pleasures of being without limitation. *Dhāraṇā* purifies the mind and leads to mastery over it. *Yamas* and *niymas* strive for the transformation of the three lower chakras.

Svāmī-jī once told me:

> *The higher chakras are like the top of the mountain, frozen in ice, when the fire of the lower centres burns strong because they are purified, then the ice can melt and awakening takes place.*
>
> *Svāmī-jī Vidyānand*

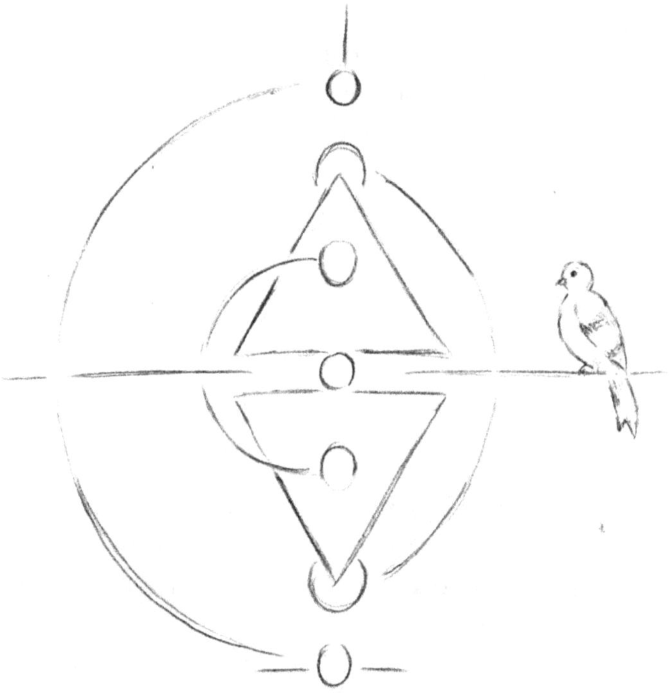

WHAT YOU SHOULD KNOW ABOUT THE CHAKRAS

Nothing.

The chakras are mystical centres. Both their function and reality exist within the realm of the mystical. They are, but they live in our experience and not in our words. They cannot be fully described or understood, as is the case with objects within reality.

Imagine trying to explain what it means to see to a man who has never opened his eyes. You would tell him of every colour and shape, shadows and tricks of the of light. This may well amuse him, but it would be a pointless exercise. As the wonder of sight stems only from its direct experience and the information about reality that one can extract from it, it would be infinitely more useful and enjoyable to simply open one's eyes and experience. Do not think or try to understand. Understand once you have experienced. You should meditate or work on the chakras simply because they are gateways to the world that lies beyond. You need willpower and persistence – that is all there is to it.

This is why you should know nothing. Forget everything you have learned and everything I have told you. Just live the mystical experience and be. Turn yourself into an empty vessel so that you can be filled. The world is vast, and full of many delicious waters which wish to fill you. Don't be afraid.

By dissolving away the mind in the end of the twelve (any chakra, twelve fingers apart) of one's own body. In all respects, the goal which is the one ultimate reality manifests well established for the adept whose mind is thus made firm and unwavering. One should cast one's mind into the end of the twelve in any way and wherever one may be in every moment, so for one whose normal mental activity has ceased by this practice, he experiences an extraordinary state of consciousness within a few days.

Vijñāna-Bhairava-Tantra (50–51)

WESTERN ANATOMY OF THE HUMAN BODY

THE MUSCULAR SYSTEM

The muscular system is strongly regenerative. Proper training at all ages can help build it. A muscle can only contract, not actively stretch. Consequently, intense strength training will always shorten the muscle. To achieve strength while avoiding this shortness, the yogi must stretch his muscles in equal proportion to the application of strength. Every tension must be followed by an active stretch. This is not to say that strength is unimportant. Indeed, it can build willpower and clarity of mind. When muscles are properly tuned and flexible, the body can be massaged from the inside, and toxins and waste can be more easily discarded. When the muscles are stiff or weak, the body will become lifeless and poisoned, and the mind weak and clouded.

What helps

Āsana, sports, and stretching. Stretching should last longer than two minutes, but should not be forceful. Three to four weekly sessions should be sufficient. It is advisable not to undertake strenuous *āsana* on a daily basis. Instead, one should take day to rest after a strong practice. Heavy physical labour is unnecessary for progress and could be seen as an expression of a mental disturbance. In short, maintain a balance between calmness and action.

THE SKELETAL SYSTEM

The skeletal system can be divided into bones and their joints.

The bones themselves require little yogic attention – every student ought to already know if their bones are weak or strong. Usually, even strong yoga practice cannot harm a bone that is normally constituted. Practicing excessively, however, and not giving the body time for regenerative rest can lead to weak bones. This phenomenon is well known. Be mindful that physical practice is a means for yoga, not a means for itself. This way, excessive physical practice becomes obsolete.

The joints are more sensitive and require special care. The cartilage that forms the surface inside the joints is sensitive and, unlike muscle, not very regenerative. Harmful forms of stress inside the joint lead to the slow, and irreversible, degeneration of this sensitive structure. This degeneration is typically discovered too late – the joint does not usually inflame even under stress. As such, care is required.

Harmful forms of stress in the joint include:

- Abnormal axis of pressure at the joint (incorrect knee rotation).
- Fast movements under high physical pressure (e.g., power yoga, professional dancing).
- Shockwaves of pressure on the joint (e.g., martial arts or combat sports).

What helps

Resting and times of repose after physical activity. Soft smooth movements can be highly beneficial. Movements made under pressure must be slow. No beating of the body. While we should do our best to be helpful, never stop children from playing in their rough and tumble fashion.

THE ENDOCRINE SYSTEM

The endocrine system is distributed throughout the body. It is the expression of the body's interaction with the demands of the world. Inner and outer activity, as well as stress and rest, are all influences mirrored in the activity of hormones. Hormones regulate growth, tiredness, wakefulness, hunger, rhythms of waking, sleeping, acting, stress and fear, release and calmness, attachments and love, and the activities of the immune system and metabolism.

What helps

The endocrine system is positively influenced by constructive decisions. Life very much depends on what you aim for. You have nothing to fear when you live for the right goals. When you take the right actions, no stress will torment you. What more can you do than act in the right way? *Yamas*, *niyamas*, and sleep.

THE NERVOUS SYSTEM

The nervous system is where experience is generated, memory created, and the world controlled. *Buddhi* (intellect), *ahaṃkāra* (ego), and *mānas* (the sensual mind) are created by our extraordinary nervous systems. *Sāṃkhya* identifies it with *prakṛti*. *Prakṛti* is nature, and the nervous system is a creation of nature.

The brain is the nervous system's most powerful structure. The brain is twofold: one hemisphere is adapted to the old – it likes to look backward – while the other hemisphere is suited to the new – it always looks forward. Much like our political affiliations, the first is located on the right, while the second is to the left. One enjoys historical biographies, the other likes to read science fiction. One is the known world, the other is that which is unknown.

The nervous system is naturally healthy when the old and the new are in harmonious balance. The thin line between them is where profound learning and growth can occur. Our nervous system has evolved in a more or less continuous surrounding. As such, we grieve for the stimulation of the new because we believe deep within us that it is rare. We are designed for a largely unchanging world in which novelty is a special gift.

Today we live in a world of constant change, the significance of the old begins to fade. We are overstimulated by change, excited by its magic. Change creates instinctive excitement, which could be seen as the body's reaction to facilitate learning. For instance, we all know the exhilaration that comes with a first kiss or the fresh smell of a newly-visited foreign country. However, excitement is not synonymous with good. Productive living is only possible in long-term decisions and in a deep understanding of the world one lives in – an understanding impossible to achieve under rapidly changing circumstances. The nervous system will remain in an addictive state of excitement in the face of the new, while profound understanding will be challenging. Relationships stay superficial if they are too frequently changed. Inner peace is hard to gain when the demands of the world are uncertain.

In these times, health of feeling and thought can be established when an unchanging surrounding is created. This situation will place the overstimulated mind into a state similar to that of chemical withdrawal. This state however, is the base for one's healthy development in long lasting creativity, profound strength of thought, and happiness.

What helps

Clear and unchanging rhythms of sleep and waking. Clear rhythms of eating and acting. Unchanging social surroundings with a few important close friends. Stable relationships. If these guidelines are respected, one will be amazed by how clear and creative the mind will become.

THE DIGESTIVE SYSTEM

The digestive system is awe-inspiring. Eons ago – quite possibly at the beginning of multi-cellular life – the body learned that it could not protect itself against microbes by simply excluding them from its system. It understood that it was vastly outnumbered by the staggering volume of different bacteria, protozoa, and mushrooms which surrounded it. The body realised that creating a symbiotic and friendly relationship with them would be more effective than maintaining an antagonistic stance. As such, the body decided to settle them inside its most sensitive area so as to gain their protection. This was an extraordinarily smart move.

Today, the human intestine is colonised by an astonishing 100 trillion symbiotic bacteria. This makes up a mass of between half and one kilogram (or, three pounds) of live bacteria in an adult's intestine. The most important are the lactose bacteria planted in the human intestine from the milk of the mother. There are several others that appear only in the human intestine and are not found anywhere else in the nature. They are absolutely human exclusive symbionts.

The diversity and strength of this microbiome is said to:

Create a healthy metabolism. Protect against excessive weight. Protect against anxiety and depression. Protect against allergies and chronic sickness.

These microbes, along with the body, have adapted to human food. The food they need to be strong is in parts as ancient as their relationship to the human body. Therefore, altered or synthetic food harms both the microbes and the human body.

What helps

Massage the intestines with proper movement, walking, and *āsana*. This will help its self-purification. Eat only unaltered natural food, nothing synthetic (vegan or otherwise), and no over-sugared food. When you eat: leave one third of the stomach empty; fill one third with water and one third with food.

THE IMMUNE SYSTEM

The immune system is closely related to the digestive system. This is partly due to the microbes in the intestine stimulating, and strongly interacting with, the immune system. If the immune system is weak, microbe communities can become toxic for the body. Toxic communities can simultaneously weaken and irritate the immune system. The first and most important interaction of the immune system with its surroundings is its relation to the intestine.

The immune system is special in a multitude of ways. As with the nervous system, the immune system can act on memories created through experience. The immune system memorises all substances and microbes it ever encounters. It knows them by their actions and understands whether they pose a potential threat. Whenever anything organic enters the body, through the skin or lungs for example, the immune system must not only know what it is, but how to deal with it. Many of these responses were learned long ago. These memories are written in our genetic code and can be traced back to the beginning of life. The immune system thus has a highly intimate relationship to all life. It knows all kinds of microbes in the water, soil, and air. This relationship is so ancient that it is difficult for us to comprehend. The immune system needs playful interaction with these well-known microbes to grow healthy. Children raised in farmhouses, where they are exposed to dust, animals and nature, develop a far stronger and calmer immune system than those raised in scrupulously clean environments.

If the immune system is exposed to situations misaligned with its evolutionary programming, such as a sterile city house, it will become agitated and start to build unnecessary defences against plants, animals, or even its own body. These overreactions of the immune system are an expression of its inability to interpret synthetic environments. Allergies may be frequent in our world, yet they are virtually unknown in agricultural societies. This can be understood when we grasp that the immune system needs these other organisms – they are vital to us.

The immune system's learning process, when it is most vulnerable to irritating influences, occurs in childhood. Children, more than others, should eat natural food, be exposed to country air, play in the mud, and drink from the river. Interestingly, this is exactly what they do if unconstrained by their parents.

It has been proven, even for adults, that a simple walk in the forest or a bath in the river is as stimulating for the immune system as doctor-guided ozone therapy.

What helps

Stand up early in the morning and walk up the mountain on a sunny day. Swim in a lake, a river, or the sea. Take a cold shower in a waterfall. Walk for hours in the forest. Play like crazy with a wet dog. Expose the body to nature and the life that is within.

THE RESPIRATORY SYSTEM

The respiratory system is crucial to your overall health and energy. Breath is life and the better one can breathe, the more alive one will feel and be. Shallow breath is a sign of weakness whereas deep breathing is a sign of strength and life.

The lungs are sensitive organs, though they have a remarkable ability to clean themselves (millions of tiny hairs - the cilia move the dirt out of lungs on a daily basis). The biggest danger for lungs is infection. For instance, a dangerous bacterial infection can rapidly lead to death. As such, the body has developed many protective habits and layers around the lungs to ensure their function and protect their integrity.

The most important protection for the lungs and the overall body's vitality is the correct breathing process itself.

Breathing through the nose humidifies air which enables the lungs to retain liquid. It also warms the air so that the lungs maintain their ideal temperature. When air passes through the nose, dust particles in the air are removed before entering the sensitive bronchial area. The nose inhibits fast breathing because less air can rush into the lungs – the channel is smaller, which reduces the speed of breath. Since the body cannot receive large amounts of air rapidly, it must breathe more deeply so as to increase its own contact surface with the air in the lungs, leading for greater oxygen absorption. This deeper form of breathing increases the lung volume in the long term and allows the body to receive more oxygen, even in moments when breathing through the mouth becomes necessary (such as strenuous physical activity). Moreover, when a greater volume of the lung is used, it becomes better ventilated and bacteria cannot easily rest in untouched pockets.

What helps

Breathing through the nose deepens breathing. This way, the lung can extend its volume, purify its pockets so as to make the body stronger, faster, and generally healthier.

THE REPRODUCTIVE SYSTEM

The reproductive system is highly sensitive in both men and women. Women typically suffer the immunological challenge of keeping their sexual organs free from disease but, generally speaking, they can effectively guard their fertility. This is different for men whose bodies are more sensitive to environmental toxins and whose fertility is less stable. Males have a higher metabolic rate and require more food than females. Moreover, the production of sperm consumes a significant amount of energy, which must be supplied through the environment. These two factors increase male exposure to the environment and the possible absorption of poison. Modern agriculture uses many female hormones to facilitate growth in animals. While these hormones act as poisons to the male body, they leave the female body largely untouched. Many European men suffer breast growth, gaseous bellies, fatty hips, and low sperm counts – all indications of oestrogen intoxication. As men typically avoid speaking of their problems, data on this has been somewhat scarce. Since 1973, sperm-cell density has decreased by 50–60% in European males. It is predicted that most European men will be infertile by 2060. Whoever has not appreciated how truly shocking this fact is should read that sentence again.

Agriculture, air pollution, and plastic additives are responsible for this terrible fact. The desire to appear strong, while being terribly afraid of seeming weak, causes many men to stay silent about this fact and fail to act for their own good.

The human reproductive system is hugely energy intensive. For both men and women, massive amounts of physical and mental energy are spent on ensuring sexual fitness and finding a suitable partner. Some think of nothing other than sexual pleasure, or do only what quantitatively increases their sex lives in the short run. For both men and women, energy conservation and protection is an issue. That said, the issues between men and women differ slightly.

The male body expends much energy in providing liquid and sperm for sexual interaction. Every day a large amount of physical energy is needed to be ready for sex at a moment's notice. The male mind is focused on potential sexual interaction at almost any time of the day. Some men suffer from this condition without realising that they are losing their path and wasting their time pursuing women. The sexually obsessed fail to arrive anywhere meaningful in their lives as their minds are far too preoccupied with gratifying momentary pleasure. Physical and mental depletion is an issue men should be vigilant of.

Women have slightly different issues here. The woman's concern is not to pursue sex like men do. This is because women are the ones who choose and, usually, if women want sex they can have it. This circumstance is entirely different for many men who suffer terribly from never finding a sexual partner. As proof of this fact, every human being has twice as many female than male ancestors.

Women risk infection from numerous sexual diseases that pose smaller risks for men. Frequently occurring urinary infections for women can pose serious health risks connected to sexual interaction. If a woman escapes falling sick, she may fall instead pregnant. The dangers of pregnancy should not be understated, and many women feel forced to depend on a man or society so as to alleviate the great burden of childcare placed on their shoulders. Woman typically must carry the responsibility for children. This explains the meticulousness with which they choose sexual partners, and why security and responsibility are important features in their choice of man.

Nobody neglects the great joy of sex and child-rearing. However, as both men and women profit from regulated sexual interaction, society has always invested a great deal of energy into limiting sexual freedom and protecting the family. The yogic commandment of *brahmacarya* is also an expression of this.

What helps

Simply brought to the point, healthy food ensures sexual potency, helps avoid environmental poisons and purifies the body. Proper exercise, like *āsana* and sports, increase testosterone levels in men and protect against estrogen intoxication.

Sexual self-control and stable relationships make life for women safer and help men realize their full potentials so they can be helpful for women and create a future for themselves and their families.

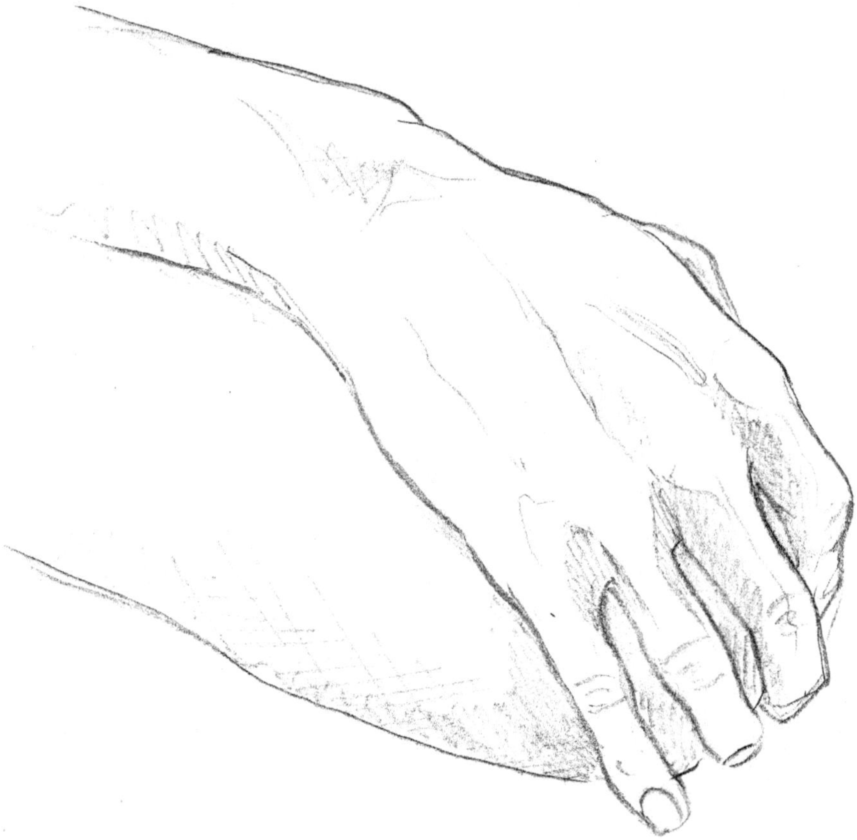

PRACTICE

Practice is the means for experience.

But practice is no means for itself.

Practice is the tree, insight the fruit.

One has to aim to bring forth one's truth.

One should not aim to bring forth the practice.

One should live what he discovers.

One should not live in the practice.

Practice is a means, remember that always.

Yogi Yogrishi

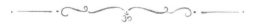

YOUR MEANS

We as teachers have the responsibility to infuse the practice with life. To live what is alive in the practice, and never to practice what is dead. Teaching yoga is no means for spirituality, because spirituality does not live in yoga. It lives in your wakeful being that is performing yoga. You are the soul of the teaching. The teaching is dead without your soul.

You alone.

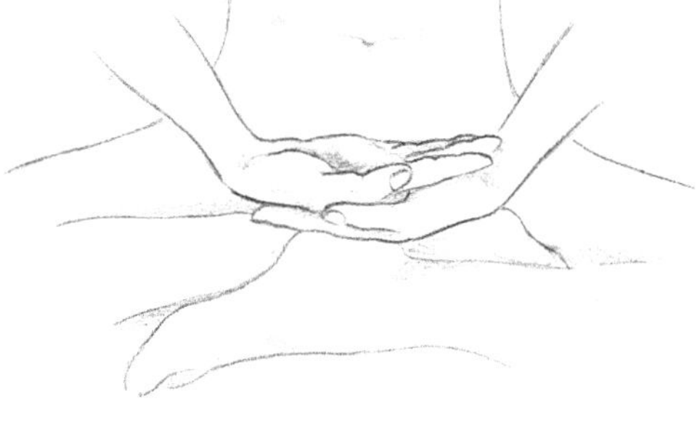

ATTITUDE AND ATTAINMENT IN PRACTICE

> *Then by the penetration that takes place, all the impurity of the universe is destroyed. This is indeed the cessation of māyā whereby the soul, free of māyā becomes like pure gold. The eleven signs of attainment (by means of Kuṇḍalinī) that manifest then are as follows.*
>
> *Trembling, Possession, Shaking, Lucid sleep, Rolling of the eyes as if inebriated, Sensation of ants crawling in the body, Dancing on one limb, Speaking in the Kaula language, Tears bursting forth, Jumping like a deer, Roaring like a lion.*
>
> *Manthana-Bhairava-Tantra (13:100–102)*

I could easily have placed this chapter at the beginning of this book – or anywhere else, for that matter – due to its relevance. We all practice because we want to be successful on the path. There is a certain way and attitude in any practice that brings about success, and there are signs of successful attainment.

Attitude

The most true and all-pervasive characteristic of life is that we cannot comprehend what is beyond our mind's reach. We are limited by the knowledge and implications of our own existence. We are surprised to be alive and will be surprised when we die. We cannot lead ourselves because, individually, we do not know ourselves.

Your eyes see what they see, your ears hear what they hear, and your mind knows what it knows. The world beyond is the truth that cannot be comprehended by the *paśu*, the fettered soul. The world will always be larger than our comprehension. Doubt, the ever-present companion on the path, is the most natural result of not knowing what is beyond the horizon. Doubt cannot be avoided because it is the result of the ignorance of the limited individual self. How could it be otherwise?

However, there is a way. The right initial attitude is that by which you feel profoundly motivated to practice. It is not you who is the willing agent, but rather it is the world through you. Since it is not your will that chose the way, individually you have nothing to worry about. You need neither justify nor doubt. If doubt arises, throw it on the fire of the great consciousness. It is the all-pervasive essence that wills this way through you. Walk each step from the heart. The heart knows, even if the mind does not.

Hindrances to Practice

> *Sickness, apathy, doubt, carelessness, laziness, hedonism (attachment), delusion, lack of progress, and inconstancy are all distractions which, by stirring up consciousness, act as barriers to stillness. When they do, one may experience distress, depression, or the inability to maintain steadiness of posture or breathing.*
>
> *Patañjali-Yoga-Sūtras (1:29–31)*

Many hindrances discovered on the path are due to one's limited nature. These hindrances cannot be avoided, but must be walked through gracefully.

Sickness

Sickness is not a question of fate, but of attitude. Being sick is normal, just like breathing and dying. Being sickly is holding a mindset that withdraws you from the world. One can flee from responsibility by being sick. Children know this all too well.

Apathy

Apathy is one's unwillingness to engage in the demands of the world. It is being dead while being alive. It means to be absent from live. Its root is fear.

Doubt

Doubt is caused by an inability to see one's own situation in the world. You can never know for sure. As knowledge, like the mind, is limited, you must simply surrender.

Carelessness

If you do not care, you cannot love. Resentment is its root. If you are resentful, you are murderous. The good will not come to you.

Laziness

Laziness saps energy. Without energy there can be no belief. Straighten out your intentions, and fight gravity.

Hedonism (Attachment)

Hedonism is one's pain at not being loved and fulfilled by the world. If you are lonely and sad, you will consume as much as you can. Pleasure consumed in this manner is an endless vortex leading to worsening depths. Mind, time, and life will be lost on the way.

Delusion

It is your responsibility to know. It your responsibility to discern. You can see, open your eyes.

Lack of Progress

Progress is not within practice. Progress is within your action inside of practice. You yourself will cause it. Be alert.

Inconstancy

Stay on the path. Where do you go? Sometimes it is best to choose. Choose now.

Signs of Attainment on the Path of Kundalini Yoga

Attainment in kundalini yoga is clearly defined: it is the coming and going of Śakti, who slowly or suddenly transforms the practitioner. The unspoken truth is that true Kundalini Yoga is always a process of ecstatic trance. When the yogi discovers Kuṇḍalinī, he will lose himself in much the same way as one engaging in a passionate relationship. Once the yogi has lost himself with the fullness of his heart, he will discover the greater ecstasy beyond. Why should it be different? Do we all not strive to passionately fall in love? This human intimate search for love is nothing more than the search for the nectar of your own true being.

Therefore, allow yourself to fall in love.

Initially there is a momentary experience of blissfulness themed as ānanda, it is the result of a touch of one's perfectness. Such initial step in uccārayoga is termed as ānanda (ecstasy), a flash of the experience of one's blissful self. Then at the next step there is the rise of another state termed as ubhāva, being due to the momentary rise into a position or a state of formlessness (upward jerking of his physical form). Then at the third step the physical form of the yogi is caught in a state of troubling, due to the feeling of looseness in his old age identity with his physical form, caused by a sudden fixation on his divine powers. Then a state of drowsiness appears in a disable. It being termed as nidrā, or sleep. It is the result of calming down of all outward tendencies in the yogi concerned. In this way, the notion of the self dissolves in the nonself, and the notion of the nonself dissolves in the self because the self is of the nature of all. Then the yogi experiences great expansion, having firmly rooted himself in the truth, upon which a whirling around takes place. All of these are the stages of consciousness.

Tantrasāra (5)

ĀSANA

Āsana should be stable and calm, make yourself soft and deep. The āsana shall love you, and you shall love the āsana. You have to talk to another, understand each other. It's always about understanding.

Yogi Pankaj Badoni

INTRODUCTION

Āsana means throne. A seat, yes, but one fit for a king. The king possesses the power to rule the world. He decides, and he acts. Likewise, the *āsana* as a throne refers to the place in which you are royal, where you can decide, determine, and act. Any *āsana* must be performed from this place of power. Power is Śakti and the highest Śakti (Parāśakti) is Kuṇḍalinī. Therefore, any *āsana* (throne) is a position from which to royally and clearly hold Kuṇḍalinī.

Āsana is not only king but also teacher. The Śakti that dwells in *āsana* can brake individual limitation and make one rise to the spheres beyond. Your *āsana* can know if you do not know. Therefore somehow you are not the one doing the *āsana*, but you give space within your body for the *āsana* to take its *seat*. The *āsana* is teacher, the Goddess, Supreme Power. When you do *āsana* remember that you do nothing, your pose is nothing more than bowing in front of the great teacher. You essentially embody the supreme, you make it speak though your limbs, position and breath.

There are said to be 8,400,000 *āsanas* that can be practiced – as many as there are species on our planet. According to Śivas explanation in the *Śiva Saṃhitā*, of these 8.4 million, 84 are said to be good, of which only 32 are especially useful for humans.

Unsurprisingly, *padmāsana* is said to be the best.

Possibly this wishes to impress upon us that every *āsana* resembles an energy found in nature and is eventually incorporated in the spirit of an animal as well. Animals, not possessing the same type of minds as us, can only reflect innocently on the forces of nature. With no mind to hinder them, they can enjoy their own nature to the fullest. Consider the greatness of the warrior, the determination of the eagle, the vital superiority of the tiger, the magic of the snake, the smoothness of the cat, the deep force of the crocodile. A directed mind can allow a human being to possess animalistic force or, conversely, it can cloud all forces and plummet to lower depths. The *āsanas* resemble these *prāṇas* in the human body so that the body can mirror the energy of nature.

> *There are eighty-four hundreds of thousands of āsanas described by Śiva, These postures are as many in number as there are numbers of living creatures in the universe*
>
> *Gheraṇḍa-Saṃhitā (2:1)*

Āsanas are performed in order to transcend the body and its limitation. This may seem ironic to us at first as most modern *āsanas* are performed in order to possess a beautiful body for impressing others. Nevertheless, *āsana* seeks to purify the body and free it from sickness and lethargy. A body free from suffering is invisible, just as pure children do not feel their bodies, they simply move through space and time as if gravity were forgotten. In the same way, one can detach from one's physical needs, and rise to greater freedom by strengthening and purifying the body using *āsanas*.

> *Āsanas are spoken of first, being the first stage of haṭha-yoga. One should practice the āsanas, which give [the yogi] strength, keep him in good health, and make his limbs supple.*
>
> *Haṭha-Yoga-Pradīpikā (1:14)*

MODES OF PRACTICE

Dynamic

Dynamic *āsanas* are frequently used in commercialised, western Kundalini Yoga. In traditional yoga, these *āsanas* are intended to remove energy blockages in the pranic body, or to activate liquid circulation or respiration. Dynamic movements are especially useful when the body is stiff or unopened. The elderly, beginners, or those with unsteady minds should regularly practice these types of exercises. Dynamic *āsanas* should be seen as preparatory for deeper *āsana* practice.

Static

Most *āsanas* are initially considered static since their original forms and functions are immobile, as resembling energies which ought to be contemplated. To perform a static *āsana* and use it for meditation purposes, one must first be strong and flexible. Therefore, the successful static performance of most *āsanas* is an advanced practice.

Duration

Beginners should hold an *āsana* as long as it is comfortable, and from there slowly extend their individual boundaries. Once the *āsana* can be held for long periods, one can start sinking into its specific flavour of energy. The duration affects the level on which the *āsana* works on the practitioner. The longer the hold, the deeper the effect. Advanced practitioners can hold *āsanas* for hours beyond their comfort barriers. This method of practice is frequently used in Kundalini Yoga to stimulate the pranic body.

RULES OF PRACTICE

Breathing

Typically, when people begin practicing yoga, their bodies are unaccustomed to effectively performing *āsanas*. Such people tend to breathe through their mouths, grasping for oxygen. It is of the utmost importance to remind the practitioner to breathe through the nose. Breathing through the nose will induce a meditative state, strengthen the *prāṇa*, increase lung volume, protect the lungs, and smooth the practice. The practitioner should synchronise their breathing and movement. The rules are as simple as they are useful:

Whenever you move or leave a position, breathe in.

Whenever you are still or enter a position, breathe out.

Whenever you emphasise strength, breathe in.

Whenever you stretch, breathe out.

These rules are guidelines and can be changed if the proper dynamic necessitates it. Movement should harmonise with breathing. This will protect from injury, increase the success of stretching, and strengthen the *prāṇa*.

Breathing should be even and unlaboured. The more equal the duration of inhalation and exhalation, the better (*samavṛtti* instead of *viṣamavṛtti*). This rule does not apply to highly experienced practitioners.

Awareness

Every exercise is a full process of integration. Body, mind and energy must cooperate. If awareness is absent, the mind cannot collaborate with body and energy. Should this be the case, there will be no effect on *prāṇa* and mind, and the body will risk injury. I know a practitioner who practiced the headstand after having drunk a beer. He broke a vertebra and is now paralysed on one side of his body. Yoga *āsanas* are strong and intense, their transformative effect on the body far surpasses gymnastics. Without full awareness, the *āsana* can be highly destructive.

Awareness is mindfulness – the presence of one's mind in the occurring process. *Prāṇa* is said to be filled by mind. If the mind is present, *prāṇa* can become still. If the mind is absent, there will be no effect on *prāṇa*. Since everybody practices yoga for achievement, it is wise to sacrifice any desire to let one's mind wonder and instead rigorously fix one's attention on the practice. If not, one would do better to engage in another activity.

Symmetry and counter pose

As the body is mirrored along a left-right vertical plane, most *āsanas* must begin on one side. The practitioner must then perform the same *āsana* on the other side to ensure bodily symmetry. *Āsanas* are very powerful; performing them one-sided would destroy bodily symmetry and lead to sickness.

Āsanas can favour either strength or stretching. To ensure a symmetry of action, strength and release must exist in equal proportion. Whenever you stretch, feel the strength first.

Most *āsanas* squeeze or stretch, and strengthen or open, very specific parts of the body while leaving others untouched. As with symmetry, the rule of counter pose suggests that each *āsana* be accompanied by another which inverts its effect. Much like forward and backward bend (*paścimottānāsana* and *matsyāsana*), this helps the body find its centre and stay in alignment.

Food

One should eat after *āsana* practice, never before. The last meal should have been eaten about three hours past. There are no food restrictions for practising *āsanas*; anyone can practice, vegetarian or carnivore. However, lighter diets are more conductive to obtaining better results as the body is not kept busy digesting such foods as meat, which produce toxins.

Time and place

One should not practice irregularly but have a fixed time and place. One should refrain from practicing in the afternoon or before lunch. *Āsana* brings one to a state of trance which, at the wrong time of the day, can ruin one's rhythm. The morning is the optimal time, at *brahmamuhūrta*, just before sunrise. Alternative times are noon, sunset, and midnight. Do not practice under the full sun at noon. Instead, seek out the shade and practice there. Avoid practicing in high winds. The ground must be strong and firm. The best places are solitary, cool, and protected.

CONTRAINDICATIONS

Whenever the body is in an abnormal state, care becomes crucial. Abnormal conditions include: sickness, injury, pregnancy, or all chronic disturbances to a balanced body. The teacher's wisdom and attention to proper instruction is invaluable here. A vital maxim to follow is to never assume that students do what is good for them. People often meekly follow instructions, even when they are painful and dangerous.

Inverted *āsanas* (i.e., head under the hip) are especially effective, but forbidden for people with certain conditions. Pregnant women, or people with heart conditions, glaucoma, ear infections, very high blood pressure, brain complications, among other conditions, should abstain from these *āsanas*.

Old age is no contraindication. However, sickness as a result of old age can be.

TEACHING METHODS

The āsana practice should be carried by the spirit of quality and not quantity. Because it is not the posture itself but the awareness within that creates the transformation. Take five postures per class and embrace them with conscious surrender.

Yogācārya Pandey Ji

The Class

The class is an ancient ritual. Contemplate on and consider that the yoga room is a temple, the candle the ritual fire, and the goddess is invoked through the power of mantra. You are the priest guiding this holy ceremony. You create a space in which the subtle process of realisation can be bodily perceived through every posture, breath, and gaze. Everything is steeped in meaning. Every detail is holy and important. You are the one who must imbue this spirit with form. It is through your deeper understanding that this can occur. Be aware of this responsibility and let it become a reality. If you do not bring the people fire, who will?

Geometry

The best form for your class is a circle. You should arrange yourself happily with whatever is present.

Start

People should rest in silence for a few seconds when they enter the room.

Chant the mantra, *Oṃ*, when any other mantra seems inappropriate. The mantra invites the divine spirit to guide the soul of the class. Not using any mantra is yoga only when one invites the divine spirit with the mantra of silence.

When the students appear fit and alert, *prāṇāyāma* can be used to start the class. If the students appear tired, begin with standing *āsanas*.

The Body

The body of the class needs a direction, much like how a film or play has a beginning, middle, and end. There are a wealth of journeys to choose from, each introducing, elevating, and settling its special character. A class can have a predefined theme, such as a focus on the back or the shoulders. However, even then a directional line should move through the class, from beginning, middle, to end.

In this manner, every class consists of three and a half parts. It has its root, its heart, its finishing realisation, and its contemplative section in which the experience is integrated.

For the first years of teaching, it would be wise to copy the classes composed by experienced teachers so as to better understand the flow of instruction. With experience comes knowledge, and your preferred flow and energy will crystallise. In the end you will have to follow your own nature.

If you create your own class in the first years of teaching, make sure that each session has a guideline or theme. Think every class through, *āsana* for *āsana*, to create a reasonable flow of energy. Unconsidered classes are unlikely to generate special insights for either you or the students. If you do not yet feel the energy, you cannot pick the correct *āsanas* throughout the class. Remember that you will be in a trance during your class, making it impossible to plan the next sequence while in this state. In such circumstances, use the morning *sādhana* sequence as an anchor.

Themes

Some possible themes are:

The lower back.

The shoulders and the heart.

The back and the head.

The hips.

The root and the belly.

The belly and the heart.

The heart and alignment.

Standing, flying and alignment.

More complex themes, such as immunity, compassion, or self-confidence are possible by placing the correct focus on each exercise. This is known as *saṅkalpa*, the inner goal in any exercise. No exercise can yield an inner result without *saṅkalpa*. The *saṅkalpa* is the soul of the exercise. It is repeated by each practitioner silently within themselves before the class.

Ailments of Your Students

Always be attentive to your students' inabilities. You can ask your students whether they have any physical impediments before starting a class. Usually, however, the students themselves will inform you when they need special care. Never ignore their needs, no matter how much you love the class you have crafted. If the student's border is self-created, it is up to them, not you, to see or remove it. The student must be the one to make the first step. When the student wants to grow, then you can help them, never before.

Old age, pregnancy, sickness, and injury must be taken seriously. The teacher must exercise caution.

Your Own Ailments

You are imperfect? You don't stretch like B.K.S. Iyengar? No problem, do not be ashamed, take pride in that! The practice of *āsanas* is a way, not a goal. Perfection is reached when you walk the path with dignity and effort, not when the *āsana* itself is perfected. Whenever you are imperfect despite your greatest efforts, encourage everyone else to walk with you. Amateurs would not climb a mountain when the master is already at the summit. They climb the mountain when the master climbs with them, stone by stone.

Your own bodily imperfection will help others feel at home – it is the sacrifice you make for your students' comfort.

> *If siddhāsana is perfected and the breath is carefully restrained in kevalakumbhaka, what need for all the other āsanas? When siddhāsana is accomplished, we can enjoy ecstasy of the meditative state (unmani avastha), the moon and the three bandhas follow without effort naturally.*
>
> *Haṭha-Yoga-Pradīpikā (1:32)*

BODILY ALIGNMENT AND TYPES

Introduction

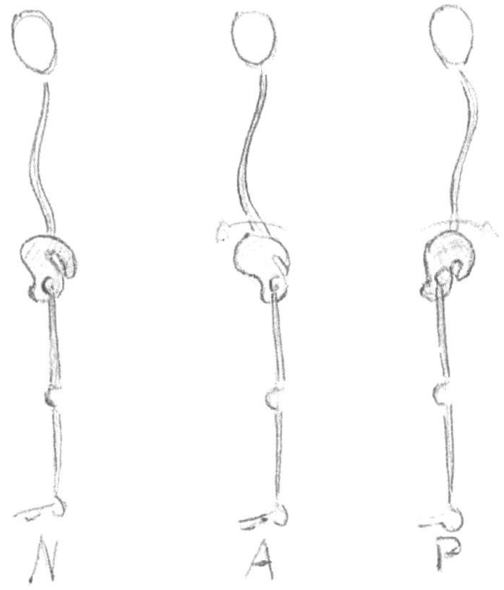

Of all the areas of the body, the hips (pelvis) seem to be the most important for overall physical health. The reasoning behind this is that the curve of the spine, the pressure on the feet, and the rotation of the thighs are directly connected to the positioning of the pelvis. The pelvis is thus the key to posture and energy. Rotating the pelvis correctly leads to the conservation of energy and alignment of the body, which in turn allows health to blossom.

We should also take care to discuss minor areas of the body, and how to align one's hands and feet inside each posture. All of this is relevant. First and foremost, we will deal with the pelvis as the understanding of this area and its impact on the body removes the major hindrances to a free energy flow.

Three Types of Pelvic Rotations

Type N – Neutral rotation of the pelvis. The pelvis is upright. This is what should be aimed for.

Type A – Anterior pelvic tilt. The pelvis is turned forward. This type is common among women.

Type P – Posterior pelvic tilt. The pelvis is turned backwards. This type is common among men.

Why the frequency of these types varies by sex is not fully clear to me. It may be related to slight anatomical differences.

Furthermore, two types of spinal curvatures occur frequently with the aforementioned pelvic tilts. These curvatures are the body's attempt to shift the upper body into a neutral position over the pelvis and thus reduce the tilt's unbalancing effects. They constitute a bodily deformation. These are a *lumbar lordosis* (inward curve) and a *thoracic kyphosis* (hunchback).

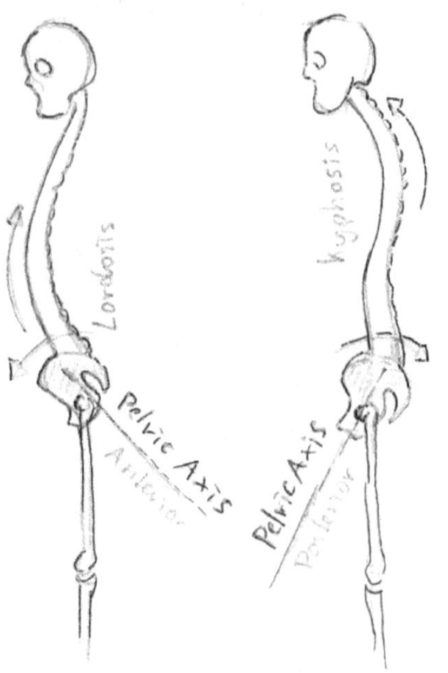

These two types of spinal adaptions correlate with the pelvic tilts. Whereas the forward tilted pelvic Type A can occur with either lumbar lordosis or thoracic kyphosis, Type P is always joined by thoracic kyphosis.

The reason for this in Type A is that a backward tilted pelvis (Type P) cannot further increase a backward bend of the spine as this would destabilise the body. However, a forward tilted pelvis (Type A) can increase either a natural S-curving (*thoracic kyphosis*) or reduce the natural S-curving for a single extended curve (*lumbar lordosis*).

Type A: Anterior Pelvic Tilt

Type A connects to an inward rotation of the thighs and an inwardly directed breathing pattern.

The inward rotation of the thighs is explained through the forward rotating pelvis pulling the femur inwards. This results in inwardly directed feet and inwardly pressurised knees. Since the pelvis rotates forward, the spine corrects the upper body's forward tilt by increasing its backward turn at the chest (thoracic spine). This results in an overall backward bend of the spine, thereby supporting an inward breathing pattern. Type A can also occur in combination with a *thoracic kyphosis*. In this case, the forward bend of the upper spine supports an outward breathing pattern. In both cases, the inwardly rotated tibia will press the inner part of the foot on the ground more strongly than the outer – a phenomenon known as 'pronation'. It is typical for Type A.

Type A is more of an *iḍā* than *piṅgalā* pattern, though it can still occur in *thoracic kyphosis* (*piṅgalā* related, Type C) as the body's compensatory reaction to an *iḍā* dominance.

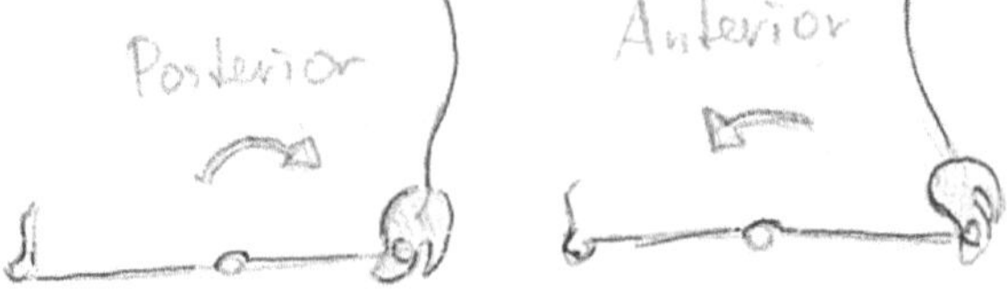

However, real balance cannot be achieved this way. This type suffers from low energy and introversion. The mind stays passive and unable to expand or control the energy. People of this type must practice a backward bend of the pelvis in all related *āsanas* so as to help balance their breathing. Stretching the body correctly and naturally will help induce a positive meditative state of mind.

Type C

For Type C, the pelvis must also find a backwards tilt. However, unlike Type A, people of Type C must practice a deep inward breathing pattern as well as a backwards bend of the upper spine. This will align the energy correctly.

Type P: Posterior Pelvic Tilt

Type P is also connected to an outward rotation of the thighs and an outward directed breathing pattern.

The outward rotation of the thighs is explained through the backward rotating pelvis pulling the femur outwards. This results in outwardly directed feet and outwardly pressurised knees – the obverse of Type A. Since the pelvis rotates backwards, the spine must correct the lower spine's tilt by increasing its forward turn of the chest (thoracic spine). This results in a stronger S-curve of the spine and an outward breathing pattern. The outwardly rotated tibia will press the outer part

	Type N	Type Anterior	Type Posterior	Type C
Spine	*Balanced*	*L. Lordosis*	*T. Kyphosis*	*L. Lordosis, T. Kyphosis*
Pelvic tilt	*Neutral Pelvis*	*Anterior*	*Posterior*	*Anterior*
Hip joint	*Neutral*	*Internal rotation*	*External rotation*	*Internal rotation*
Tibia	*Neutral*	*internal rotation*	*External rotation*	*Internal rotation*
Foot	*Neutral*	*Pronation*	*Supination*	*Pronation*

of the foot on the ground more forcefully than the inner (known as 'supination'). It is typical for Type P.

Type P is closer to *piṅgalā* than *iḍā*. People of this type suffer from extroverted energy and restlessness. The mind stays active yet unable to settle the aroused energy. This type must practice a forward bend of the pelvis in all related *āsanas* so as to help balance breathing. Correct stretching will naturally induce a peaceful meditative state of mind.

Pelvic Postural Alignment

Considering the above, the importance of achieving a correct postural alignment from the pelvis outward is abundantly clear. Once the pelvis can find a neutral position, various body parts automatically align. Furthermore, the energetic patterns that one carries throughout the day are supported by these bodily types. When corrected, the underlying energetic disturbance can surface and be released. It is highly recommended for every true seeker to understand that one's pelvic position can either induce or hinder a meditative state.

Body and mind are once again in indivisible unity.

	Type N	Type A	Type P	Type C
Nadis	*Suṣumnā*	*Ida*	*Pingala*	*Pingala Compensation*
Prāṇa	*Samāna, Equal*	*Apāna, Inbreath*	*Prāṇa, Outbreath*	*Prāṇa, Outbreath*
State of mind	*Meditative*	*Introverted*	*Extroverted*	*Fluctuating*

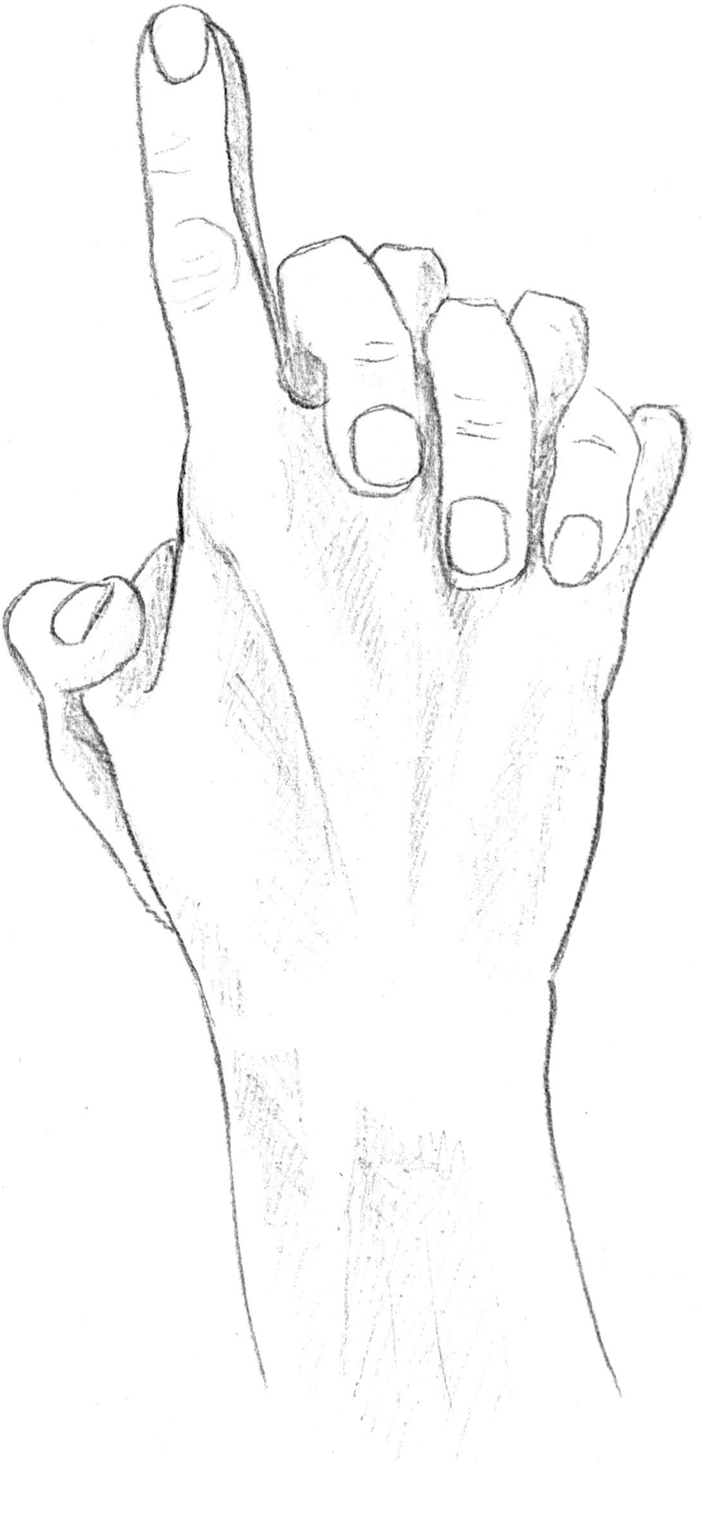

KRIYĀ

INTRODUCTION

Different to *karma* (the result of an accomplished action), *Kriyā* is an action's dynamic force. In yogic practice, *kriyā* is commonly understood as an action, or a set of actions, aimed at achieving a particular goal.

And yet it is so much more than that. Patañjali teaches us that *kriyā yoga* is the first step to *sādhana* – the way to the goal. Patañjali refers to the fact that the unlimited threefold cosmic energy is blocked by the absence of *kriyāśakti* – the power of action. Awakening *kriyāśakti* allows one to overcome the causes of suffering and thus walk the path to liberation. *Kriyā yoga* is therefore that yoga which awakens the universal power of action.

Yoga of Action (Kriya Yoga) has three components:

Tapas – discipline (heat or intensity),

Svadhyaya – refinement (self-study),

Ishvara Pranidhana – surrender to God

Its purposes are to disarm the causes of suffering and achieve samadhi.

Pātañjalayogasūtra II (1–2)

Therefore, all *kriyā* should be performed with this orientation. *Kriyā* is always full of passionate intensity, self-awareness and full of surrender to the supreme goal. This is the right place for your heart.

It is important to highlight that every class you teach must be a *kriyā* in itself. This means that each exercise within a class must find a natural order in which the energy can flow constructively and awaken *kriyāśakti*. To achieve this flow, each exercise must be a natural answer to its predecessor. This 'answer' can only be found if one possesses a clear vision of where the class should lead you to. This oneness of your vision, the class, and your skillful action requires a wealth of experience, as well as a long and deep journey into yourself until you find the strength to lead others on your own secret paths up the mountain. Until you have reached this point, I would advise you to study our *sādhana*, classes, *āsanas*, *mudrās*, and the great masters' *kriyās*.

OUR MATSYA KRIYĀS

I have learned many *kriyās* in the style of Yogi Bhajan. He was always very strict in the timing and order of the *kriyās*' performance. Performing an exercise in a predefined manner helps the student discover their boundaries and overcome their individual attachments. Krishnamacharya, the grandfather of modern Ashtanga (*aṣṭāṅga*) Yoga, once said that success in yoga cannot be achieved by following one's likes or dislikes, as this only serves to change an exercise according to one's own limitations. All this is indeed true for those students who cannot listen to the subtle voice inside their hearts.

Just in this case we will make an exception, because I believe in you.

I want you to discover the hidden blessing that is you, which I suspect (and hope) that you can already feel. I want you to discover your nature, because this nature, in its highly personal flavour, is what the world thirsts for. It is your duty to reveal it to the world.

There is just one commandment on this higher path of practice: You must always, and by all means, seek out the expression of you that is the highest, most lovable, truest, clearest, and most desired on your way to a brighter world. Do not be overwhelmed; achieving this is easier than you might think – you must simply act from your heart. In doing so, all will be achieved with ease. By acting contrary to your heart, it will be impossible to achieve regardless of how hard you try.

Therefore, I invite you to change and play in a loving manner with all the *kriyās* I have prepared for you. The classical *āsanas* are used here, so they can be easily integrated in any *haṭha* and *kuṇḍalinī* class. All of these *āsanas* can also be performed with *kapālabhāti* and *bhrāmarī* in any static posture.

Bīja Nyāsa

We can perform *bīja nyāsa*, which is to place a sound inside the body, at the end of each class. As this can be the same in each class, I have expounded it here separately. In this *bīja nyāsa*, we place the seed sounds of the five elements inside the venerable *suṣumnā* and let their vibration expand. We invoke their energy. Please consult the mantra section for the correct performance of this *nyāsa*. To form the correct sound, I would advise you to either search for a qualified teacher, or come to me for help.

Sit in meditation posture with your hands outstretched and firmly fixed. Perform *mūlabandha* at the beginning of each sound. Place the seven notes in each chakra. Simply make yourself vibrate with sound. Then, successively place the exoteric *bījas* for each element in the centres.

The last step invokes the elements through a mantra. For this, chant Oṃ at *mūlādhāra*, and pull the perineum, then ascend the *bīja* through the body and expand above in Ma (the supreme mother). Finally you can venerate the body of the Goddess by uttering these five *bījas* successively through your body.

Oṃ Aim– Oṃ Hrim– Oṃ Śrīm– Oṃ Khapharem– Oṃ Hasrauum

Alternatively, you can perform the chakra transformation from the mantra section. At the end, perform *namaskāra mudrā* and breathe deeply.

Centre	Svara	Bīja	Invocation
Mūlādhāra	*Sa*	*Laṃ*	*Oṃ Laṃ Ma*
Svādhiṣṭhāna	*Re*	*Vaṃ*	*Oṃ Vaṃ Ma*
Maṇipūra	*Ga*	*Raṃ*	*Oṃ Raṃ Ma*
Anāhata	*Ma*	*Yaṃ*	*Oṃ Yaṃ Ma*
Viśuddha	*Pa*	*Haṃ*	*Oṃ Haṃ Ma*
Ājñā	*Dha*	*Kṣaṃ*	*Oṃ Kṣaṃ Ma*
Sahasrāra	*Ni*	*Śrī*	*Oṃ Śrī Ma*

Remember the Teacher

All *kriyās* should be practiced with the teacher. Nothing can be achieved in the teacher's absence.

The teacher is both the means and goal. Every action begins with, is pervaded by, and finally rests in, the teacher. Without this teacher, Kundalini Yoga can be harmful and nothing will be attained. Always remember the teacher, both in the beginning and the end.

This teacher is your heart. The one teacher, *manonmanī*, the place beyond mind.

Before you even chant the mantra, take a few breaths with your hands folded in front your heart. Sink into the cavity of your innermost being. Repose at the bottom of your heart. Silently remember the teacher. The flame, beautifully burning without smoke. An eternal light in the dark, illuminating the path.

Here I present some of our *kriyās* and exercises how we practice them in the class. If you want to discover more *kriyās* and classes to inspire your practice, you can look at my book: "Kriyas and Classes in Kundalini Yoga: Classes and Kriyas to inspire and energise your Hatha and Kundalini Yoga practice". ISBN-13: 979-8830464215

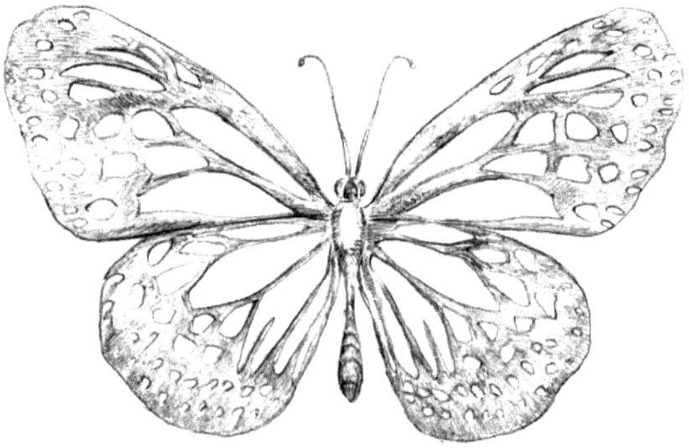

KUṆḌALINĪ-STAVAḤ - HYMN TO THE GREAT GODDESS

This hymn to Kuṇḍalinī is from the Rudrayāmalottara-tantrasya, The Tantra of the Divine Couple. It is a beautiful veneration of the great Goddess that is the divine power of action (*Kriyā Śakti*) and the way to liberation. It shall be chanted in the early morning or at noon, to worship Kuṇḍalinī as the rising energy in all undertakings and the heart of all things.

If this chant becomes your *sādhana* it can open your heart, make you sway in love, make you drunk with passion for her, who is life and love for everything within it. It can lift you into unbound joy, it is the refreshing beams of moonlight, the warm rays of the morning sun. The gentle kiss of your lover. Innocently fall in love with it.

This eight verse invocation is a powerful means of awakening Kuṇḍalinī. Following is an interpretive translation of this sacred text.

Important note: If you want to learn how to chant this mantra, visit the hidden section on our school's website where you can listen and learn this mantra and others mentioned in this book.

yogamatsya.com/mantra-downloads

1st Verse

Oṁ

janmoddhāra-nirīkṣaṇīha taruṇī vedādibījādimā

nityaṁ cetasi bhāvyate bhuvi kadā sad-vākya-sañcāriṇī

māṃ pātu priya-dāsa-bhāvaka-padaṃ saṅghātaye śrīdharā

dhātri tvaṁ svayam ādideva-vanitā dīnātidīnaṁ paśum

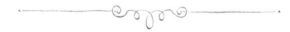

The great Goddess Kundalinī is always searching to liberate spiritual seekers in this world from the cycle of suffering. She is the ever-young yet ancient origin of spiritual knowledge, as well as the seed-mantras. She lives in the mind of the sages. Sometimes it is her that speaks in the voice of the sages true teachings to earth. O Creatrix! You are the beloved wife of the primordial God, bearer of beauty and auspiciousness: please protect me, a bound soul, more distressed than the most distressed. Please raise me, so I can be your beloved servant, and that I may be united with you.

2nd Verse

raktābhāmṛtacandrikā lipimayī sarpākṛtir nidritā

jāgrat-kūrma-samāśritā bhagavati tvaṁ māṁ samālokaya

māṃsodgandha-kugandha-doṣa-jaḍitaṃ vedādi-kāryānvitam

svalpa-svāmala-candra-koṭi-kiraṇair nityaṁ śarīraṁ kuru

You have a red lustre and you are nectarean moonlight. You exist in the form of all sounds. You sleep in the form of a coiled serpent. When you awake, you enter the central channel. O blessed Goddess, you open all eyes in this world! This body is bound to actions; it is flawed with bad odors, odors arising from the flesh. Please make this body eternal with just a fraction of your millions of exceedingly pure moonbeams.

3rd Verse

siddhārthī nija-doṣa-vit sthala-gatir vyājīyate vidyayā

kuṇḍalyākula-mārga-mukta-nagarī māyākumārgaḥ śriyā

yadyevaṃ bhajati prabhāta-samaye madhyāhna-kāle'thavā

nityaṁ yaḥ kula-kuṇḍalī-japa-padāmbhojaṁ sa siddho bhavet

Perfection is achieved through wisdom; the city of the liberated ones on the path of embodiment is attained through the Goddess Kundalinī; the false path of illusion is vanquished through the radiantly powerful Goddess. If one wishes to attain perfection through her grace, purifies mind and body, regularly worships at the time of early morning or at midday, the radiant words of this recitation of the Kula Kundalinī, this one becomes successful on the path.

4th Verse

Vāyvākāśa-catur-dale'tivimale vāñchā-phale mūlake

nityaṃ samprati nitya-deha-ghaṭitā śāṅketitā-bhāvitā

vidyā kuṇḍala-mālinī sva-jananī māyā kriyā bhāvyate

yais taiḥ siddha-kulodbhavaiḥ praṇatibhiḥ sat-stotrakaiḥ śaṃbhubhiḥ

O you imperishable one, You are contemplated eternally in your symbolic form in the four-petalled lotus at the root: that is the space of prana, where the fruits of all desires reside. Those who are initiated into the family contemplate You as wisdom, as the Coiled One, as Self-born, as the power of all creation and as the power of action, they worship You with beneficent sacred hymns.

5th Verse

dhātā-śaṅkara-mohinī tri-bhuvana-cchāyā-paṭodgāminī

saṃsārādi-mahā-sukha-praharaṇī tatra sthitā yoginī

sarva-granthi-vibhedinī sva-bhujagā sūkṣmātisūkṣmā parā

brahma-jñāna-vinodinī kula-kuṭī vyāghātinī bhāvyate

Remaining in the mūlādhāra, that Yoginī enthralls even the Creator and Śiva. She unveils the true nature of reality in the three worlds, and with the greatest of ease, she destroys the cycle of worldliness and the experience of being bound. Contemplate her as One who pierces all the inner knots; the One who sleeps in the body; the One who herself is coiled; the Supreme Goddess Parā, subtler than the subtlest, who is absorbed in the knowledge of the Absolute; the One who defeats all ignorance.

6th Verse

vande śrī-kula-kuṇḍalīṁ tri-valibhiḥ sāṅgaiḥ svayambhū- priyāṁ

prāviṣṭyāmbara-mārga-citta-capalāṁ bālābalāṁ niṣkalām

yā devī paribhāti veda-vacanā saṃbhāvinī tāpinī

iṣṭānāṁ śirasi svayambhu-vanitāṁ saṃbhāvayāmi kriyām

I bow to the supreme Kula Kundalī, who is the lover of the Self-born One who surrounds him with her perfect form and her three folds. She has entered the sky of consciousness through the central channel and She enlightens the mind. She is like a young woman, pure and complete. This Goddess shines, her words true knowledge; She creates everything for those who love her and destroys the ignorant. I worship her - the wife of the Self-born One - as the Power of Action at the beginning of all things.

7th Verse

vāṇī koṭi-mṛdaṅga-nāda-madanāli-śreṇi-koṭi-dhvaniḥ
prāṇeśī rasa-rāśi-mūla-kamalollāsaika-pūrṇānanā
āṣāḍhodbhava-megha-rāji-janita-dhvāntānanā sthāyinī
mātā sā paripātu sūkṣma-pathagā māṁ yogināṁ śaṅkarī

The Goddess of speech emanates the primal sound, which is like the ecstatic rhythm of drums, her sound is as intoxicating as the humming of millions of bees. She is the source of prāna, and all life. Her perfect face, full of absolute joy, is like the blooming of a lotus rooted in the ocean of nectar. Her face is dark like the deep blue shining in the cloudy sky at the onset of the month of rains. She supports the whole world. May that Great Mother, who moves within the central channel of consciousness protect me thoroughly. She is the guide of all yogis.

8th Verse

Tvām āśritya narā vrajanti sahasā vaikuṇṭha-kailāsayor
Ānandaika-vilāsinīṃ śaśi-śatānandānanāṃ kāraṇām
mātaḥ śrī-kula-kuṇḍali priya-kare kālī-kuloddīpane
tat-sthānaṁ praṇamāmi bhadra-vanite mām uddhara tvaṁ paśum

Those who give their hearts to you, they immediately go to the place where the Gods reside. You revel in pure bliss. Your face is like the refreshing joy of a hundred moons. You are the source of creation. O Mother, O sacred Kula Kundalinī, O beloved form of Śakti, you fill everything with affection, you are the light and power of the Family of Kālī, I bow to the root where you dwell; You rescue me, a bound soul.

kuṇḍalī-śakti-mārga-sthaḥ stotrāṣṭaka-mahā-phalam

yaḥ paṭhet prātar-utthāya sa yogī bhavati dhruvam

If one practices steadfast the path of Kundalinī Śakti, Rises early in the morning, and recites this auspicious eight-verse hymn, he will certainly be a yogi.

kṣaṇād-eva hi pāṭhena kavi nātho bhaved-iha

pavitraḥ kuṇḍalī-yogī brahma-līno bhaven-mahān

Just by reciting this prayer, one becomes a great poet in this world. The yogi practicing kundalini yoga, purifies his heart, becomes great and one with Brahman.

iti te kathitaṁ nātha kuṇḍalī-komalaṁ stavam

etat stotra-prasādena deveṣu guri-gīṣpatiḥ

O lord, thus have I given you the beautiful hymn of the Goddess Kundalinī. By its blessing one becomes praiseworthy, like the light of gods.

sarve devāḥ siddhi-yutā asyāḥ stotra-prasādataḥ

dvi-parārdhaṁ ciran-jīvī brahmā sarva-sureśvaraḥ

By the radiant light of her hymn, all gods are given power, and Brahma, the lord of all, lives for countless ages.

Oṁ śrīgurubhyo namaḥ

MATSYA MŪLĀDHĀRA KRIYĀ

The action for strengthening the *mūlādhāra*. *Mūlādhāra* is the golden fire of your presence, it is your will be to, the very basic strength and vitality.

Perform alongside easy breathing pauses between the exercises.

60 – 90 minutes

Sūryanamaskāra

Salutations to the sun. The sun is red when he rises. He is earth and fire unified in a mystical marriage. Stability and loving passion conjoined, rising to nourish the world. Perform this *sūryanamaskāra* with a *kapālabhāti* pulse from the navel for each position. Do not stretch! Each position should only be slightly touched by the hand of the rising sun. Stay dynamic and open.

Inhale when you change positions, exhale sharply and pull the navel when you touch each position. Take a shower in the sun's rays.

Practice 12–108 times.

The twelve positions of *Sūryanamaskāra* and its corresponding *bījas*.

Hrāṁ	– *Pranāmāsana*	– *Prayer pose*
Hrīṃ	– *Hastottānāsana*	– *Raised arms pose*
Hrūṁ	– *Pādahastāsana*	– *Hands to feet pose*
Hraiṁ	– *Aśva Sañcalanāsana*	– *Horse riding pose*
Hrauṃ	– *Parvatāsana*	– *Mountain pose*
Hraḥ	– *Aṣṭāṅga namaskāra*	– *Eight points salutation pose*
Hrāṁ	– *Bhujaṅgāsana*	– *Cobra pose*
Hrīṃ	– *Parvatāsana*	– *Mountain pose*
Hrūṁ	– *Aśva Sañcalanāsana*	– *Horse riding pose*
Hraiṁ	– *Pādahastāsana*	– *Hands to feet pose*
Hrauṃ	– *Hastottānāsana*	– *Raised arms pose*
Hraḥ	– *Pranāmāsana*	– *Prayer pose*

197 Sūryanamaskāra

Oṃ mitrāya namaḥ – I salute to you who you are the friend of all!

Oṃ ravaye namaḥ – I salute to you who you are Ravi, the protector

Oṃ sūryāya namaḥ – I salute to the sun who is the source of all good.

Oṃ bhānave namaḥ – I salute to you, who you are full of rays of light.

Oṃ kaghāya namaḥ – I salute to you who you walk across the sky

Oṃ pūṣṇe namaḥ – I salute to you, who you guard all things

Oṃ hiraṇyagarbhāya namaḥ – I salute to you, who you are the golden womb of live

Oṃ marīcaye namaḥ – I salute to you, who you are the sparkling dust of light

Oṃ ādityāya namaḥ – I salute to you, who you are the beginning of all

Oṃ savitre namaḥ – I salute to you, who you bring everything about.

Oṃ ārkāya namaḥ – I salute to you, who you are the ray of fire

Oṃ bhāskarāya namaḥ – I salute to you, who you are the source of all light.

Every single one of the 12 positions of the sūryanamaskāra, is guarded by one of these mantras. May you do the salutation to the sun fast or slow – carry them in your heart.

Vajrāsana

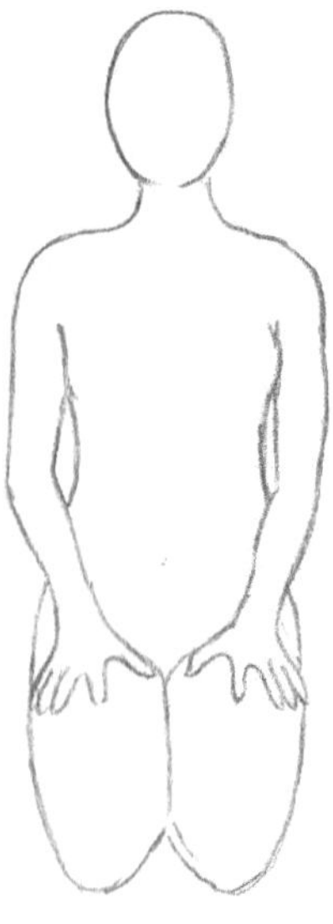

Thunderbolt pose. Sit in *vajrāsana* (sit on your heels), or any favorite sitting posture, centre yourself. Elongate your spine and deeply start to chant the *bīja* of *dhāra* (*Laṃ*). Whenever *Laṃ* is chanted pull *mūlabandha* and move the *bīja* through your body.

Practice at least 5 times with contraction of *mūlabandha*

Then start with an gentle *bhastrikā* while moving your belly in and out. Choose a speed that allows your lungs to fill and empty themselves completely. Allow your body to become hyper-oxygenated. In the end breath in and hold with and extended abdomen. Then exhale and contract your abdomen. This is *udara śakti vikāsaka* also known as *ajgari* – the female panther. It is a very powerful tool to bring the energy in the centre, awaken Kuṇḍalinī and induce a meditative state of mind.

Practice 5-30 times deep *bhastrikā*, *ajgari* and then relax.

Nauka Sañcālanāsana

Boat rowing pose, Sit with your legs straight in front of your body, your upper body erect. Breath in open your chest and clench your hands just like if you would grasp the oars of a boat. Breathe out and lean forward as far as you can, bend the knees if necessary. When you breath in, lean as far back as possible bringing the fists next to your shoulders. Do this in a dynamic circular movement, breath deep.

Perform *nauka sañcālanāsana* more than one minute, with strong deep breathing

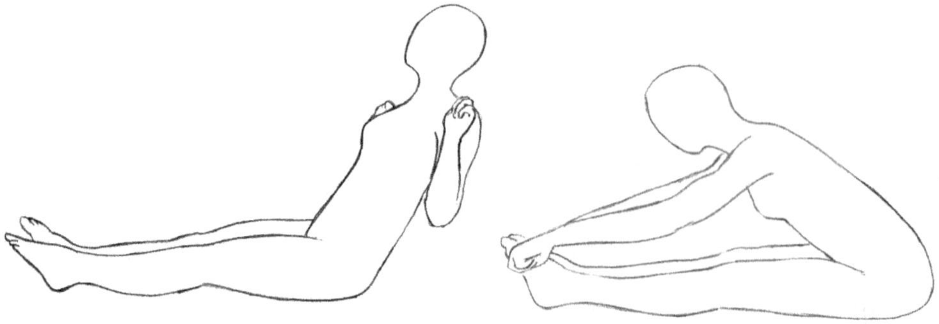

Cākī Cāḷaṇāsana

Churning the mill pose. Sit with the legs wide apart and stretch out your arms horizontally over the ground, interlock your thumbs or all of your fingers, just like if you would hold a stirring stick.

Breath in and elevate your torso, exhale and move forward in circular grinding motion, exhale and move backwards. The circular motion must originate the hip while your spine remains straight. Keep the arms parallel and straight throughout the exercise. Inhale and stretch in the centre, change direction after a while.

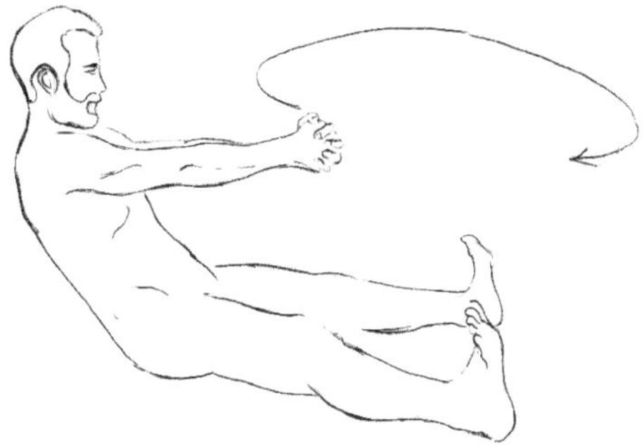

Move slowly with deep breathing for at least one minute each direction.

Titali Āsana

Butterfly pose. Come into the butterfly pose. First, playfully perform the butterfly quickly and dynamically for one minute.

Stretch up your spine. Feel the centre and pull yourself up. Enjoy the creative energy underlying this posture. Pull your perineum inward and perform *bhastrikā*. Feel the sky above. In the end breathe in deeply, breath out deeply and hold, this is *ajgari*. Contemplate the centre.

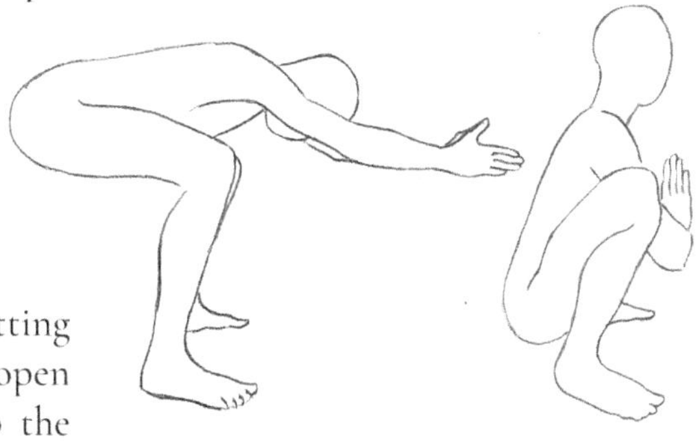

Finally, very slowly bend forward, your head touching your toes, breathing deeply.

Namaskārāsana

Salutation pose. Come into squatting pose, perform *namaskāra mudrā*, open your knees with your elbows, keep the spine straight, and breathe deeply. This *āsana* can be performed with dynamic movement. Breathe in, stretch the upper body and keep your arms horizontal. Breathe out and come back into squatting with your spine straight. Keep the hands in *namaskāra mudrā*.

Enjoy and perform this for 30 – 60 seconds.

Kāṣṭha Takṣanāsana

Wood chopping pose. After relaxing your feet, come back into squatting pose, interlock your fingers into a fist and stretch the arms in line with your back. Breathe in and raise your arms. Forcefully push them to the ground, pull *mūlabandha*. One can chant "Ha" when chopping down.

Fix your eyes firmly on the ground and apply a strong pace to your breath.

Perform this for over one minute. In the end perform *bāhyakumbhaka*, outer retention.

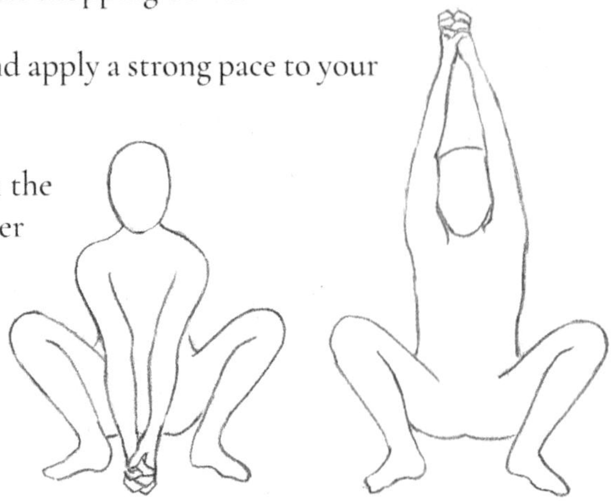

Vāyu Niṣkāsana

Freeing the wind pose. From this squatting pose, hold the inside of your ankles with your thumbs above, and fingers below your feet.

Inhale in squatting pose, straighten your back and tilt your head backwards, gazing upward.

Hold the breath for three seconds inwardly and perform *mūlabandha*.

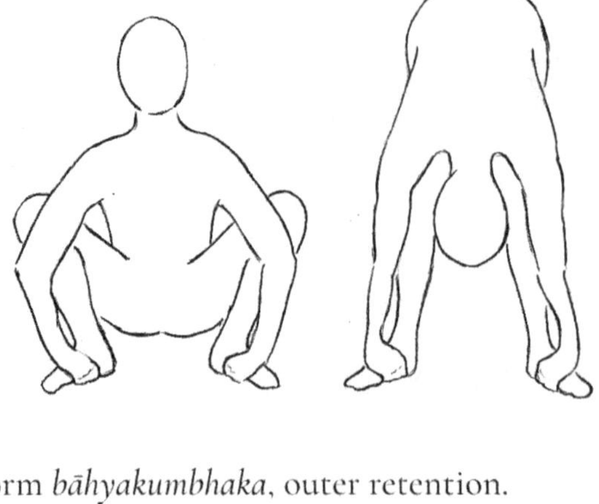

Then exhale, straighten your legs and bend forward gazing inwardly. Hold your breath outwardly for three seconds and perform *mūlabandha*.

Move in the rhythm of your deep breathing for over one minute. In the end breathe in deep and then out, perform *bāhyakumbhaka*, outer retention.

Śaithalyāsana

Animal relaxation pose. While sitting in *siddhāsana*, stretch over your knees and breathe deeply. Bend forward by breathing out. First left, then right, stretch up in the centre. Invert the folding of your legs.

Śaithalyāsana - Change and turn your left leg outward, your foot will be behind the buttocks while the right leg stays inward with the foot touching the thigh. Again, bend forward over the right leg, breathing out. Breathe deep. Next, come up and place your right hand on your left knee and rotate to the left. Breathe. Stretch up in the centre. Change legs. *Śaithalyāsana* will centre your siting position.

Practice five deep breaths for each side.

Ardha Matsyendrāsana

Matsyendras pose. First, come to rest until your body feels still. Put your left leg over your right thigh, right foot on the left and left foot on the ground on the right side of your body. Hold your knee and feel the beauty of this posture. When you feel its beauty, gently use your breath to rotate to the right. Breathe deeply, massage

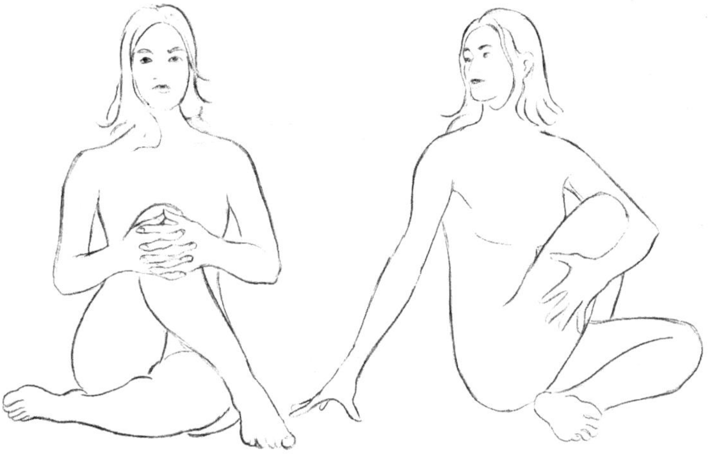

your intestines. Change sides.

Perform this for one minute for each side. Breathe deeply or use gentle *bhastrikā* and *ajgari*.

Uṣṭrāsana

Camel pose. Move into *uṣṭrāsana* or to *ardha uṣṭrāsana*. Push yourself deep into the *āsana* and try to fall into the sky. Take 10 deep breaths.

Śaśankāsana

Rabbit pose. Then gently come to *vajrāsana*, open your knees, stretch up and bend forward to *śaśankāsana*. Surrender. Stretch your arms.

Then, apply *mūlabandha* and begin with one minute of *bhastrikā, ajgari* and in the end *bhrāmarī* with your forehead on the ground.

Jānuśirāsana

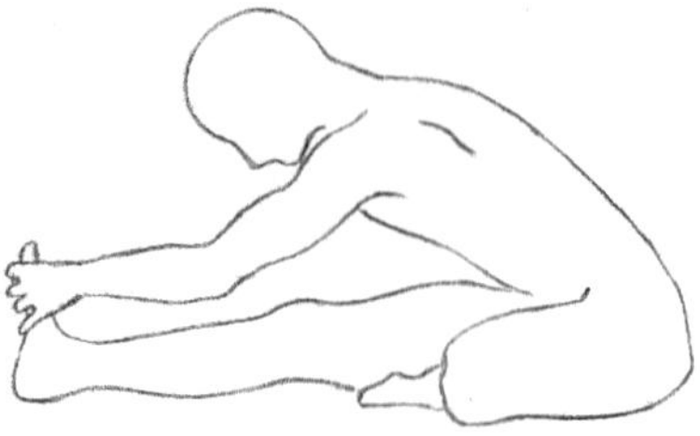

Head-to-knee pose. Place your heel in the perineum. Practice five times with deep breathing, then stretch.

One minute of *bhastrikā, ajgari* and in the end *bhrāmarī* for each side.

Jānuśirāsana (variation)

Head to knee pose. Turn the left leg outward and place your foot next to the buttocks. Keep the knees together, stretch the other leg and perform *jānuśirāsana*. Change sides.

One minute for each side while breathing deeply and using *bhrāmarī*.

Matsyāsana

Fish pose. Lay back and support your buttocks with your hands. Stretch your legs and arch up your chest.

Practice three times with deep breathing, then one minute of *bhastrikā and ajgari.*

Paśćimottānāsana

Back stretching pose. Practice with deep breathing, *bhastrikā, ajgari* and in the end *bhrāmarī.*

Mahāmudrā

This is the great seal. It is the attitude of energy and can only be understood with love. While it requires intensity, it cannot be performed brutally. It is the energy itself that must be awakened, so it must be a celebration, not a dry exercise. If you discover yourself performing this without passion, stop immediately and realign your intention. Begin again while dancing with the Goddess. Celebrate!

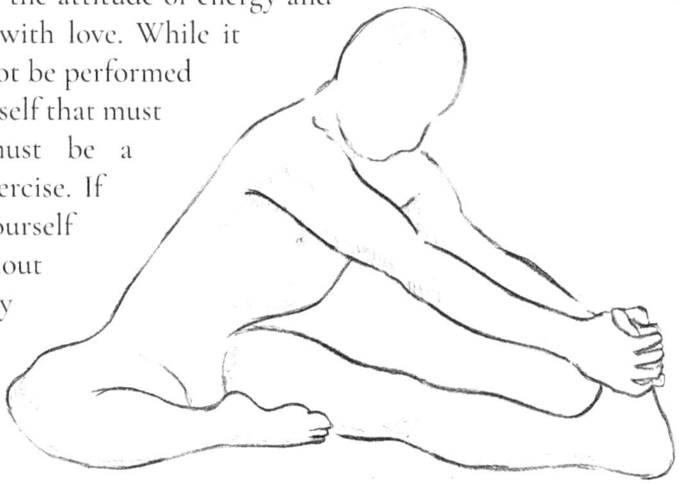

This is *pratyāhāra*, making it an internal process. It is not your body and its twitching alone that you observe. This *mudrā* occurs within. Turn your gaze inwards. Internalize yourself...

Sit in *daṇḍāsana.* Stretch your right leg out, sit on your left heel and let it press against the perineum. If this is difficult move into *jānuśirāsana.* Make yourself stable and comfortable. If necessary, let your buttocks be supported from the side. Sit straight and lean forward with your forehead facing front (not down). See the internal sky above. Hold the big toe of your right foot with both hands. Breathe deeply. Breathe in as deeply as you can, then pull *mūlabandha* forcefully. Hold the breath as long as is comfortable. Then, very slowly, breathe out. When the breath is still within you, pull *mūlabandha* hard. See the energy accumulate and rise to the sky. Enjoy the bliss.

Perform for as long as possible. Change sides, reverse legs. Feel at home. This is the giver of great energy. Remember that it happens within.

Alternative: Maṇḍūkī Mudrā

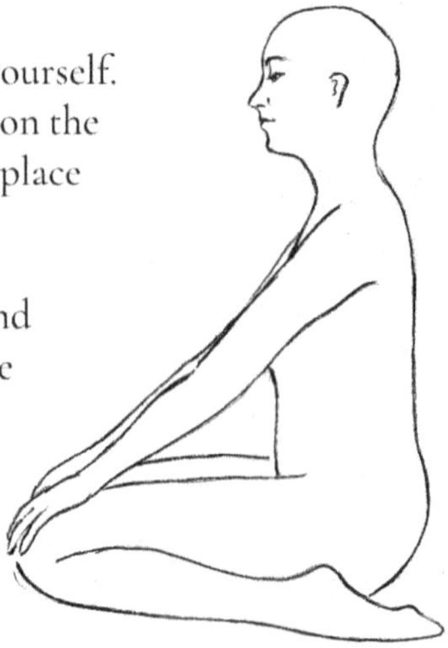

Frog pose. Sit in *maṇḍūkī āsana* without straining yourself. Turn your feet outward so that your buttocks if firmly on the ground. If you cannot perform this without straining, place a pillow underneath.

Rest your hands on your knees, keep your spine and arms straight, and stay completely relaxed. The purpose of this exercise is calmness. Open your eyes, perform *nāsikāgra dṛṣṭi* and let your mind become fixed. If your eyes are tired, relax them and then continue. Breathe slowly and rhythmically, like a gentle wave.

Concentrate on *mūlādhāra* in silence.

Perform for as long as possible. Feel at home. This is the giver of great peace.

Bīja Nyāsa

Placing the seed syllables. Perform your *bīja nyāsa* with heart.

Śavāsana

The corpse pose. Lay supine on the ground. Surrender completely.

Contemplate. I am what I am. I am being.

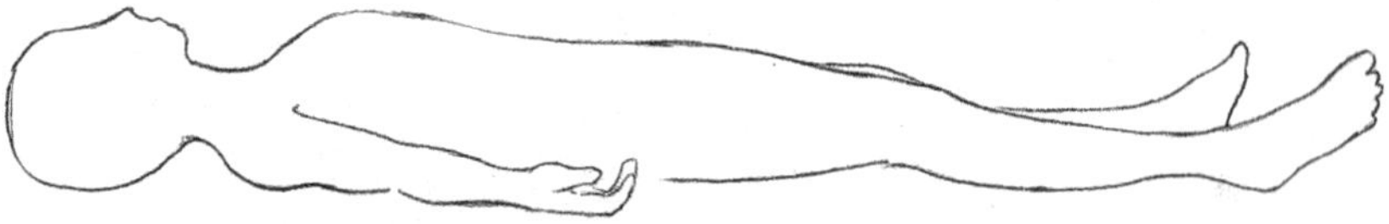

Summary

Vajrāsana, Laṃ & Bhastrikā	Thunderbolt pose with bellows breath.
Nauka Sanchalanāsana	Rowing the boat
Cākī Cāḷaṇāsana	Churning the mill
Titali Āsana	Butterfly pose
Namaskārāsana	Salutation pose
Kāṣṭha Takṣanāsana	Chopping the wood pose
Vāyu Niṣkāsana	Wind releasing pose
Śaithalyāsana	Animal relaxation pose
Ardha Matsyendrāsana	Half spinal twist.
Uṣṭrāsana	Camel pose
Śaśankāsana	Hare pose (rabbit pose)
Jānuśirāsana	Head to knee pose
Matsyāsana	Fish pose
Paśćimottānāsana	Back stretch pose
Mahāmudrā	the great seal
Bīja Nyāsa	Placing the Seed sounds
Śavāsana	The corpse pose

SVĀMĪ VIDYANAND PURIFICATION SĀDHANA

Purification *sādhana*. It is a *kriyā*, it unblocks the universal power of action

This *sādhana* was given to awaken to the energy of divine mother, it is gentle and loving. It must be performed with devotion, then it will cover you with the warm hand of your ever expanded being.

I have given the minimum times of 30 seconds *kapālabhāti* and 3 times *bhrāmarī* in each posture. Know that you can expand them as much as you want. My teacher told me, that if one holds each position one minute with deep breathing, one minute with *kapālabhāti*, one minute with *bhrāmarī* and one minute with the mantra "Oṃ Mā" from the heart, then this Kriya becomes a powerful means of awakening Kuṇḍalinī.

Approximately 60 minutes.

Nāḍiśodhana

Nāḍiśodhana should be practiced with full awareness, or not at all. There are many ways of creating breathing patterns, such as changing the length of the inhalation, exhalation and *kumbhaka* (holding of breath) in a certain proportion. This does not concern the new practitioner. Simply keep the lengths of the in- and outbreaths equal in duration. One can use a mantra like Oṃ to count the time the in- and outbreaths. The breath should be deep and can be strong. Pull *mūlabandha* whenever the breath turns and allow yourself a short *kumbhaka* (though no longer than two seconds). This will stimulate the *nāḍis* and help purification.

When you sit for your *sādhana*, you have nothing else to do, so do nothing else...

Practice 10–20 rounds of this every morning.

Kapālabhāti

Breath of fire. Gently pulse your navel in the exhalation and keep a steady rhythm. When you practice *kapālabhāti* , imagine a golden egg surrounded by subtle electric fibers. Imagine it vibrating up slightly when you push air out and moving down slightly when you breathe in. When you feel the stimulation of the navel point, observe a fine stream of energy being generated in the pelvis and expanding beyond the forehead. At the end, pull *mūlabandha* and retain the breath inside.

Practice for one minute every morning.

Sūryanamaskāra

Salutations to the sun. *Sūryanamaskāra* can be done with deep breathing, with either one breath in each position or as many as one needs to find the right pace.

Each of the 12 positions of the *sūryanamaskāra* is said to be connected to one primal aspect of the sun, these aspects are mirrored in their sound form by 12 *bījas*

Hrāṁ	– *Pranāmāsana*	– *Prayer pose*
Hrīṃ	– *Hastottānāsana*	– *Raised arms pose*
Hrūṁ	– *Pādahastāsana*	– *Hands to feet pose*
Hraiṁ	– *Aśva Sañcalanāsana*	– *Horse riding pose*
Hrauṃ	– *Parvatāsana*	– *Mountain pose*
Hraḥ	– *Aṣṭāṅga namaskāra*	– *Eight points salutation pose*
Hrāṁ	– *Bhujaṅgāsana*	– *Cobra pose*
Hrīṃ	– *Parvatāsana*	– *Mountain pose*
Hrūṁ	– *Aśva Sañcalanāsana*	– *Horse riding pose*
Hraiṁ	– *Pādahastāsana*	– *Hands to feet pose*
Hrauṃ	– *Hastottānāsana*	– *Raised arms pose*
Hraḥ	– *Pranāmāsana*	– *Prayer pose*

Inhale and change the position, exhale and utter the corresponding *bīja*. Carry these mantras in your mind or on your lips when you move through the aspects of the sun.

If you are an advanced practitioner and you wish to shower in the rays of the sun, perform this *sūryanamaskāra* with a gentle *kapālabhāti* pulse in the navel for each position. Each position should only be slightly touched by the hand of the sun, not pulled violently. Stay dynamic and open.

Practice 12–36 times each morning.

Jānuśirāsana

Head to knee pose. Practice three times with deep breathing. Stretch.

30 seconds of *kapālabhāti* and three times *bhrāmarī*. On each side.

Titali Āsana

Butterfly pose. Practice three times with deep breathing. Stretch.

30 seconds of *kapālabhāti* and three times *bhrāmarī*.

Paśimottānāsana

Back stretch pose. Practice three times with deep breathing. Stretch.

30 seconds of *kapālabhāti* and three times *bhrāmarī*.

Pāda Prasara Paśimottānāsana

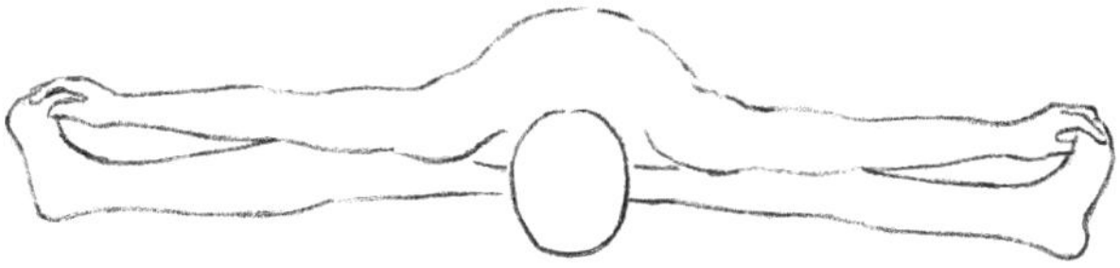

Open legs back stretch pose. Practice three times with deep breathing. Stretch.

30 seconds of *kapālabhāti* and three times *bhrāmarī*.

Mārjārīāsana

Cat pose. First, move in a dynamic cat–cow posture about one minute. Inhalation–up, exhalation–down.

Then look up in the cat and start with 30 seconds of *kapālabhāti* After this go into cow and practice three times *bhrāmarī*.

Parvatāsana

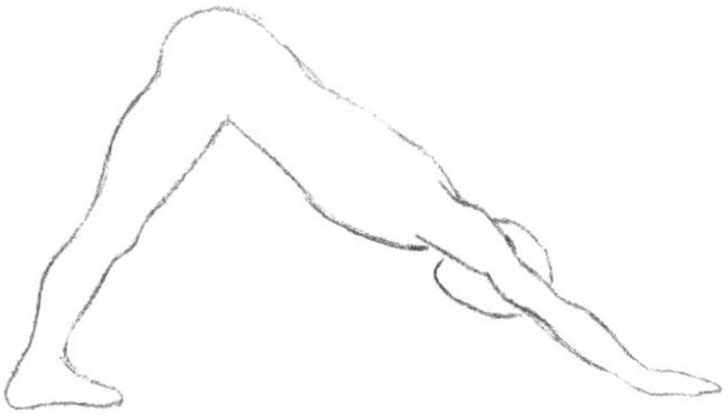

Mountain pose. Move gently into *parvatāsana* and practice three times with deep breathing.

30 seconds of *kapālabhāti* and three times *bhrāmarī*.

Vajrāsana

Thunderbolt pose. Sit and relax in *vajrāsana*. Open your chest. Stretch your arms. Practice three times with deep breathing. Pull *mūlabandha*.

30 seconds of *kapālabhāti* and three times *bhrāmarī*.

Uṣṭrāsana

Camel pose. Move to *uṣṭrāsana* or *ardha uṣṭrāsana*.

Practice three times with deep breathing, and about 30 seconds of *kapālabhāti* .

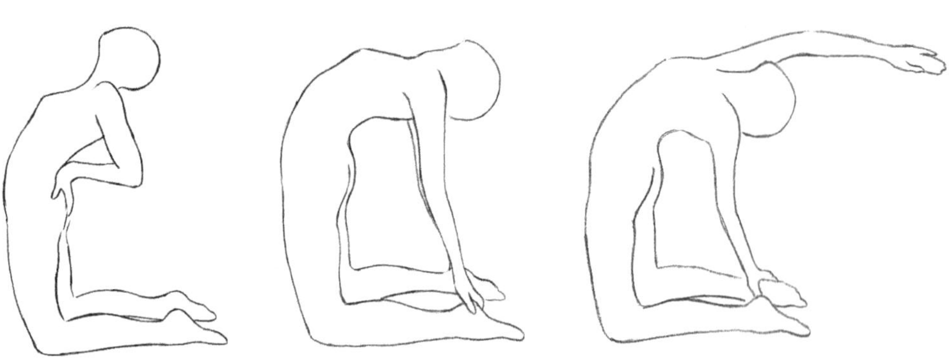

Śaśankāsana

Rabbit or hare pose. Through *vajrāsana*, open your knees, stretch up and move into *śaśankāsana*. Surrender yourself. Stretch your arms. Practice three times with deep breathing.

30 seconds of *kapālabhāti* and three times *bhrāmarī*.

Silently chant the mantra of the Divine Mother.

Bīja Nyāsa

Sit in meditation posture with your hands outstretched and fixed. Perform *mūlabandha* at the beginning of each sound. Perform our *bīja nyāsa*.

Finally, perform *namaskāra mudrā* and breathe deeply.

Śavāsana

Lay on your back with your palms facing upwards. Contemplate the following:

I am you. You are me. We are one

Summary

Nāḍiśodhana	Psychic Network purification
Kapālabhāti	Cleansing the skull breath (shining face)
Sūryanamaskāra	Salutations to the sun
Jānuśirāsana	Head to knee pose
Titali Āsana	Butterfly pose
Paścimottānāsana	Back stretch pose
Pāda Prasara Paścimottānāsana	Open legs back stretch pose
Mārjārīāsana	The cat pose
Parvatāsana	Mountain pose
Vajrāsana	Thunderbolt pose
Uṣṭrāsana	Camel pose
Śaśankāsana	Rabbit pose
Bīja Nyāsa	Placing the seed sounds

SŪKṢMA VYĀYĀMA - PAVANMUKTĀSANA I

Anti-rheumatic exercises - *āmavātī rodhaka vyāyāma*

The *pavanamuktāsana* series was first introduced in the west by the teacher swami Satyānanda, which led many people to believe that it originated there in the Bihar school of yoga. But this is a misconception, as the *pavanamuktāsana* belongs to a much older tradition that was taught as a part of the *sūkṣma vyāyāma*, the subtle yogic exercises, which had already been established through the teacher Dhīrendra Brahmacārī.

The way that this *pavanamuktāsana* is offered here is different than originally taught by Satyānanda. Here they are rendered as they are taught in our Kundalini Yoga tradition. This anti–rheumatic series is far more than a series against joint pain. It is a very energetic series that can break energy blockages and stimulate the spinal fluid. It can also expand consciousness and has strong healing properties for the mind and body. Since this series works strongly on the flow of energy along the spinal cord, it is advisable to relax in *śavāsana* in between the exercises and whenever a tickling sensation occurs. This helps to calm the nervousness system and to integrate the energy.

Since these exercises are supposed to be subtle and work with one's energy body rather than with the physical, one should practice them with firm focus on breath and rhythmic movement.

Approximately 60 – 90 minutes.

Prāraṃbhik Sthiti

Base position. Sit straight up with your legs stretched out, place your hands either on your knees or behind your buttocks with your fingers facing backwards. Make sure your spine is straight and your posture embodies energy.

Pādāṅguli naman

Toe bending. Sit in base position with your legs stretched out and the feet slightly apart and focus on your toes. Keep your face open and your eyes firmly fixed on your toes. Wherever your eyes wonder there you go. Since these excises are subtle it is important that you remain where you are supposed to be. Bend your toes forward and back towards your body with rhythm of your breath. Your breath should be deep and intense throughout the exercise, this will stimulate the *prāṇa* and make it flow.

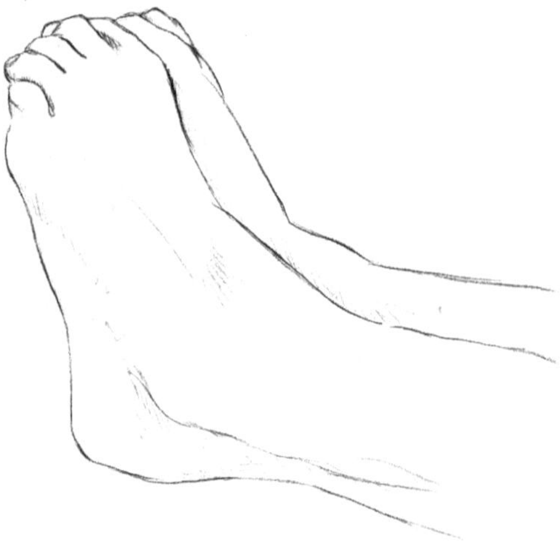

In the end inhale bend the toes towards your body enter, hold the breath. Then exhale bend the toes away from your body centre and hold the breath outside.

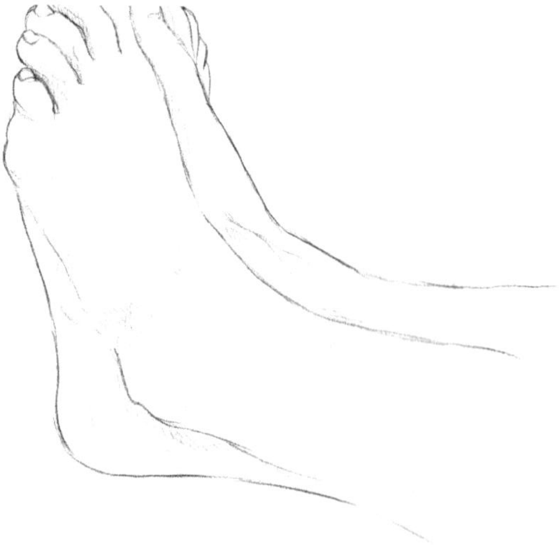

Deep, rhythmic breath, 1-2 minutes.

Note: Holding the breath is called *kumbhaka*, one should hold the breath with *mūlabandha* and as long as comfortably possible. Hold the breath till a sensation of silence or the lightening emerges from the centre. In my opinion the only difference between hatha and kundalini yoga is the diligent focus on *kumbhaka*. When *kumbhaka* is performed with complete concentration, even the simplest exercise turns into kundalini yoga.

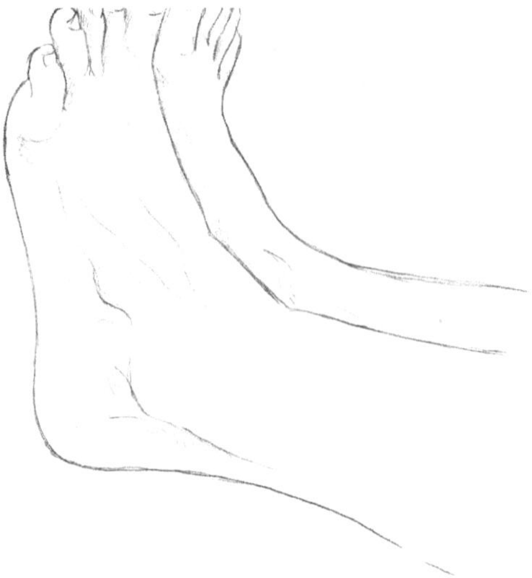

Kulph naman

Ankle bending. Remain in the same position and start to bend your feet from the ankle forward and backwards in the previously described manner. Keep the breath rhythmic and passionate. In the end hold the breath in in the inhalation, and gently pull the center during the exhalation.

Deep, rhythmic breath, 1-2 minutes.

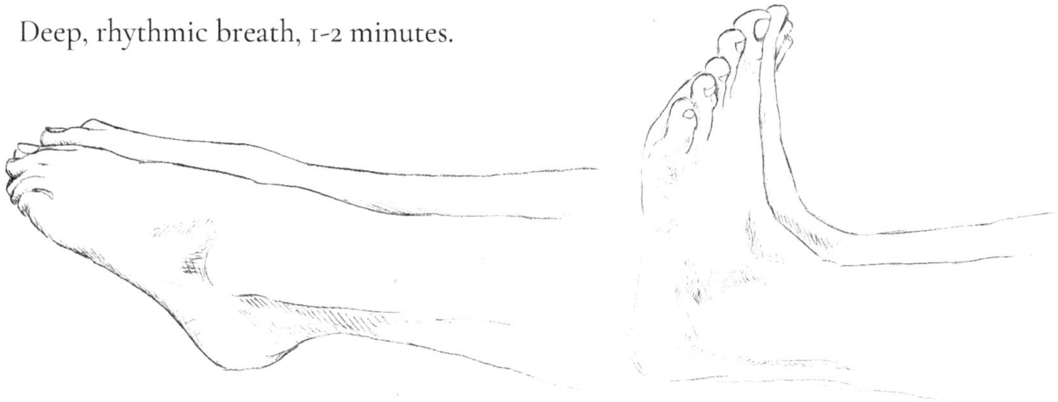

Kulph cakra

Ankle rotation. Remain in the same position with the feet closed and touching one another. Start to rotate both of your feet from the ankles. Observe the rotation with maximum attention. Observe with an innocent but unbroken attention just like a child would observe a new and fascinating toy. Be gripped by it. Nothing is simple, let the magic unfold. Synchronize with your breath. After a while change direction.

Step2. Open your feet slightly just 20 cm apart. Start to rotate your feet from the ankles in opposite directions. Synchronize the breath. Keep the breathing deep. When you finish, inhale and move the breath gently into the center and pull the feet up. Exhale, hold and push the feet down. Change directions and repeat.

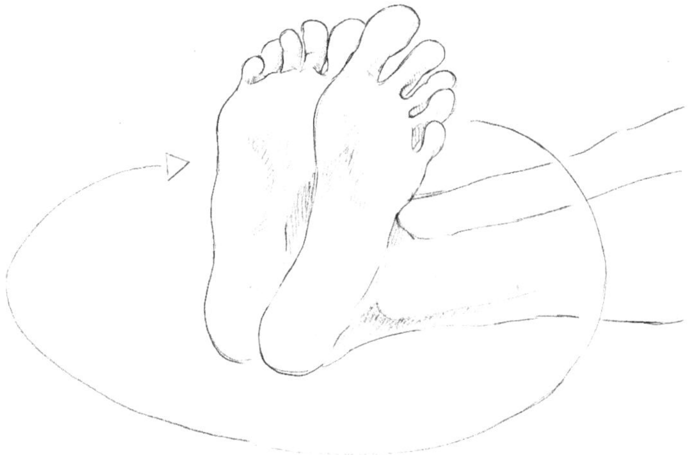

Deep, rhythmic breath, 1-2 minutes.

Kulph ghūrṇan

Ankle crank. Take your right knee with both hands, elevate the knee and pull it to the chest, push the knee outwards and gently take your right ankle and lift it on top of the right thigh.

With your right hand hold firmly your ankle, you must feel that you have strong grip. Take the fingers of your left hand and one after the other interlace the fingers of your left hand with the toes of your right foot.

Once you are in this position elevate your spine and open your chest, look deep inside, and start to slowly and deeply to rotate your right foot with the rhythm of your breath. When you inhale move the foot up, when you exhale push it down. Be aware the movement is deep, and the foot itself is not actively involved in the movement. pay full attention like a curious child.

In the end inhale, hold and take time. Exhale hold and take your time, then relax.

Gently move the leg horizontally outwards, then bring the knee up to the centre and stretch the right leg, repeat the same procedure on the other side.

Deep, rhythmic breath, 1-2 minutes on each side.

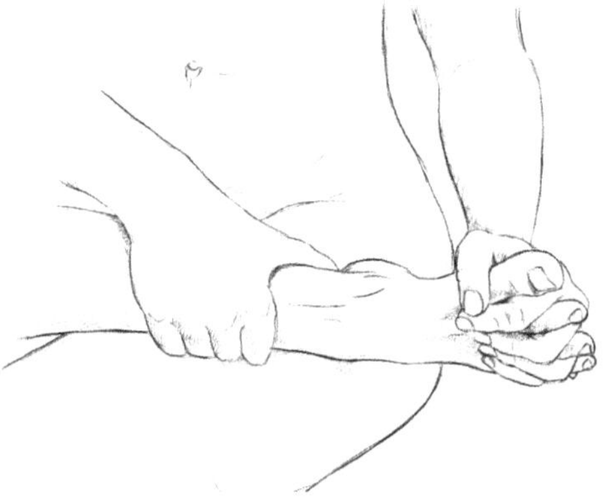

Jānuphalak ākarṣaṇ

Kneecap contraction. Sit again in the base position with your legs stretched out. Bring your hands on your knees, your thumbs and index fingers rest on both sides of your kneecaps.

With the rhythm of your deep breathing contract the muscles of your thighs so that the kneecaps move upwards. Hold the breath and the kneecaps gently after the inhalation. Then exhale slowly and relax them. Enjoy the internal massage of your knees - vitality will flow.

Deep, rhythmic breath, 30sec. - 1 minute.

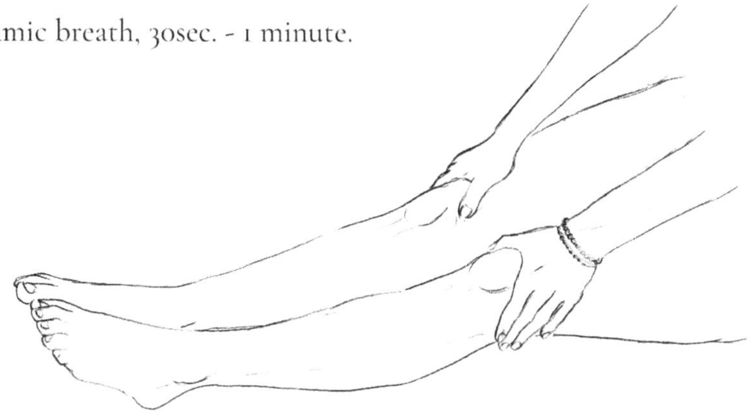

Jānu naman

Knee bending. From the base position, bring both hands underneath your right knee and interlock your fingers with the palms turned upwards. Then pull your knee towards your chest and exhale while you lengthen your spine. Inhale and stretch the leg out over the ground with your arms stretched out as well. Look at your toes. With a deep rhythm start to stretch and bend your knee. <Keep your chest open. Breathe deep and allow the rhythm to carry you away. In the end, inhale, stretch and hold. Then exhale, contract and hold. Breathe and lower your leg to the ground. Repeat on the other side.

Deep, rhythmic breath, 1-2 minutes on each side.

Jānu cakra

Knee rotation. Just like in the previous exercise interlock your fingers under your thigh, open your chest and pull the knee up. Gently start to describe a circle with your foot and lower leg but keeping the thigh in position, the thigh will rotate gently outwards and inwards but without moving up or down. Synchronize with your deep breathing, so the leg is stretched in inhalation and bend in exhalation. In the end deeply inhale, exhale, hold pull the knee to the chest and relax.

Concentrate on this movement, it is meditative by nature.

Deep, rhythmic breath, 1-2 minutes on each side.

Ardha titalī āsana

Half sided butterfly pose. From the base position with the legs stretched out, elevate the right knee, move it to the side and let the right ankle rest on the left thigh. Again, interlock your fingers of your left hand with the toes of your right foot starting from the little finger and small toe, one after the other. Straighten your spine and relax your face if you wish close your eyes and gaze inwards.

Slowly start to pull your leg to the chest and inhale. Exhale and push it to the ground. Move your hand in circular motion around your knee pulling and pushing it gently. Gradually become faster and more rhythmic and gaze inwards. After a while, inhale and straighten your spine. Hold the breath inside and gaze into the silence. Exhale

gently and push the knee to the ground and hold the breath there.

Move your foot outwards, the knee upwards, and then straighten the leg. Repeat the same procedure for the other side.

Deep, rhythmic breath, 1-2 minutes on each side.

Pūrṇa titalī āsana

Full butterfly pose. Sitting in the base position with the legs stretched out, bring both of your knees to the chest just like in *bījāsana*, and contemplate the centre. Elevate the spine and feel the sky above you. Then after a few breaths, open your knees slightly and bring the hands between your legs. Interlock your fingers, with your hands holding your feet, and allow your thumbs to close over your big toes. Then let your feet rest on the ground and straighten your spine.

Gently start to move your legs up and down like a butterfly flying. Keep the breath deep. Move slowly and then faster and in the end, slowly again. The breath doesn't need to be synchronized with the movement. Smile and enjoy flying like a butterfly. In the end, inhale, stretch, exhale and bend forward. Remain in the stretch for a few breaths.

Fly joyfully 2-3 minutes.

Śroṇi cakra

Hip rotation. Again, come into the same position as in *ardha titalī āsana*. Let your right-hand rest on your right knee.

Slowly and with an open face and focus, start to rotate your knee in a circle. Synchronize your breath with the movements. When you inhale, the knee moves upwards. When you exhale, it moves downwards. Move with the highest attention, this happens inwards. After a while change direction.

Move your foot outwards, the knee upwards and then straighten the leg. Repeat the same procedure for the other side.

Deep, rhythmic breath, 1-2 minutes on each side.

Makra vyāyāma

The crocodile exercise. From the base position bring your knees up and feet on the ground. Open your legs so your feet are about 40cm apart. Bring your arms behind your body, fingers pointing backwards, arms stabilize the torso upwards.

Inhale and open your belly and chest. Exhale and let your legs fall to the left while turning your head to the right. Inhale and bring your knees again upwards and your head turning to the centre. Exhale let your knees fall to the right and your head turns to the left.

Move in this manner with deep, rhythmic breath, from one side to the other. 1-2 minutes.

Step 2. Then close your feet and knees like in the illustration above and perform the same exercise but with closed legs, this way the stimulation will move up the spinal cord.

Move with deep, rhythmic breath, from one side to the other. 1-2 minutes.

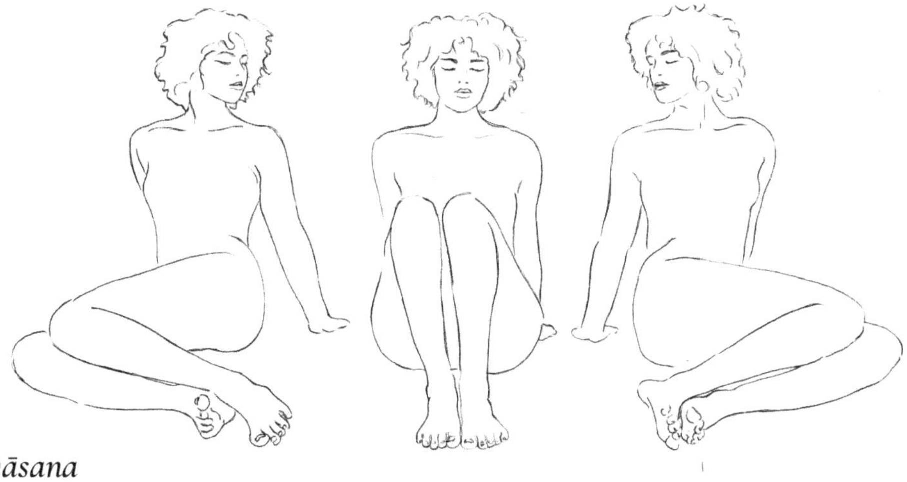

Śavāsana

Lay on your back with your palms facing upward. Let the vibration settle in silence. This exercise stimulates the spinal channel like no other. Deep rest for at least 2 minutes is mandatory.

Muṣṭika bandha

Hand Clenching. Sitting in the centre in *sukhāsana*, stretch out your arms to the front and open your fingers wide. Gaze forward firmly with your face open. In the exhalation clench your fist with your thumbs inside, in the inhalation open the fingers wide again, choose a good rhythmic pace. In the end inhale open your hands hold and gaze inside. Then exhale slowly.

Deep, rhythmic breath, 1-2 minutes.

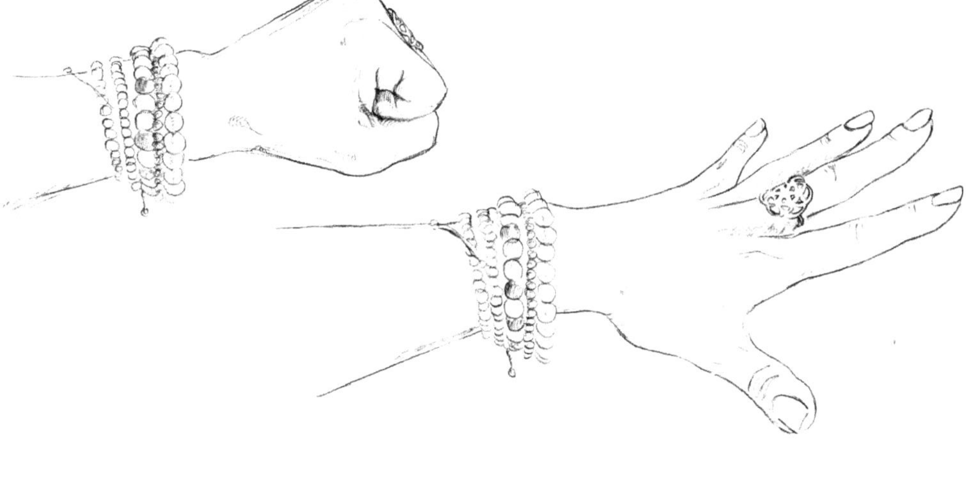

Maṇibandha naman

Wrist bending. Still sitting in easy pose with your arms stretched out horizontally in front of you. Close your fingers but keep them stretched out and start to bend your hand from the wrist. Inhale push your palm forward and your fingers up. Exhale and bend the hand down from your wrist. Also here choose a good rhythmic pace. In the end inhale push the palm forward and hold. Exhale slowly and relax.

Deep, rhythmic breath, 1-2 minutes.

Maṇibandha cakra

Wrist joint rotation. Still sitting in *sukhāsana* with your arms stretched out horizontally in front of you. Bend your left hand down at the wrist as you support your left arm with the right just under your elbow. With the left arm still

stretched out, close your fingers and form a fist with your thumb clenched inside. Very slowly and clearly start to rotate the fist from the wrist, with the palm facing downwards at all times. Synchronize the movement with your deep breathing. In the end, inhale, bend the fist upwards, contemplate the center and hold. Exhale slowly and relax both arms.

Invert the posture and repeat the exercise.

Deep, rhythmic breath, 1-2 minutes on each side.

Kaphoṇi naman

Elbow bending. Bring both arms to the side, palms up and inhale, this opens *mahā-prāṇa* – the great Energy. Then bring both arms to the front and open the fingers slightly, so to form a cup like shape with them. In the exhalation bend the elbows so to bring the hands to the shoulders. In the exhalation stretch them again. Choose a good rhythmic pace. In the end stretch the arms out and hold. Exhale slowly and relax.

Deep, rhythmic breath, 1-2 minutes.

Skandha cakra

Shoulder rotation. Open your arms to the side, palms facing upwards. Bring your hands on your shoulders with the fingers in cup shape. Inhale and very slowly bring your elbows up till your hands are behind your neck, slowly in course of this inhalation bring the elbows behind you and make the arms rotate backwards and downwards. Describe a full circle. When your arms come forward exhale and contract the chest, when the arms move further let the elbows touch each other in front of your face. Rotate with deep breathing slowly in one direction, then change directions.

Deep, rhythmic breathing, 1-2 minutes in each direction.

Grīva sañcālana

Neck movements. Straighten your spine and gently start to move your head to the left when inhaling and then to the right when exhaling, breath slow and deep. After a while invert the breathing. When you move your head, pay attention to explore the maximum range of movement.

Then come to the centre and start to rotate your head gently along the chest and neck. Role your head slowly and consciously from one shoulder to the neck, to the chest, to the opposite shoulder. Synchronize your breath with the movement. After a while reverse the movement. Sink into the movement.

Move your head in deep, rhythmic breathing, 1-2 minute in each direction.

Jālandhara bandha

The lock of the infinite source of cosmic nectar. Inhale and move your head to the neck, feel the pressure in your neck, close your eyes and rise. Imagine a bright light burning on your forehead. Hold the breath deeply in your body and be silent. Exhale slowly and put your chin to the chest, look inside and bow down in front of the great sky. Hold the breath outside.

Move very slowly in this manner 3 - 5 deep breaths. Welcome home,

Śavāsana

Lay on your back with your palms facing upwards. Contemplate the ocean of live, your home.

Be thankful

CONTEMPLATIONS

These meditations are all creative contemplations, *bhāvanā.* They emphasize openness. They are *śuddha vikalpa*, pure thoughts. They are a modification of mind but yet they lead to the true self. Behind the image is the true reality, the one state of being.

Imagine that anything that you can perceive is nothing but the consciousness that it perceives. Because without that consciousness it would not be. Therefore anything is just consciousness. This is the nature of all. With firm conviction observe this thought.

The total plenitude of the absolute is everywhere and therefore in all beings. Whenever you see anything or anybody, no matter how ordinary that person my be. With firm conviction stabilize your mind in the thought that this person is fully pervaded by the absolute.

The whole world or anything that you perceive is just an illusion like a magic show. Firmly stabilize your mind in this thought and simply become happy.

Whenever you see another person concentrate on this person's heart with on pointed awareness. This heart is just like the heart of God.

Listen with an open ear to your heart. There is a sound there that is just like a rushing river, without beginning or end. Listen to this sound it is your most inner blessing.

When you sing any mantra or *bīja* concentrate on the sound, just when it fades away. When your mind is fully fixed on that sound fading, you can travel with it into the transcendental void – supreme freedom.

Imagine all around you till the very edge of the universe and beyond, in all directions, above and below, everywhere just space till eternity, focus on this with firm conviction.

Imagine the fire of time rising from your feet, step by step consuming everything, from your body, the room, the country, till the whole universe, what remains? Focus on this with firm conviction. It is the truth.

Remember the most beautiful scene of love and passion that you ever experienced, imagine these kisses and touch on your skin. Focus on this rising joy with one pointed concentration, till the secret bliss beyond your bliss will make you dissolve.

See that space that is your body, see that space that is the world. Visualize that all this space is just pervaded by the bliss of your own self. with clear conviction expand into this bliss.

Anyone is fully loved and embraced by at least one person, and even a person who may appear as the greatest jerk, is still embraced fully by his own parents. Who can say which degree of love is objectively justified? Who can say that the moment you don't love someone is more important, than the moment you do?

Therefore, it should become clear as the day to you, that it is your choice alone that makes someone lovable or not. Take your chance. Allow yourself innocently to love any person you encounter deeply. Make your mind that whoever you may see is the most lovable creature in the world. Focus with all your power on this thought. They deserve it. And you will become supremely happy.

RELAXATION

ŚAVĀSANA

The corpse pose. You should not consider yourself aware of everything that happens inside your mind or body. Relaxation is the state which allows for the integration of the changes made to your system. These changes occur in every yoga session, whether consciously witnessed or not. One must pass through a state of complete surrender to relinquish the old so that the new can find its place. Relaxation is that state in which the old can be washed away — the deeper the relaxation, the more of the old that drifts away and the more of the new can enter.

The wold is so full of beauty, the secret of yoga is to make one empty so that this overflowing beauty can enter. The more full we are, full of thought and self, the less the one unbound state can enter. Letting go of whatever you think you are, doesn't mean to loose anything. It means to gain the whole world. Death is the greatest letting go, and the ground for the greatest new. Considering death from this perspective, its just a deeper and all encompassing relaxation, a relaxation that frees you from whatever you are, and makes you gain the unbound. Perhaps this is why relaxation is so difficult; because something has to die, so that the new can enter your being. Let no one tell you that *śavāsana* is merely lying down, it is an exercise. Performed correctly, *śavāsana* is an exercise in dying. When death is performed correctly, the great unknown, which is the beauty of the world can fill you. *Śavāsana* is the last *āsana* (or throne) in every class, as being the last it is the highest. Perform it correctly!

DEATH

Death in general is misunderstood. Everybody is afraid of it. The elderly are shut out from society. Instagram is full of beautiful men and women but completely devoid of the beauty of old age. This is a symptom.

It is the symptom of a world that cannot die. A world that cannot die must live at any cost. Life at any cost means death for everybody else. As we cannot relinquish growth, everything else has to shrink to nothingness. As we cannot let go of the need to consume, the oceans must be consumed instead. Since we cannot let go of our need for meat, animals must be put to death. The more life and pleasure one wants to consume, the more life and pleasure that person must rob from somewhere else.

Yet the first victim has still not been named, which is one's self. By fearing death or clinging to life, you yourself are the first one to die. Life must be lived and cannot be borne, for fear is a burden. One cannot live when one is afraid of life's greatest destiny. All life must end and merge with the unknown. Its destiny is to dissolve like salt in the ocean. Once death is understood as the final destiny, life becomes meaningful, and every moment precious. How could you waste a single moment when you understand how precious and finite they are? How could you feed your greed when you already know that everything you have must one day be given?

In this spirit we should practice surrender. We should be able to let go of all, even ourselves. Behind this lies the great secret of the practice of *śavāsana*.

Life doesn't belong to us.
Every life is just borrowed from earth and one time it has to be given back. All things have to be given one day, so give with gratitude.

Yogi Yogrishi

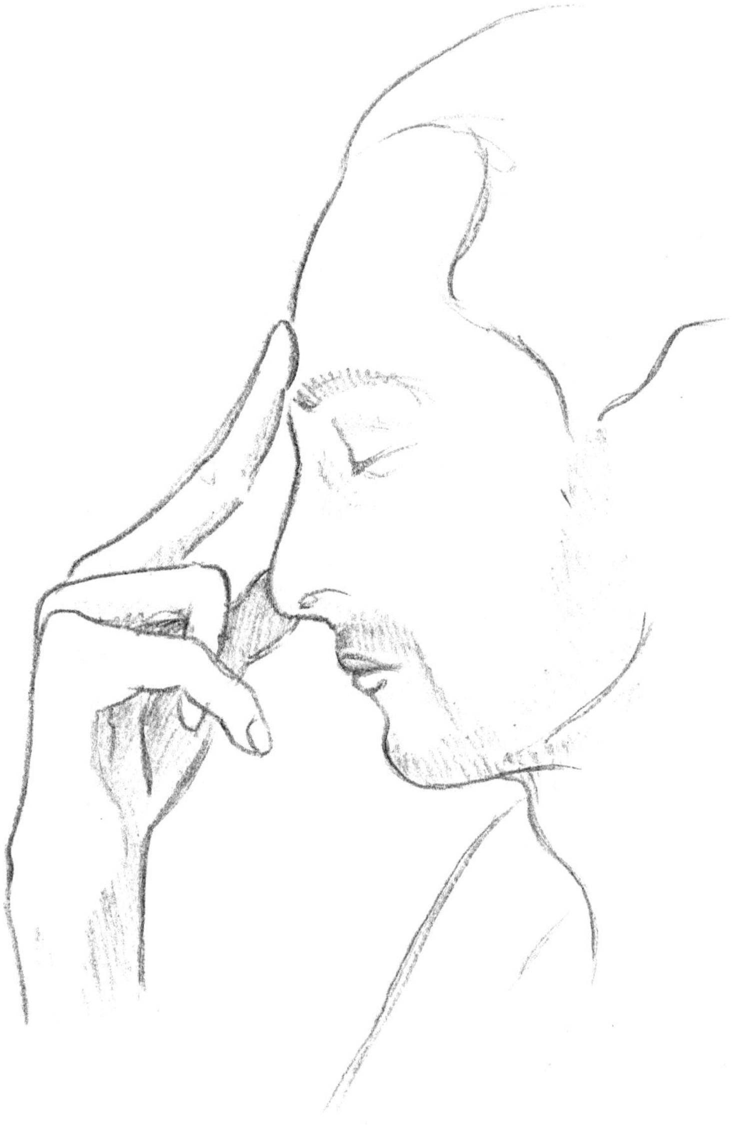

PRĀṆĀYĀMA

Other prāṇāyāmas give specific benefits, whereas Nāḍiśodhana gives all the benefits. As you have faith so will the benefits be with prāṇāyāma. With devotion to the Lord Narayana one should always eat satwic food.

Yoga-rahasya (1)

INTRODUCTION

Prāṇāyāma, meaning *'prāṇa-ayāma'* (*prāṇa*, energy + *ayām*, expansion) or *'prāṇa-āyāmaḥ'* (*āyāmah*, restrain, control, stopping), is the science of controlling one's own vital energy (*prāṇa*) through breathing techniques.

Āsana is usually only practiced in preparation for *prāṇāyāma*. It is said that, once a person is ready for *prāṇāyāma*, all of the benefits of *āsana* can be attained with *prāṇāyāma* alone. While *prāṇāyāma* is of crucial importance for all yogic practices, it most especially so for Kundalini Yoga techniques. There are numerous *prāṇāyāmas*, all of which favour different pranic movements and their corresponding effects on body and mind. Some generate energy, others move it. Some cool energy while others clean the channels through which this energy flows. There are seven different terms in *prāṇāyāma* which we should familiarise ourselves with:

Pūraka	Exhalation
Recaka	Inhalation
Antara kumbhaka	Retention after inhalation
Bāhya kumbhaka	Retention after exhalation

Kevala kumbka	Spontaneous (meditative) breath retention
Sahita kumbhaka	Conscious (forced) breath retention
Samavṛtti	Same length
Viṣamavṛtti	Different length

Prāṇāyāma is defined by six attributes which outline its practice. Patañjali briefly describes the essence of *prāṇāyāma* in his *sūtras:*

As the movement patterns of each breath --
inhalation, exhalation, retention -- are observed as to
duration, number, and area of focus, breath
becomes spacious and subtle.

Pātañjalayogaśāstra, (2:50)

The first pillar is focus, which is applied on exhalation (*bāhya*), inhalation (*ābhyantara*), and retention (*stambha*). All *prāṇāyāma* begins with exhalation, as one must first become an empty vessel in order to be filled by the greater energy. Inhalation is the second step, and is the filling of the pure inner space with the energy of the practice. Retention is the timeless contemplation about the energy created. Breath is meant to be long (*dīrgha*) and subtle (*sūkṣmaḥ*) – qualities which are both the means and the goal of achieving expansion.

Expansion in subtlety and spaciousness is attained through the framework that mind and body creates. This framework is the place (*deṣa*) of focus, the number (*saṃkhyābhiḥ*) of breaths, and the time (*kāla*) of practice. The *deṣa* is your internal gaze as well as your outer focus. The number (*saṃkhya*) is the clear and protected framework of counts in which your breath moves in and out. It is your rhythm, both in terms of the pace of your specific practice and the daily routine in which your practice takes place. *Kāla* is both the hour of practice and its length.

Keep these basic attributes of *prāṇāyāma* in mind when proceeding with this chapter.

HOW TO PRACTICE

Prāṇāyāma is not simply breathing.

Attention is key to *prāṇāyāma*. Without attention, *prāṇāyāma* is useless. This applies more strongly to *prāṇāyāma* than to *āsana*. The greater the distraction during performance, the higher the concentration required. Attention can be painful at first, but with effort this dissipates. When the mind wanders, contemplate: one should do fully what one is doing and nothing else, because what is done if you don't do what you do?

So, do it fully.

No strain but surrender

Just as energy cannot be forced into existence, neither can consciousness. When people apply force it is because they are impatient for the good to enter on its own. Why do these people believe the good will not come when one is ready? Why should the Absolute restrain his blessing when your heart is open? There is no good reason to believe in this restraint. All good things are here. Either one is ready to embrace them, or one is not, but if one strains to attain them quickly, all one will achieve is delay.

When practicing *prāṇāyāma*, give yourself completely to the practice. Instead of straining, fix your position to show your beauty. Instead of wanting, pay proper attention to the flow of your breath. Furthermore, overstraining – especially in *kumbhaka* (retention) – can be harmful. *Prāṇāyāma* is the manipulation of *prāṇa*. This changes the way you feel, perceive, and think. Your body and being need time to gently adapt to this. Remember, Rome was not built in a day.

> *Four things are necessary in practicing prāṇāyāma. First a good place; second a suitable time, moderate food, and lastly purification of the nāḍis. Practice of yoga should not be attempted in a far-off country (loss of faith), nor in the forest (no protection), nor in a city or in the midst of a crowd (exposure). If one does, so he loses success.*
>
> *Gheraṇḍa-smahita (5:4)*

Preparation and Posture

Begin by practicing *āsana* before starting with *prāṇāyāma*. Sometimes you will find that 10 minutes of *āsana* is sufficient. This will open the body and remove tension.

Choose a comfortable sitting *āsana* and fix your body to it. Ensure that the body is straight and unbending. Avoid unnecessary movements, such as fidgeting or looking at others. The body is a vessel and energy cannot accumulate during *prāṇāyāma* if one is not steady. Be firm, stretch your arms, and fix them forcefully. The position taken should resemble strength, beauty, and ease. If pain occurs, one should move so as to subdue it and then return to the position. There is no use in suffering, as this will not help one's attention. If one is able to pay proper attention, moving a painful leg will not corrupt one's focus.

Food and surroundings

There are many restrictions surrounding *prāṇāyāma*, perhaps because it is highly arousing, and being polluted is unhelpful when one wants to stay centred.

Prāṇāyāma should be attempted only after one has firmly decided to transform one's being. If this decision is made, a proper vegetarian diet and a pure lifestyle should pose no problems. If you find these to be problematic, ask yourself what you really want. Then strongly act according to the answer. This way the mind becomes directed. Thought, speech, and action are aligned.

> *One should be vegetarian, enjoying sweet and nutritious food. One should not eat before prāṇāyāma. One should rise up. One should avoid superfluous company and entertainment. He who practices without moderation of diet, incurs various diseases, and obtains no succes (...). Half of the stomach should be filled with food, one quarter with water: and one quarter should be kept empty for practicing prāṇāyāma.*
>
> *Gheraṇḍa-saṃhitā (5:16-22)*

Place and time

Prāṇāyāma should be performed in the early morning before sunrise at *brahmāmuhūrta*, or at noon or sunset. *Prāṇāyāma* should be avoided less than two hours before going to bed as its arousing nature can prevent sleep. *Prāṇāyāma* should be done alone and in a silent space where one can deeply contemplate breathing. The best environment is a clean and well-ventilated room. *Prāṇāyāma* should not be practiced under direct sunlight, except at dawn under the gentle rays of the early sun.

Kumbhaka

Kumbhaka refers to the techniques of holding one's breath.

Since the body is a mirror of the macrocosm, day and night, sunrise and sunset find their proper expression in the body's function. Respiration is said to mirror nature's movement of energy throughout the day. Inhalation relates to the dawn, retention to dusk, and exhalation to the night. Retention after exhalation is the sunrise in the early morning. From there on, the circle repeats again. Since the hours of sunrise and sunset are holy, so must be the time between breaths. When breath is still and unmoving, it is referred to as the *kumbhakas.*

Some say that *prāṇāyāma* begins with proper *kumbhaka.* Indeed, the *Haṭha-Yoga-Pradīpikā* makes no distinction between *prāṇāyāma* and *kumbhaka*, as the former must also be the latter. This means that when the moments between the breaths are sufficiently expanded and enjoyed, the raising of consciousness can take place.

Iḍā and *piṅgalā* also refer to night and day, and therefore to exhalation and inhalation. *Suṣumnā*, either sunrise or sunset, also resembles *kumbhaka.* Indeed, *kumbhaka* is used to bring the *prāṇa* into *suṣumnā.*

The highest stage is the spontaneous stopping of the breath as a result of realisation, not as its means. *Prāṇa* could flow freely into *suṣumnā*, rendering breathing itself unnecessary as body and mind would rest in the mysterious – and simultaneous – stage of sunrise and sunset. When combined, inhalation and exhalation are *yuj.* This is the goal of yoga. This is *kevalakumbhaka.*

> *When kevalakumbhaka without inhalation and exhalation has been mastered, there is nothing in the [inner] world that is unattainable for the yogi. Through this kumbhaka he can restrain the breath as long as he*

likes. Thus he [gradually] attains the stage of Rāja Yoga. Through this kumbhaka, Kuṇḍalinī is aroused and then the suṣumnā is free from all obstacles; but without Hatha Yoga there can be no Rāja Yoga, and vice versa. Both should be practiced until Rāja Yoga is perfected.

Haṭha-Yoga-Pradīpikā (2:70–75)

Mantra in Prāṇāyāma

Prāṇāyāma is very often used with mantras or *bīja*. The *Yoga-rahasya* considers all *prāṇāyāma* conducted without mantras to be inferior to those conducted with them. Mantras are used to fill the gaps in the breathing process, and measure the time of breathing and retention. Filling these gaps helps fix the mind on the higher goal. Some use the *gāyatrī* mantra to measure the length of the in- and outbreaths. Oṃ is typically used to measure breathing.

Initially, one can silently repeat Oṃ five times when inhaling and five times when exhaling. This will fix the mind and even the breath. Similarly, *'Oṃ Namah Śivaya, So-Haṃ, Oṃ Yaṃ Ma'* or *'Oṃ Mā'* can be used.

Prāṇāyāma is of two types, one done without mantras and the other with mantras. One should choose the appropriate manta for individual requirements. Sagarbha is with mantra and Vigarbha is without mantra. The smritis (texts) say that prāṇāyāma done with mantra is commendable while the other is considered inferior.

Yogarahasya (1)

THE PRĀṆĀYĀMAS

Yogic Breathing

Yogic breathing is deep and holotropic. Each breath gently fills the lungs to their utmost capacity. In- and outbreaths must be even in length (*samavṛtti*). One can feel the pleasure of oxygen entering the lungs, like a delicious liquid entering the throat when parched. The air softly fills the lungs from the top down. The belly gently extends outwards. When maximum inhalation (*recaka*) is reached, one must gently be aware of the space in between the breaths. This place is beyond breath. It is energy. For a brief glimpse of this, be aware of your retention after inhalation (*antara kumbhaka*). You must feel it. Then gently breathe out (*pūraka*) for the same length. Let your belly move inward again and lengthen yourself. When you reach maximum exhalation, gently feel *bāhya kumbhaka*. Hold this for a moment, and feel the inner sensation of joy.

Some dismiss yogic breathing as easy, but it requires fully expanded lungs and some concentration. If you find yourself struggling, perform it more playfully. The lung must be able to deeply open and close to its full and natural volume. This is achieved through three preparatory stages.

Stage One

Place your hands at your side, just over your hips so that your fingers can touch your belly. Breathe deeply. Move your belly inward during the exhalation and outward during the inhalation. Breathe to your full capacity.

Stage Two

Place your hands at your side, right at your ribcage so that your fingers are underneath your breast. Breathe deeply. Move your chest inward during the exhalation – one can tuck in the chin as well. Expand your chest in the inhalation (open the chin at this point). Breathe to your full capacity.

Stage Three

Place your hands just behind your neck, interlace your fingers, and pull gently to the side. Breathe deeply. When breathing in, open your chest wide. When you have reached the maximum inhalation, breathe a little more just at the very top of the lungs. When you exhale, contract your chest and close your elbows in front of your face. Breathe into the top of the lungs.

Nāḍiśodhana Prāṇāyāma

Nāḍiśodhana (psychic network purification) is the most important, useful, and gentlest *prāṇāyāma* of all. The *Yogarahasya* of *Nātamuni* says that all of the possible benefits of *prāṇāyāma* arise from this one alone. Moreover, the Yoga-*yājñavalkya* dedicates a whole chapter solely to this *prāṇāyāma*. It is the *prāṇāyāma* that purifies the channels of the subtle body, thereby transforming it into a vessel sufficiently worthy for consciousness. Sit straight and relax your body. Stretch out one arm over your knee in *chinmudrā* with the palm facing upward. The other hand should be brought up in front of your face. Put two fingers on your forehead, gently massaging the third eye while the thumb and ring finger are at both sides of the nose so as to regulate air flow. Make the air flow into your left nostril and wonder at this gentle stream of life. Hold the air for a brief moment. Then exhale the air through the right nostril. When the air has left your body, and you have reached the utmost exhalation, perform a very gentle *bāhya kumbhaka* and keep the air outside. Then, inhale once more through the right nostril, hold, and exhale through the left side. This is one round.

Perform *kumbaka* in a gentle manner at each turning of the breath. While the length of each breath is unimportant, you must ensure that they are equal. Nor does it matter for how long you perform *kumbaka* but, again, it must have an equal length in *antara* and *bāhya*. Perform *mūlabandha* at each *kumbaka*. Your success in this *prāṇāyāma* is irrespective of how much you strain or on the complexities of your in- and outbreath ratio. It depends on your attention and love for your practice alone.

> *Having inhaled the air through the left nostril filling up the abdomen, then meditating on the fire in the belly with its flame in the Dehamadhya and meditating on the seed letter of fire Raṃ, which is established in the region of fire, he must exhale slowly through the right nostril. Then one who is determined and wise, inhaling the air through the right nostril, must again exhale slowly through the left nostril. One should practice this in solitude six times every day at the three sandhis (in the morning, afternoon and evening) for three to four months or three to four years.*
>
> *Yoga-Yājñavalkya (5:17-20)*

Kapālabhāti

Kapālabhāti (the shining skull) is a *satkarma* – one of the six purification exercises – as well as a *prāṇāyāma*. It moves the *prāṇas* and purifies them when they mix with the fire at the navel. *Kapālabhāti* is performed from the *kanda*, the navel point. *Kanda* is commonly misunderstood as *maṇipūra* chakra. In some yogic schools, the *nāḍis* all originate from there. It has the form of a golden egg, is situated underneath the navel, and is the centre of bodily pranic force. From there, the *prāṇas* expand upwards. The great sun makes them rise.

Sit straight, open up your face, and feel the sun rise on your forehead. Pull *mūlabandha* very gently. Push the air out and move your navel inwards. When the breath relaxes, you will inhale naturally rather than actively. Pulse your navel in and out. Feel the pulse massaging your lower belly. The rest of your body should be relaxed. Your face stays open and released. The pace can be accelerated until a comfortable rhythm is reached. Imagine this little golden egg moving upwards upon exhalation and imagine it moving downwards when the breath relaxes. Imagine a stream of golden light rising to the sky.

Inhale and exhale like the bellows of a blacksmith. This is kapālabhāti and removes all ailments due to kapha.

Haṭha-Yoga-Pradīpikā (2:35)

Śītalī Prāṇāyāma

Śītalī (cooling breathing) is like a friend, gentle and comfortable, that you invite into your home to relax. This friend will talk to you decently, calmly, and lovingly. They will make you drink delicious waters, nourish your mind and body, and leave you feeling whole, calm, and as clear as crystal.

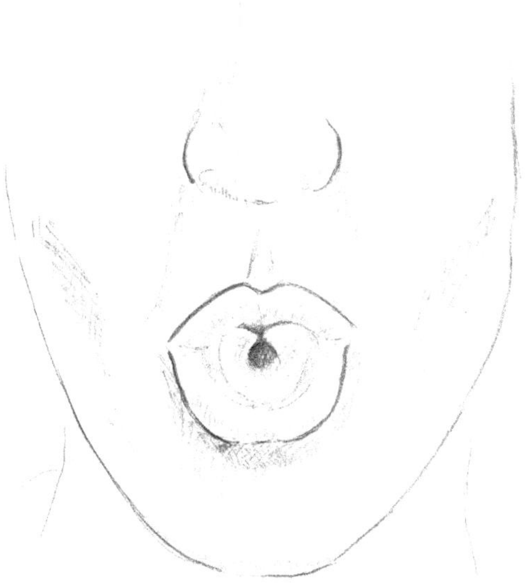

Sit straight and gently tuck in your chin. Stick out and roll your tongue. I realised this is not something everyone can do so, if this is hard for you, try to pull out your tongue a little and roll the sides up as much as you can. Then, slightly press your upper lip against your tongue so that its sides are fixed with your mouth and they roll in naturally. This should help you succeed.

Once done, inhale, slightly raise your chin, and imagine yourself sucking in the air as if it were a delicious drink from the sky. The air is as cooling and white as milk. It drops down from the moon above you. Drink this air and enjoy it. When you reach maximum inhalation, retain the air inside for the briefest of moments. Pull in your tongue, lower your chin, and deeply exhale through your nose. Keep in- and outbreaths at an equal length. This is one round.

> *The wise inhales through the tongue, then follows kumbhaka and exhalation through the nose. This kumbhaka, called śītalī, removes illnesses of the spleen, fever, gall bladder trouble, hunger, thirst, and the effects of poison, like snake bites.*
>
> *Haṭha-Yoga-Pradīpikā (2:36-57)*

Bhrāmarī Prāṇāyāma

Bhrāmarī (bee breathing) is said to bring about an unsurpassed level of joy in the practitioner. It can be likened to a wedding with one's self. It is the great joy being expressed in the sound that resides in the heart, that is like an eternal rushing river. *Bhrāmarī* is a way of being, meaning it is thus a body. When one practices *bhrāmarī*, one should imagine being a body made of nothing but this sound, and yet this is not an audible sound in one's ear. Instead, it is a subtle sound that one cannot hear. Whenever you make a humming sound, listen to that which is behind it – the inner sound of the pure pleasure of pure being.

The great *nāda* (primal sound) is everywhere in the body, though some parts are closer to it than others. *Nāda* appears in the central channel of *suṣumnā*, or *sárasvatī nadí*, that is said to have 'sound in her womb'. The heart is said to be the seat of *śabda-brahman*, the god in sonic form.

> *Inhale rapidly, producing the sound of a male bee. Then*

exhale with the sound of a female bee. This is followed by kumbhaka. The great yogis, by constantly practicing this, experience indescribable happiness in their hearts. This is bhrāmarī.

Haṭha-Yoga-Pradīpikā (2:67)

The Heart Bhrāmarī

Sit straight and bring your hands in front of your heart, one over the other. Tuck your chin in gently and feel your spine like a staff raised to the sky. Settle in your chest, like a shiny ball falling into the cavity of your heart to the point of maximum repose at the very bottom of your being. You are home.

Pull *mūlabandha* to fix the energy and begin performing this sweet humming sound gently in your heart. This sound is joy in essence, it is your inner honey. Stay focused and listen to the sound beyond what is audible – the music of your heart. Expand that sound from your heart, breath by breath. The sound will expand until it reaches its maximum extension throughout the world of which you are a part, and all is a part of you.

The Suṣumnā Bhrāmarī

Feel this graceful *suṣumnā* that begins from your perineum and runs to the top of your head. It is a line without dimension, incredibly thin, which stretches throughout the universe. Untouchable, it is only realised by its own means. Let us set it into vibration.

Sit straight. Perform *ṣaṇmūkī mudrā*. Close the gates to your face with the fingers of both hands. Close your ears, mouth, and eyes, and place your middle fingers adjacent to your nostrils. When you have closed the channels of your senses, fall inside of yourself. *Pratyāhāra*. There is no world outside, only within. There is only this one endlessly thin line, stretching throughout the universe, this graceful stairway to heaven. Start with *bhrāmarī prāṇāyāma*. Understand that sound as being the very nature of *suṣumnā*. See that sound as being like golden light vibrating within. This is your body, enjoy.

Ujjāyī Prāṇāyāma

Ujjāyī (victorious breathing) is the invincible breathing of the one who has mastered the fire and has therefore mastered the mind. It originates from the *viśuddha* chakra, from where you are enthroned over the world. It is the spacious breath. Space is the master, space pervades all.

Sit straight and gently tuck your chin in. Avoid pressing too hard, but feel your neck rising to the sky. Imagine that silver disc shining inside your throat. Start breathing deeply in *ujjāyī*, joined by the sound of lolling waves or fire burning in the wind. It is a clearly audible sound, emitted from the throat. With every exhale, imagine a silvery light shining from your throat and expanding in space. When you

inhale, feel that silvery light collected again in the centre of your throat. Feel that space in front of you. It is eternal. Expand in that space with each breath and recollect it again in your throat when you breathe in. Become spacious. Become invincible.

> *With closed mouth inhale deeply until the breath fills all the space between the throat and the heart, to the tips of the lungs. This creates a noise. Do kumbhaka and exhale through the left nostril. This removes phlegm in the throat*

and enhances the digestive power of the body. This is ujjāyī and can be practiced walking or sitting, it keeps diseases away from the individual organs and the Nāḍis, especially diseases that are due to kapha.

Haṭha-Yoga-Pradīpikā, (2:51-52)

Bhastrikā Prāṇāyāma

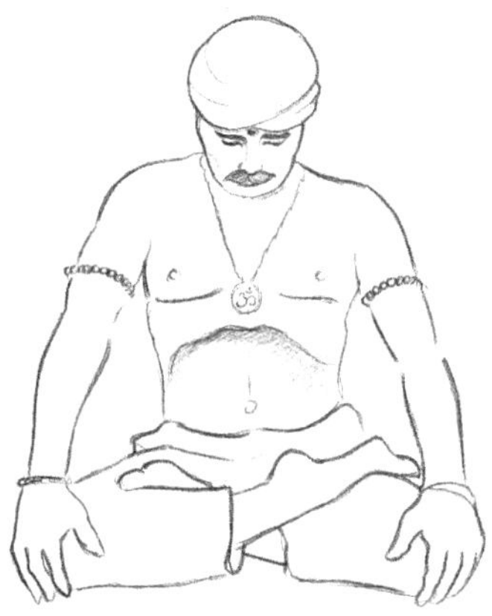

This 'bellows breathing' is a remarkably strong *prāṇāyāma* that is, in many ways, a yogic secret. *Bhastrikā* awakens *Śakti–Kuṇḍalinī*, and purifies and strengthens like no other breath. *Bhastrikā* can lead to mastery and completely expand ones being. *Bhastrikā* is fire, fire is light, fire is *suṣumnā*, fire is consciousness. It runs the house and warms the kitchen. It sheds light on the altar, guides the ritual, and clarifies the deity. Yet we must be careful, for the fire can also burn the temple to ashes and drive a person to madness. Fire is a force, and any force must be guarded with consciousness.

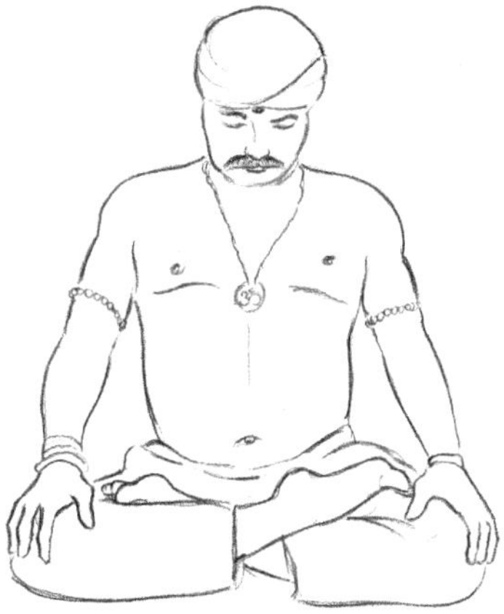

Bhastrikā is an advanced *prāṇāyāma*. My teacher, Sanjeev Pandey Ji, taught me four variations of *bhastrikā*, which I will describe in further detail shortly. It is worth remembering that it is hardly possible to achieve a profound insight into *bhastrikā* when it is not practiced with an experienced teacher's guidance. The teacher may show you the secrets and transmit energy with their presence that you would be unlikely to discover alone. This is something that I also had to experience myself.

Bhastrikā is the bellows that blows on the fire. It is equally strong as an inhalation or exhalation. It is often mistaken with *kapālabhāti* due to its similar appearance. The crucial difference is equal strength of exhalation and inhalation. It is first practiced in this threefold form. One side after another.

Iḍā bhastrikā – Sit up straight, elevate your head, and venerate your solar plexus. Imagine the sun rising in front of you, and show pride and gratitude. Close your right nostril and perform *bhastrikā* 30 times through your left nostril, and finally inhale and exhale. Take time to relax before continuing.

Piṅgalā bhastrikā – Perform the same process but close the left nostril.

Madhya bhastrikā – Then perform *madhya bhastrikā* (central bellows breath) one last time in the centre through both nostrils. Keep straight. Once done, perform *Sūryabheda kumbhaka.*

Sūryabheda kumbhaka – At the end of your *bhastrikā* practice, exhale slowly from the left nostril. Inhale slowly from the left, exhale from the right, in from the right, and hold in *antara kumbhaka* (the sun). Repeat the whole pattern with internal retention 2–4 more times and then relax. The number of retentions can gradually be increased every 2 weeks from 5 to 10 to 20. Performing *Sūryabheda kumbhaka* after *bhastrikā* is necessary for controlling the powers awakened by this powerful *prāṇāyāma. Ajgari* has the same effect.

Śārdūla Kriyā -Ajgari

This exercise has many names, some call it *śārdūla kriyā* – the exercise of the Panther because it makes one strong and clear like this mystical cat. Dhīrendra Brahmacārī referred to it as *ajgari,* sometimes transliterated *ajagari,* which is naming its nature as being that of a large and powerful snake – a boa.

Ajgari or *śārdūla kriyā* is a way to unite with one's own energy. Full of force, it centres the *prāṇa*, carrying a great silence, like the panther. *Ajgari* can be performed in almost all positions, making it highly useful for centring the energy during a yoga class. However, it should be avoided in balancing *āsanas. Ajgari* is usually preceded by *bhastrikā*, but it can be combined with almost any activating modification of breath, like *kapālabhāti. Ajgari* centres, and whenever this is desired or necessary, it can be done. However, of all the *prāṇāyāmas, bhastrikā* needs either *sūryabheda kumbhaka* or *ajgari* to return the energy to the central channel. Dissipated yogic energy can make one nervous and angry, and destroy the practitioner. *Ajgari* protects from these dangers.

After an activating *prāṇāyāma*, inhale deeply, slowly expand your belly, and fill yourself with air. Hold this air until you feel the energy settling in silence. Hold for about 5–20 seconds.

Then exhale deeply, contract all your muscles, feel the tension, and pull your belly inwards. Take time to pull your belly in and move the diaphragm upwards against the spine. Perform a gentle, false inhalation and move the diaphragm even deeper to explore this internal space. This is *uḍḍīyānabandha*. Hold for another 5–20 seconds. Then inhale deeply, straighten your body, and relax. Contemplate the centre in silence.

Seated in the vajrāsana posture firmly hold the feet near the ankles and be against the kanda. In the posture of vajrāsana the yogi should induce the kundalini to move. Then he should do bhāstrikā-kumbhaka. Thus the kundalini will be quickly awakened. Then he should contract the 'sun' [through uḍḍiyānabandha] and thus induce kundalini to rise. Even though he may be in the jaws of death, the yogi has nothing to fear. When one moves kundalini fearlessly for about an hour and a half, she is drawn upward a little through the suṣumnā. In this way she naturally leaves the opening of the suṣumnā free and is carried upward by the prana current, in this way one should daily move the kundalini.

Haṭha-yoga-pradīpikā (3:121–122)

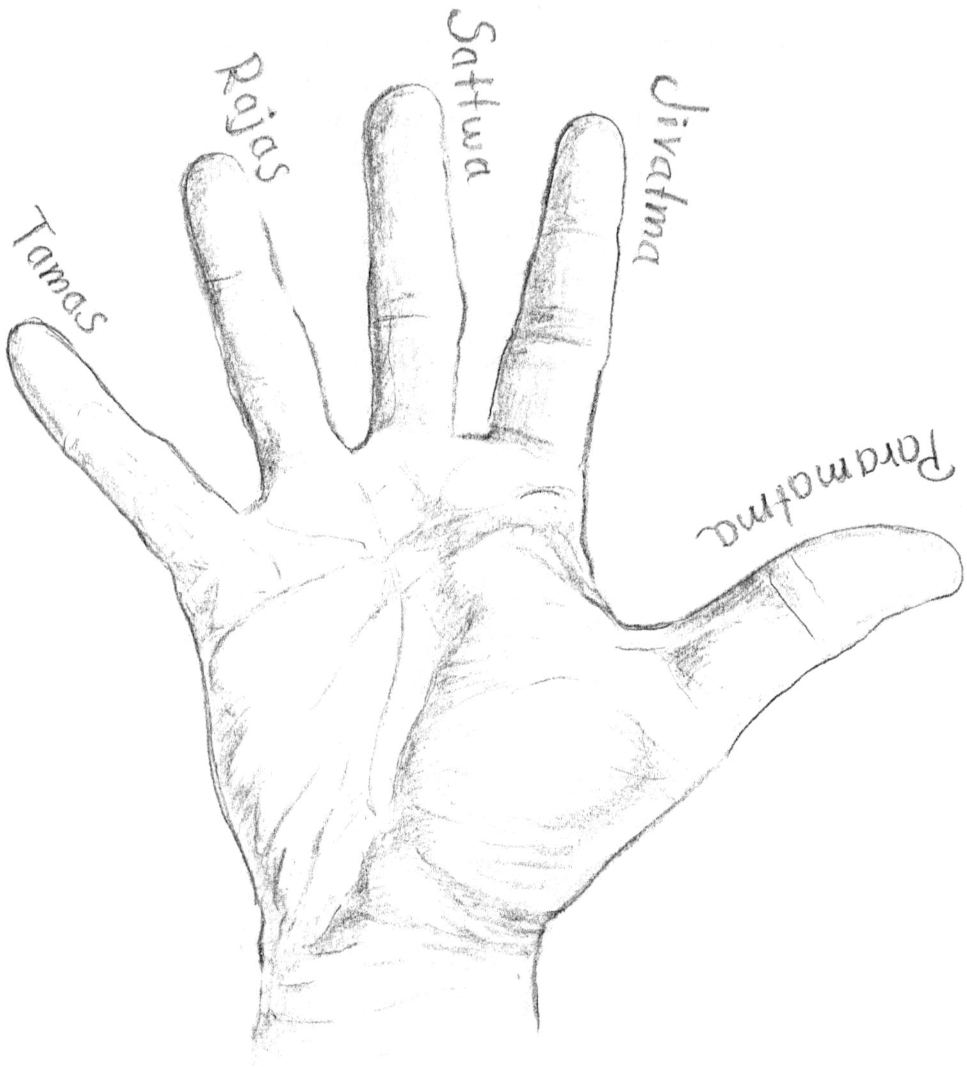
Tamas
Rajas
Sattwa
Jivatma
Paramatma

MUDRĀ

According to the etymology of the word mudrā, it means that which gives (da) or bestows bliss (mud), that is, the attainment of the essential nature of things and, through the body, the Self. This is why mudrās are called thus in the scriptures.

Tantrāloka (32:3)

INTRODUCTION

Mudrā, meaning 'seal' or 'gesture', is a posture using various body parts to resemble a certain flow of energy. The *Kulārṇava-tantra* excellently translates *mudrā* as that which generates joy or delight. Indeed, all *mudrās* should be practiced as resembling joy.

In the time of the ancient tantrics, the *mudrās* were first and foremost hand gestures resembling the energy of the deity worshiped. The *mudrā* was considered the outer form of the inner flow of the deity's energy. When this divine energy would manifest itself in the body of the practitioner, the *mudrā* was considered to spontaneously substantiate itself, so intimate is the connection between *mudrā* and deity. *Mudrā*, in this context, transcends mere gesture – it is the energy of the deity in action. Here *mudrā* is an expression of the goddess' power of action (*kriyāśakti*), similar to how mantra would be the body of the goddess and expression of her knowledge (*Jñānaśakti*). *Mudrā* is power in action. *Mudrā* is the goddess.

The *Kubjikā-mata-tantra* explains *mudrā* as that which melts away 'what sealed the self' and identifies *mudrā* with Kubjikā. She is the aggregate of the letters which form 'having threaded together the universe', she is simlply Kuṇḍalinī herself.

Mudrā (gesture or seal) is said to be power (śakti). It will melt what has been sealed. That which is sealed is what has been hidden by the power of consciousness, which is both manifest and supreme. Gesture is that due to which one does not know (reality). As long as the soul is bound by the impurity of ignorance, he does not know the Supreme Self and Māyā continues to function. When the darkness of ignorance has been rent asunder and a man sees oneness, then that same power is called supreme, and it brings about liberation from bondage. That supreme power is one, and she exists by Śiva's will. She frees from the influence of malevolent planets and the like and melts away the currents of the fetters. The energies are called gestures (mudrā) because they release (mocana) and melt (dravana). Flight always takes place by the path of the skyfarers which is the elevated state. That energy is called Khecarī – the Skyfarer – because she transports all living beings along this path. She should be known to be one in the supreme state and is also said to be threefold. Assuming the form of letters, she is will, knowledge and action. Divided into fifty, she is said to be one. Complete in all her limbs and parts she abides in the form of the alphabet beginning with "Na" and ending with "Pha" having threaded together the universe. Thus she is called Mālinī (Kubjikā). All the mantras are sealed with this mudrā. Thus she is called mudrā and gives immediate realization. In her parts she is in the form of the Mothers (letters)

Kubjikā-mata-tantra (6/75cd–86)

In Hatha Yoga, *mudrā* is a seal of energy and an integral part of the tradition. The 11th century *Amṛtasiddhi* – Hatha Yoga's first text – teaches several important *mudrās*, though their depiction differs somewhat from the above. They are described as techniques for the preservation of life's energy, semen or *bindu*, and no mention is made of the coiled goddess. As influenced by the tantra tradition, the 12–13th century *Vivekamārtāṇḍa* (from Gorakṣa) understands the very same *mudrās* as the means with which to raise Kuṇḍalinī to attain liberation. Here again we see the special influence of tantra in ancient yoga and its transformation into Kundalini Yoga.

Now I shall teach you in brief the stimulation of the Goddess. The Goddess is coiled, making her move from her home to the centre of the eyebrows is called the stimulation of the Goddess, śakticālana mudrā. There are two chief ways of accomplishing this: stimulation of Sarasvati (suṣumnā) and restraint of breath. Through practice Kuṇḍalinī becomes straight.

Gorakṣa-shataka (16–28)

FUNCTION OF MUDRĀ

Mudrā is an expression of the goddess's energy. When a *mudrā* is performed, Kuṇḍalinī is manifested. The typically uncontrolled energy that leaves the body finds direction in the form of the *mudrā* and is returned to one's field of awareness. The *mudrā* fixes consciousness inside an experience. It further prohibits consciousness' natural inclination for dissipation. It stops its fleeing and thus makes the experience available.

HASTA MUDRĀS

Hasta mudrās are hand gestures. The fingers represent the elementary forces of existence. The first three fingers mirror the three *guṇas*, which represent all nature and everything that exists as an object within it. *Tamas* is darkness and inertia. *Rajas* is desire and movement, and *sattva* is lightness and transparency. The index finger is the principle of the individual soul, *jīvātmā*. It is singular one-pointed consciousness. The thumb is *paramātmā*, the supreme all-pervasive being. Hand *mudrās* move and intertwine these energies. In so doing, one can form new relations between these forces and correctly realign the self within them.

Añjali Mudrā

Also known as *namaskāra mudrā* (or, the Gesture of Gratitude), the performance of this *mudrā* directs your energy into your being's most dominant space, the heart. It is radiant and the seat of power.

One always must perform *añjali mudrā* at the beginning and end of every yoga class. Through *añjali mudrā*, you show your possession and strength of your heart. Indeed transformation is impossible without it and, even if everything else is done well, when you forget the heart, you forget the one reason the be.

Settle your mind inside the cavity of your heart. Here you should rest. Place your hands in front of your heart and push your palms together so that you feel a slight pressure. Open your chest. Feel the gentle pressure of your thumbs against your

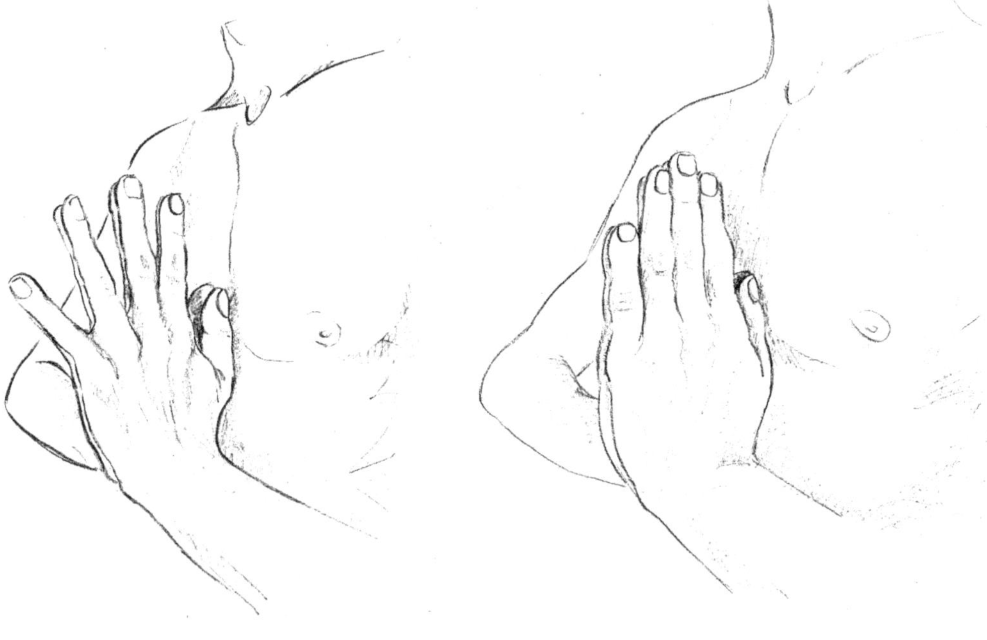

ribcage. When you open your fingers slightly, this is energy. When you close them, this is consciousness. Be grateful for all of this! There is a miraculous universe out there and you are meant to witness it. Think of how incredibly lucky you are to simply be!

Cinmudrā

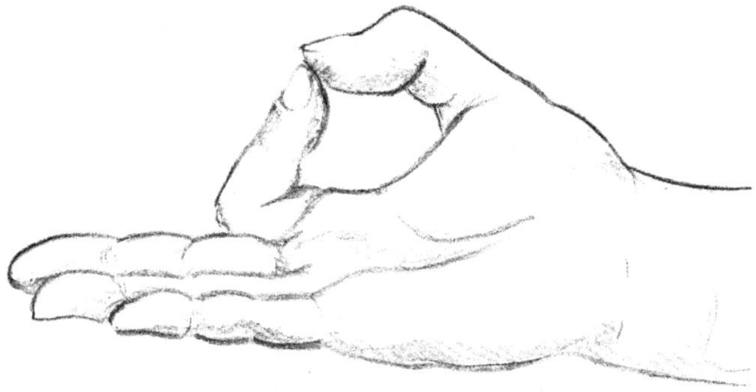

This *mudrā*, the Gesture of Consciousness, symbolises one's acknowledgment of the supreme position of consciousness. The three fingers that are spread away from body (the small, middle, and ring fingers) symbolise the three *guṇas*, and therefore the world.

When the index finger touches *paramātmāṇ*, this is yoga. It is union. Both *cinmudrā* and *jñānamudrā* are gestures of union: yoga. This *mudrā* is cit, because the union of the individual with the universal is achieved through the open hand. The hand acknowledges the formless space above, which is consciousness.

Jñānamudrā

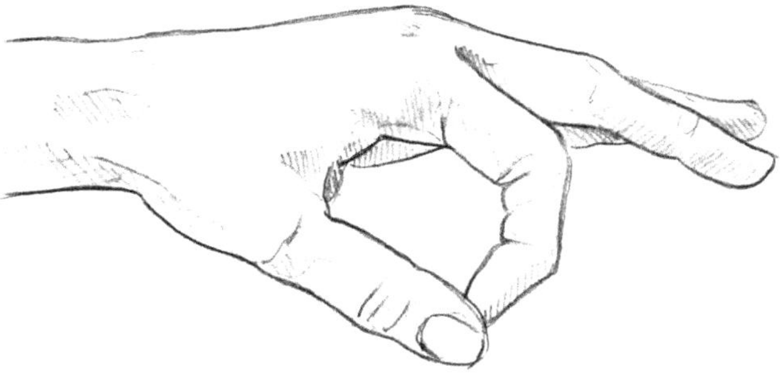

Jñānamudrā, the Gesture of Knowledge, is highly similar to *cinmudrā*. However, this time the union (yoga) of the individual soul with the supreme soul is achieved through a downward facing hand. This acknowledges the form or *śakti* below. This Śakti is the mother of all objectivity and therefore everything that can be known. It is *jñāna*, or the highest knowledge.

Bhairava Mudrā

The Gesture of the Dispeller of Fear involves resting both hands open on one's lab. They resemble profound meditation. Both palms face the sky, gazing into the supreme above. They do not want, nor aim for, anything. They simply surrender to pure being. Bhairava is the one who dispels fear by means of removing limitation. Bhairava is all pervasiveness. When you perform this *mudrā*, consider that the whole universe and your body is pervaded by nothing but one supreme consciousness.

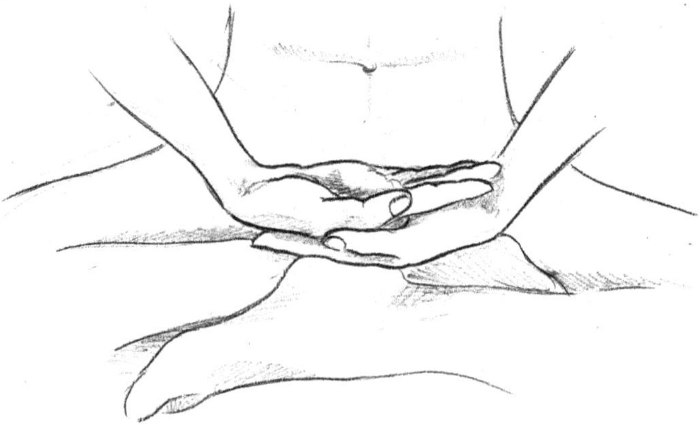

Yonimudrā

Yonimudrā, the Gesture of the Womb, is one's acknowledgment that all things are born from one source. *Yoni* means vagina, womb, or source. It is a female place, one of energy. It is an invocation of Kuṇḍalinī or the force that strives to unfold from below.

Yonimudrā resembles a triangle – the symbol of energy or Śakti. This symbol of energy is created through the connection of the individual soul with the universal. Concurrently, the three fingers (symbolising the *guṇas*) are interlaced. This means that the energy that creates the sensual outer world is bound and brought inwards. Directing the energy of the sensual world inwards for the sake of realisation is Kundalini Yoga. *Yonimudrā* is therefore more than a gesture of energy, it is a gesture of the goddess and Kundalini Yoga.

When one performs this *mudrā*, one must sit up straight, direct the energy inwards and hold the three fingers tightly interlaced. Then, gently pull them apart. Place yourself in the centre of this triangle that you have created. Use this focal point for your *dhāraṇā*. Open your chest and venerate the energy!

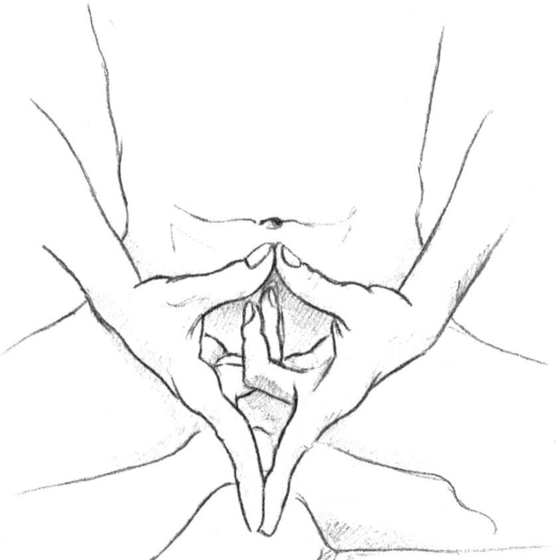

MANA MUDRĀS

Mana mudrās are seals of energy performed with the head.

Śāmbhavī Mudrā

Śāmbhavī mudrā, also called *bhairava mudrā*, is the Gesture of the Energy of Śiva in the ancient traditions. In modern yoga, it is understood as *bhrūmadhya dṛṣṭi*, which means to gaze at the point of the brow. This centre represents the command of the divine. It is where one's own will and that of the supreme are one. It is the fulfilment of one's mission in life. It is ecstasy. My master once told me that *śāmbhavī mudrā* unlocks unsurpassed joy. In my understanding, the *śāmbhavī mudrā* of today is the symbolic inward gazing of the enlightened being.

It seems to be a natural historical process that a well-understood internal vision tends to decay by slowly being reduced to an outer gesture. For instance, think of how a genuine symbol of gratitude can be reduced to a meaningless handshake. *Śāmbhavī mudrā* underwent the same process. It was originally understood as the inner mind's gaze into the divine presence while one's senses (eyes) expand outward on any object. This awareness of the presence of the divine spirit in any experience is *śāmbhavī mudrā*. It is Śiva's gesture due to his pervasiveness and omnipresence. It is expansion in perception, yet it is remaining connected to the inner core of being that is identical to the supreme Śiva, consciousness. In ancient tantra this practice was called *śakti vikāsa*, or the expansion of energy.

> *'Expansion of energy' means the flowing outward of the energy which has been hidden within, through an instantaneous expansion of the entire circuit of the sense faculties without losing connection to the centre, in accordance with the method of entering into bhairava mudrā (śāmbhavī mudrā), as in the scriptural quote. 'Attention within while gazing outward, neither closing nor opening one's eyes'.*
>
> *Kṣemarāja in his commentary on the Recognition Sutras*

Imagine you are clearly and lovingly visualising the deity in your heart. You look inside and are fully aware of this image. Your eyes remain open in interaction with the world. You internally stay fully imbued with the supreme. This is *śāmbhavī mudrā*. From this inner place you expand into the world. It is a powerful declaration of the one divine light present in all moments.

Nāsikāgra dṛṣṭi

This is the Gaze of the Tip of the Nose, for this is where the *prāṇa* of *iḍā* and *piṅgalā* move in and out. The tip of the nose is also a space closely connected to the root chakra (*mūlādhāra*) from where these two *nāḍis* emerge. Here sleeps Kuṇḍalinī, waiting to enter the centre of being (*suṣumnā nāḍi*). Focusing all of one's attention on this primal flow of energy through *mūlādhāra* is a powerful method with which to awaken Śakti. Whenever the eyes are turned inwards – as in *śāmbhavī mudrā* or *nāsikāgra dṛṣṭi* – the mind is fixed. When the mind is fixed, the natural experience hidden within the flow of energy comes to the fore, no longer shackled by the mind's obstacles. When one performs *nāsikāgra dṛṣṭi* for prolonged periods, miraculous internal experiences can happen.

The nose is a singular organ. It mirrors all of the bodily energy flow. The back of the nose mirrors *suṣumnā nāḍi*. The right nostril is *piṅgalā nāḍi*, and the left is *iḍā nāḍi*. The nose's tip is *mūlādhāra* chakra and its root is ājñā. One can thus observe and direct the activity of the three primary *nāḍis* through the nose.

Khecarī Mudrā

> *Gesture of the Skyfarer. The mind goes in void because the tongue goes to be situated in the void (khe or 'the region of sky'). Because of this, it is saluted by all siddhas. Indeed.*
>
> *Gorakṣa-śataka (67)*

Khecarī means to move into the sky. In post-classical Hatha Yoga, *khecarī mudrā* is known as moving the tongue far back into the nasal cavity in the skull—a feat which can only be accomplished by the somewhat bizarre practice of cutting the frenum underneath the tongue. Even without this practice, *khecarī mudrā* as the backward movement of the tongue can manifest spontaneously when one's mind is moving into the sky of consciousness. In early tantric scripture, *khecarī mudrā* was simply achieved my meditation over the great *khecarī vidyā*, the Skyfarer, KHAPHAREṂ.

I shall proclaim the khecarī mantra which grants success in yoga, O Goddess. Without it the yogi cannot enjoy khecarī power. Practicing the yoga of khecarī by means of khecarī mantra preceded by the khecarī seed syllable the yogi becomes lord of the khecaras (skyfarers) and dwells among them forever.

Khecarī-vidyā (1.31–32)

Khecarī mudrā is secret. One must internalise the self. There is no vision, sound, touch, nor taste – only the great space beyond. Gaze inwardly at the sky. Gently tuck in your chin. Move your tongue upwards inside the nasal cavity. Rise into this great space beyond.

The following poetic quote is from the *Manthana-bhairava-tantra*, where Kuṇḍalinī is praised as being the Goddess Khecarī, the essence of the Skyfarer. *Khecarī mudrā* is thus a *mudrā* of Kuṇḍalinī and her movement towards the sky.

She is the yogini who was in the past, is in the present and will be in the future. Then by her own free will, she is the universal energy of the wheel of khecarī. O you who are praised by the heroes, above that is the accomplishment of the energy of the Skyfarer. She moves in the sky and is herself the movement in the sky. She is in the middle between the one who moves in the sky and the movement. She is Khageśī (the Skyfaring Goddess) who is both the void and Kubjikā, the Supreme energy who moves in the void. She, Khageśī, is sixfold (the six chakras) and as suṣumnā, she is the void.

Manthana-bhairava-tantra (36:47–48)

Ṣaṇmūkī Mudrā

The gesture of the Six-Headed One. As with *khecarī mudrā*, the one reality has no need of your outward directed senses. Patañjali writes that, when the senses are withdrawn, their energy can reside utterly in the service of realisation. The mind that was previously busy processing sensual information can now turn to clearing pathways and finding the truth. *Ṣaṇmūkī mudrā* is a powerful gesture. It closes the gates of sensual perception and forces one to gaze inwards. *Ṣaṇmūkī mudrā* is also called *devī mudrā* (the attitude of the Goddess). When the gates of sensuality are closed, the great current of energy is reversed, thereby allowing one to see that all things originate within and emanate outside. Inside there is a great current of *nāda*, the eternal sound. *Nāda* is the Goddess, *nāda* is *Śabda-brahman*, the vibration of the absolute.

Begin by sitting straight and close the six gates of your body, starting with your sphincter, perineum, and genitals with *mūlabandha* and a gentle *vajrolī mudrā*. Once done, close your ears with your thumb, your eyes with your index fingers, your nose with your middle fingers, and your mouth with your ring fingers. The little fingers are placed below the lips. Breathe deeply through your nose and release the pressure of the middle finger gently while breathing. When the breath remains inside, close your nostrils and hold this breath. Feel the very centre. There is nothing in this world but this one coil of energy within. As the practice continues, listen to the sound in your centre that rises along the graceful *suṣumnā*. Venerate this sound. Feel it pierce the sky. Perform *bhrāmarī*.

> *Thus is the means for mastery over prāṇa, One with a beautiful countenance! Having assumed a posture that one is capable of staying in, with a focussed mind, then having drawn by force the senses away from sensory objects and completely controlled them, the wise one, pulling the apāna upwards, having controlled the mind by meditating on the praṇava, restrain the ears and the other*

senses with the hands. Close the two ears with the thumbs, the eyes with the pointers, and the nostrils with the middle fingers, and having thus restrained all the senses, focus on the crown of the head, till the state of bliss is experienced.

Yoga-Yājñavalkya (6:50–53)

KĀYA MUDRĀS

Kāya mudrās are performed with all of the body and, as such, are an integral part of *kriyā yoga* (yoga of the power of action). They are all highly significant for Kundalini techniques.

Prāṇa Mudrā

The Gesture of Energy. *Prāṇa* is life, it is being, it is ever-flowing. *Prāṇa* secretly resides in the heart as nothing else is closer to being. *Prāṇa mudrā* is not an invocation, but a veneration. Nothing needs to be invoked because everything is already present – it need only be appreciated. Even if you were to invoke it, but not appreciate it from your core, what good would that serve? This is a celebration. Celebrate your life.

Sit up straight in a comfortable meditation posture. Bring your hands into *bhairava mudrā*, one on top of the other, palms facing upwards. Take a deep breath and feel your lungs fill with air. Hold here. Feel your lungs empty and hold there. Then, while inhaling, elevate your hands with your palms facing inwards until they are

over the eyebrow centre. Point your fingertips to one another. Then, raise and open your arms until they are over your head so that your palms are at ear height and face the sky. Briefly hold your breath. While exhaling, bring your arms back the way they came and lower them one over the other in *bhairava mudrā*. Hold your breath in emptiness.

Follow the rhythm of your breath. The in- and outbreaths must be equal in length. Holding your breath outside or in must also have the same intensity and duration. The *prāṇas* must be balanced.

Yoga Mudrā

The world is the interplay between the outer and inner, upper and lower, and the individual with the cosmic – all reflected in this gesture of union. When opposites combine, there is a great marriage and the purpose of both is fulfilled. This is yoga. Yoga *mudrā* is to bow down in the face of two polarities and sincerely attempt to unify them. It is a marriage.

Sit in *padmāsana* or *siddhāsana*. If either of these positions is challenging for you, take a small pillow and sit in a comfortable meditation posture. Hold your right wrist with your left hand, or vice versa. Close your eyes, inhale and open your face to the sky. Exhale, and lower your body to the ground so that your forehead rests on the floor. Gently pull *mūlabandha* and feel the soft pressure on your forehead. Bow down in front of the earth. Be thankful. This is *yogamudrāsana*.

Like a dance between two forces, one can move up and down with one's breath. When one straightens the upper body, the attention moves to *mūlādhāra*. When one exhales and lowers the forehead to the ground, the attention moves to *ājñā* chakra. Unify the polarities.

Maṇḍūkī Mudrā

Maṇḍūkī Mudrā, the gesture of the frog, is the deepened version of *nāsikāgra dṛṣṭi*. It is an acknowledgment of un-mindedness. *Mūlādhāra* is the energy closest to earth. Earth is pure empty being, it is the body. Earth has two states: conscious and unconscious. Living in the body without consciousness is called darkness, but when one lives in the body with full awareness then this is called being in the moment. *Maṇḍūkī mudrā* emphasises this latter state. It is full awareness achieved by straightening oneself and being completely present. It is also a veneration of the energy of *mūlādhāra*. When *maṇḍūkī mudrā* is performed with awareness and devotion, a great peace will blanket the mind. Silence occurs and pure un-minded being can shine forth. It is a blessing.

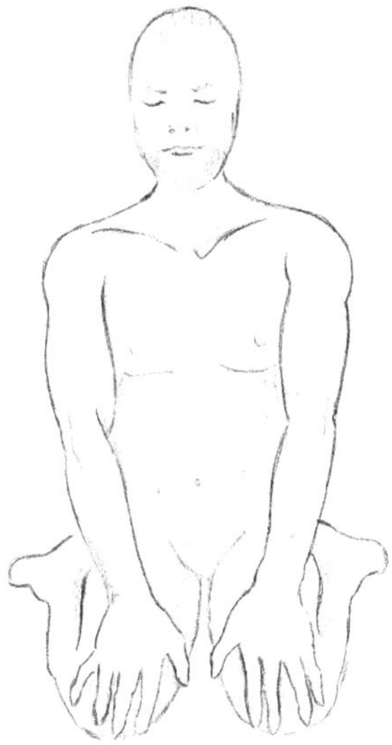

Sit straight and enter *maṇḍūkī āsana*, the seat of the frog. Your feet should rest beside your hips and your buttocks should touch the ground. Should you find this pose difficult, please do use support. Gently straighten your neck and apply *nāsikāgra dṛṣṭi*. Pull *mūlabandha* and contract your sphincter muscles. Breathe deeply. Feel comfortable. You are good. Being is easy. Being is comfortable. Nothing is to be achieved in this life, everything you have will be given away. Feel the energy

BANDHA MUDRĀS

These *mudrās* are performed with *bandhas*. Here the great gesture.

Mahāmudrā

The great gesture. Despite its name, *mahāmudrā* is very subtle. It is secret. One must understand from the outset that *mahāmudrā* does not occur outside. It requires a gaze that is completely focused on the internal. *Pratyāhāra*. It is great because it is the reverence to the one great energy and the body as its vessel. This great goddess is always present. *Mahāmudrā*

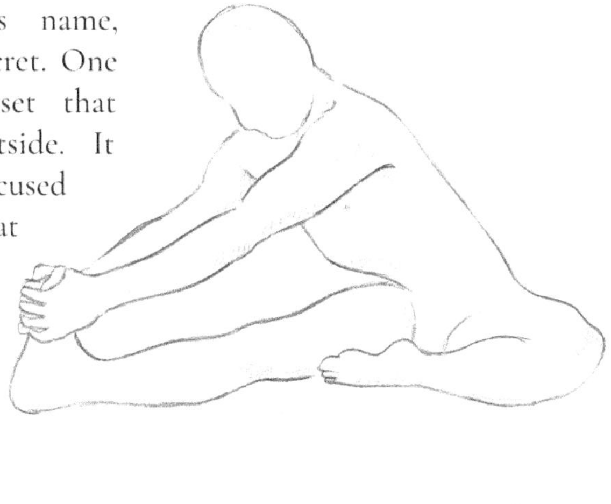

makes the body her home. There are many ways to perform *mahāmudrā*. Some emphasise the visualisation of the energy's pathway through the chakras. I will present the most simple and beautiful way here.

Settle in your heart – your only true guide and teacher. Start from *daṇḍāsana*. Sit up straight and stretch out your right leg. Sit on the heel of your left foot so that it presses against your perineum. Open your face to the front without bending down. Hold onto your big toe with your hands. Close your eyes and breathe in deeply. Once your lungs are as full as they can be, forcefully pull *mūlabandha*. Hold this breath for as long as its comfortable. Look inside, look at the energy. Move into the golden *suṣumnā*. Make this energy meet the centre. Release *mūlabandha*, then slowly exhale. This is one round. Practice five rounds on one side to begin with. Change your legs and repeat.

Mahāmudrā is an intimate *mudrā* for you and you alone. It is to meet yourself.

> *Press the anus with the left heel and extend the right leg; grasp the toes with your hand. Then practice jālandharabandha and draw the breath through suṣumnā. Thus the Kuṇḍalinī will stretch out, like a snake that has been hit by a stick. The two nāḍis become lifeless, because the prāṇa leaves them. Then exhale slowly, never fast. The sages call this mahāmudrā. It destroys death and other sufferings. Because it has been taught by the great siddhas it is called mahāmudrā, the great Mudrā.*
>
> *Haṭha-Yoga-Pradīpikā (3:10–14)*

ĀDHĀRA MUDRĀS

These *mudrās* are performed with the lower parts of the body responsible for procreation and excretion. Once mastered, these *mudrās* will grant you great vitality.

Vajrolī / Sahajolī Mudrā

Gesture of the thunderbolt. Even while following all his desires, and without conforming to the regulations of Yoga, a householder can become emancipated, if he practices the Vajroli-mudrā. This Vajrolī-yoga practice gives emancipation even when one is immersed in sensuality; therefore it should be practiced by the Yogi with great care.

Śiva Saṃhitā (4:54–55)

Sex is everything. Sex increases life, but also consumes it. Sex is the body's greatest joy, but can be a heavy burden. Sex is deadly. Sex is vitality. Why is it that, even though people are aware of this, they are hesitant to harvest its source? Water is life, it is sex. Water also has two sides: the conscious and unconscious. The unconscious side of water is a dangerous current, forever flowing downwards and eager to pull everything down with it. The conscious side of water nourishes all. It is the master of great power: the power to give life. It is like a thunderbolt that can shatter illusion. It is this magical force of sexuality that, when controlled, is the strongest of all. It can purify the yogi. It is the master of life. In the *Śiva Saṃhitā*, Śiva tells us that *vajrolī mudrā* is the greatest secret of all. It is especially secret because, unlike the others, it harvests the deepest human desires and readies their energy for realisation. Like a thunderbolt, it is an incredibly powerful tool.

Gather your attitude. Fearlessly sit yourself down and straighten up. Pull *mūlabandha* and breathe deeply. Breathe for at least one minute while contemplating deeply. Look inside yourself. Contract your genital muscles forcefully when you inhale. When you exhale, raise your belly by contracting your abdominal muscles and with *mūlabandha*. Breathe in and out in this manner until you can see the thunderbolt. You are a carrier of life.

Ejaculation of semen is death, preserving it within is life; therefore, let the yogi preserve his semen with great care

(...). The yogi certainly obtains through this practice all kinds of powers, at the same time enjoying all the innumerable enjoyments of the world. This yoga can be practiced along with much enjoyment; therefore the yogi should practice it.

Śiva Saṃhitā (4:60 & 65–66)

Aśvinīmudrā

Aśvinīmudrā, the gesture of the horse, is the contraction of the sphincter. The sphincter is closely connected to *svādhiṣṭhāna* chakra and to water. Some claim that it is connected to *mūlādhāra*, but my master taught me otherwise. As with many of life's questions, the truth may lie somewhere in the middle. The anus for some is an organ of sexual performance, which proves its connection to the waters. *Aśvinīmudrā* emphasises the upward rising aspect of the energies of *svādhiṣṭhāna*. While *vajrolī mudrā* increases the power of the lower energies, *aśvinīmudrā* makes them rise. *Aśvinīmudrā* helps the lower energies move into *ājñā* chakra, which is why it is often performed in conjunction with *śāmbhavī mudrā*, as in *siṃhāsana*.

Aśvinīmudrā is both beautiful and helpful to the practice of yoga. One should not be afraid of using this *mudrā*. The lower energies can be easily awakened through a thorough performance of this *mudrā*. Once they are made to rise, spiritual experience is close at hand.

Sit up straight and tuck in your chin. Breathe in deeply. When you reach maximum inhalation in *antara-kumbhaka*, contract your sphincter muscles. Continue doing so when you exhale and straighten your spine. Hold in *bāhya-kumbhaka*. Enjoy the rising energy. Then inhale slowly and relax completely. Enjoy this pleasant feeling.

RULES FOR PRACTICE

No fear. Only joy. Remember the heart. All other rules are useless.

BANDHA

INTRODUCTION

Bandhas (locks) are *mudrās* in that they are inner gestures. They are meant to contain, and raise, the bodily *prāṇa*. *Bandhas* are hugely important in yoga. Kundalini Yoga would be near impossible without the practice of *bandha*. It is so essential that it deserves its own short chapter.

Bandhas differ very delicately from most other *mudrās*. The *mudrās* discussed in the last chapter are concerned with special qualities of energy that are called upon or sealed in the body. The *bandhas*, however, focus more heavily on all of the energy present within the practitioner. They aim to contain bodily energy and move it in accordance with the intelligence contained in the one great Śakti.

There are said to be three important obstacles (or attachments) on the path to liberation. These are: *brahmāgranthi*, *viṣṇugranthi*, and *rudragranthi*. They constitute the primal limitations a being can have.

Brahmāgranthi	the limitation through the body and the attachment to it.
Viṣṇugranthi	the limitation through emotion or thought and the attachment to it.
Rudragranthi	the attachment to the 'I', and the limitation which arises from it.

These three knots (*granthis*) are located at three specific places in the body. The three *bandhas* correspond to their locations and are *mudrās* (gestures) that allow the energy to rise through the limitations caused by these knots.

The fist lock, *mūlabandha*, is the most important for any yoga practitioner as it serves to reverse the flow of *apāna* and fuse it with *prāṇa*, thereby allowing Kuṇḍalinī to move. It has many positive health influences and ought to be practiced regularly.

Performance

The *bandhas* are inner subjects. They are secret. I cannot explain their performance – indeed, no one can. The mere outer movement of the body and breath creates an energetic condition that grant the practitioner the necessary space from which to enter the experience. However, one must enter alone.

Similar to what we have discussed regarding freedom, *bandhas* are realised through themselves. This you must know in order to perform it. What is written here must be approached in a visionary form. It must be done intuitively. This approach is the only one that can lead to success.

MŪLABANDHA (SUPPORT LOCK)

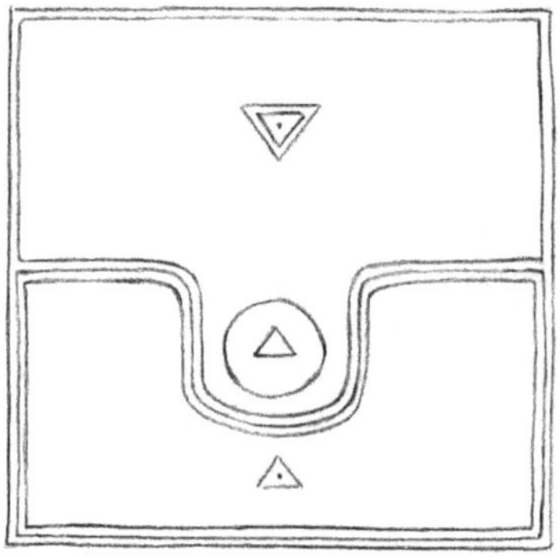

The root lock. Think of *mūlabandha* as the master key. It is the seal of primal energy. Its application conserves life and awakens energy. In *mūlādhāra*, Kuṇḍalinī exists in the form of a coil of electric energy. There she has the form of lightening, like the thunderbolt of Indra. The application of *mūlabandha* is mandatory for Kundalini Yoga as this is the easiest way to connect with the primal energy. Here she is awakened like a snake uncoiling after having been 'hit by the stick of *prāṇas*'. This form is physical and direct. The experience of Kuṇḍalinī is easily obtainable. The yogis say that the downward moving current of *apāna prāṇa* and the upward moving current of *mahā prāṇa* are reversed through *mūlabandha*. Both *prāṇas* then collide and are lifted inside the fire orbit of *maṇipūra*, after which the heat of *prāṇaśakti* mingled with fire awakens the great goddess.

Mūlabandha has many physical advantages and should not solely be performed for the successful practice of Kundalini Yoga. Everybody profits from the arousal of sexual energy though *mūlabandha*. For instance, women gain greater strength in this area, which helps them achieve and maintain a healthy and functional body after something so strenuous an event as childbirth. The female body is subject to greater transformations during menstruation and pregnancy than any which the male body is subjected to. The stabilising and vitalising function of *mūlabandha* is enormously helpful in this context.

The locations of *mūlabandha* vary by tradition. Some claim it to be the anus or underneath the navel. Others put it at the cervix for women and the perineum for men. Speaking from personal experience, the science of yoga is derived intuitively and most descriptions of *chakras*, *bandhas*, and their locations are figurative. Accordingly, it makes little sense to rigorously pursue precision. It is best to understand the visionary insight of the yogi by the same means and then apply the technique intuitively. If you can feel where the *mūlabandha* is in you, that's good enough! You've got it!

Stage one

Sit up straight but relaxed. Start to rhythmically pull *mūlabandha* (contract the sphincter muscles, perineum, or cervix). Feel the muscles contract and release in a strong pulse.

Stage two

Sit up straight but relaxed. Begin deep yogic breathing. Inhale and hold *mūlabandha* gently in *antarakumbhaka* (internal retention). Release upon exhalation. At the end of a slow exhalation, hold *mūlabandha* again in *bāhya-kumbhaka* (external retention).

> *He who regularly practices the root lock is expert in yoga. He should press his anus with the heel and forcefully contract his perineum over and over again, so that is breath goes upwards. The upward and downward moving breaths (prāṇas) becoming united by means of this lock, and nāda and bindu also, this is sure to bestow complete success in yoga.*
>
> *Dattāreya-yoga-śāstra (144)*

UḌḌĪYĀNABANDHA (UPWARD RISING LOCK)

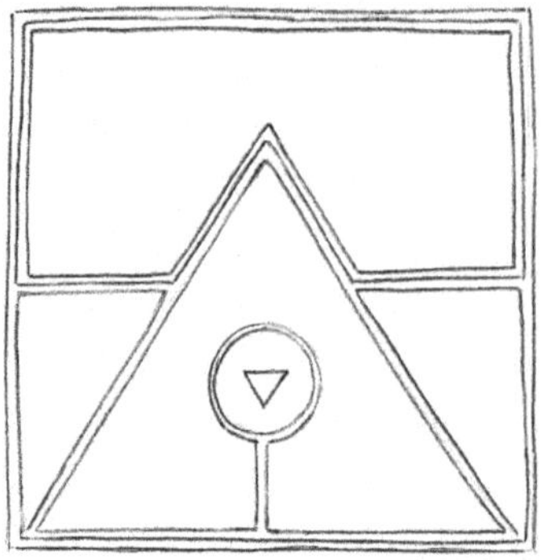

Uḍḍīyānabandha, the abdominal lock, is the great bird that flies upwards to the sky. The Western tradition might call it the phoenix; the bird which rises from the ashes, always reborn, giving life and expansion. *Uḍḍīyānabandha* is the inner movement that causes the energy to rise from the flames' orbit. It is a rising movement, it is inner freedom. *Uḍḍīyānabandha* is purifying. When performed, the mind is reduced to ashes allowing for a deeply comfortable peace. Released from fear, thought, and craving, one can instead find strength.

Physically, *uḍḍīyānabandha* purifies and activates the intestinal region. It provides great control over breathing and the abdominal muscles; it straightens the spine and improves one's health.

Sit straight in *vajrāsana* with your knees open. Straighten your arms, firmly hold your knees with your hands, and open up your chest. Stick out your tongue, and exhale deeply through your mouth while bending forward and contracting your chest. Once all of the air has left you, straighten your spine once more, then pull your arms straight with your shoulders raised and facing forwards. Now, breathe in without actually letting the air enter (your diaphragm should move inwardly and upwardly at this point). Try to inhale more deeply and push your intestines ever upwards by the force of this vacuum. Try to pull your upper belly in the direction of your spine. When you finally do breathe in again, open your chest and return to the starting position. Do this both easily and joyfully.

Look inwards and observe your diaphragm opening to the inside as if it were the sky. Look both inwards and upwards; you are the bird and the sky is your belly.

Uḍḍīyāna is easy and always thought because of its many

good qualities. Practicing it regular, even when an old man becomes young. With special effort the yogi should pull his navel upwards and push it downward. Practicing like this for six months, he is sure to conquer death.

Dattāreyayogaśāstra (142)

JĀLANDHARABANDHA (NECTAR, WATER LOCK)

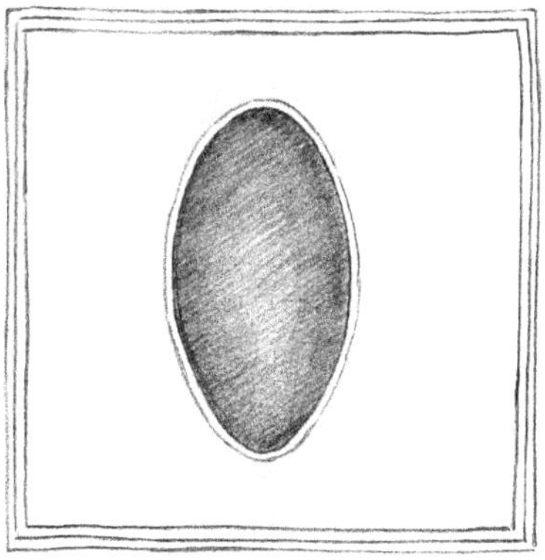

Jālandharabandha, the neck lock, is a gesture of devotion to the one source. It involves bowing one's head to the great and infinite universe above. Everything is contained in seed form in the loft space above us. This seed is like the delicious liquid from which all life springs. It is nectar (*amṛt*). This nectar descends from the moon and nourishes all life. This nectar is not solely the seed of your body, but of your being as a whole. Deep inside of you is the feeling that you only exist because you are able to experience the inner joy of connection with the vastness above. You drink from this great cosmic breast in your most hidden dreams. Your being is fed with the joy of pure existence.

This nectar, the milk of life, descends into your being. However, it is typically consumed by your individual will in *maṇipūra* – this fire scorches the innocent seed-like existence given to you from the cosmic mother. You become deluded by your own thoughts and desires.

Jālandharabandha is the gesture which aims to preserve this delicious drop of life. By performing it devotedly, you will be able to feel this innocence nourished by the drops of life. You will be able to hold the liquid in your throat and enjoy its presence in all of its fullness. It is called, for this reason, the lock of the waters as it preserves these cosmic waters from being consumed by fire.

Sit comfortably and breathe deeply. Straighten your neck to the sky and feel your head pointing upwards. Tuck your chin to your chest, not forcefully, but you should be able to feel your throat contract. Imagine yourself bowing to the great unknown. Imagine removing your head from your shoulders and simply placing it in the vastness of the sky, right in the centre of the universe. Let it rest there and breathe deeply. When you look at the stars, can you see their beauty? All the life there is, and all the life that will ever be, is contained there.

The yogi should contract the throat and firmly place the chin on the chest. This is jālandhara lock. It prevents loss of nectar of immortality (amṛta). As long as it keeps drinking the nectar of immortality that has dripped from the thousand pedalled lotus in the skull of embodies beings, the fire might not drink that nectar of immortality, the yogi should drink it himself. Through constant practice in this way, it goes by the rear pathway and makes the body immortal. For this reason, one should practice jālandhara.

Dattāreya-yoga-śāstra (138)

MANTRA

The little mother (syllables) is the seed of knowledge.

Śivasūtra (1:4)

INTRODUCTION

Mantra has a very long tradition in India. Mantras were already sung as part of the Vedic *Saṃhitās* (in the context of fire offerings) in approximately 1500 BCE. According to some scholars, the Vedas themselves (written in early Sanskrit) were often misunderstood by Brahmanical schools throughout the ages. Some schools learned them entirely as phonetic expressions of divinity. The exact spelling and creation of sound was of crucial importance as meaning was expressed entirely through sound rather than semantic elements. Once this is understood, it becomes clear why such a strong tradition of mantra recitation evolved.

The *Śivasūtra*, which can be considered the root text of non-dual tantra, says that the little mother is the source of knowledge. The little mother is *mātṛkā*, the syllable. These syllables are fifty in number and form the Sanskrit alphabet. Each syllable is initially classified as a specific expression of energy in sound form. Here, knowledge is understood as energy made manifest. This suggests that knowledge is first contained in energy or sound, much like the universe (as it is the aggregate of all knowable objects). The letters are described as 'the little mother' because the universe (born from sound), in seed form, is contained in the letters, making them just like a mother. Accordingly, the letters are expected to give life to the whole world.

This is the cosmological understanding. However, this short sentence has many more layers. The knowledge here is also the word (made from the letters/syllables). The word is related to the knowledge insofar as the word is an abstraction of a certain object of knowledge. Moreover, knowledge is that which extracts an object from an infinite reality. If we say 'apple', we may mean a real (or physical) apple. However, as every object is an expression of eternity and infinite in its properties, we can never comprehend this self-same real apple. Understanding it in its fullness would mean becoming one with that which surpasses all. The knowledge of the apple is therefore always a reduction of the ultimate reality (of the apple) into a limited object of perception (a physical apple). Knowledge is therefore limitation, as is the word.

Knowledge is bondage.

Śivasūtra (1:2)

Put differently, the word creates an object by extracting it from an ultimate reality, while at the same time limiting an ultimate reality to appear in the form of knowledge. All words are therefore the mothers of knowledge, the mothers of all objects of perception.

I feel inspired to provide a quote from the Bible here as this concept is shared by the insights of Western tradition:

In the beginning there was the word,
and the word was with God
and the word was God.

John (1:1)

The word appears first in the form of sound – which are vibrations. Vibrations are therefore understood as the source, meaning that the whole world has come into being from sound, its mother. In this view, all objects exist in a vibratory-sound form before they can take any shape within perception. *Prāṇa* must therefore also possess a phonetic expression. *Bīja* (seed syllable) is the result of this understanding. It is the seed sound of an energy, or its phonetic form. It is also the seed of the fruit (created power) and the essence of all mantra. The tantrics discovered *bīja* mantras as magical formulas of worship that invoked specific seed energies. The lengthy garlanded formulas of twenty (or more) seed syllables, the *mālāmantras*, are a further extension of this.

The *Viṣhvasāra tantra* says that *Parabrahman* (supreme soul, or God) exists in the form of sound, *Śabdabrahman* (sonic God), inside the human body as *jīvātmā*, the individual soul. This means that your very essence (and that of all) is sound. Brahman, the universal soul, is also filled with vibrations, which are his unmanifested energies. These energies are the unlettered and unformed universal sounds (*dhvani*). These are one sound, or *nāda*. Furthermore, the tantras claim that all manifestations of sound in the form of utterances would be impossible without the prior existence of that same sound in its subtle form. Existing in this subtle sphere, all mantras are different aspects of the sound which emanates from Brahman, this sound is the energy of Brahman. And since the highest energy (*parā*) is nothing but Kuṇḍalinī, all this just means that all mantras are different aspects of the great energy of Kuṇḍalinī.

Mantra is therefore recited to awaken Kuṇḍalinī in the form of mantra Śakti (the power of mantra). This mantra Śakti brings about the magical power of accomplishment through unification with the mantra's energy – a process known as mantra *siddhi* (the accomplishment of the mantra). Behind this mantra is the deity itself, Kuṇḍalinī, who can reveal herself as *saccidānanda* (truth, bliss, and consciousness).

Every deity has their *bīja*, which contains all mantra *siddhi* (fruit of the mantra) and the deity's essential power in seed form.

The meaning of a mantra is not limited to its words. *Bījas*, in particular, have no meaning at all outside of their sound body. This sound creates a form (*rūpa*) in the ether (*ākāśa*). This form, its inherent vibration, is the manifestation (*svarūpa*) of the deity itself. This clarifies why mantra is not limited to prayer. Given the chance, people could chant their own words, and yet they generally do not. They prefer to recite a mantra. The mantra is the body of a prayer, not an individual's own prayer. It is the body of a deity and must be treated as such.

In Haṭha Yoga

In modern yoga, the extensive use of mantra (as used by the tantric schools) has been largely forgotten. This is due to tantra's decline in the public consciousness and the need for transferring a mantra – and its proper intonation – directly from master to student. Most modern mantras are tantric and do not originate from Patañjali Yoga. Furthermore, the use of mantra was seen as the 'lowest of all yogas'. This is a classic example of people discarding what they fail to comprehend – an unfortunately pervasive human trait. It is highly probable that many yogis were driven to this statement as mantra brings about wondrous results in the practitioner without significant ascetic strain. This must have been a hard truth to digest for the early ascetic traditions who sacrificed so much. Since tantra is the source of Kundalini Yoga and mantra, it is wise for a Kundalini student to lend the science of mantra one's ear.

> *I praise the great of ocean of knowledge, the aggregate of fifty wheels (syllables), of which the tradition of the Deity, the current of the siddhas, has arisen by Śiva's will. I praise the awakened consciousness of the reality that is the principle of mantra, the sun of consciousness on the mountain of kula consisting of the six wheels, by whose will everything has emerged into being.*
>
> *Manthana-bhairava-tantra (3:90cd–92ab)*

OUR LINEAGE, OUR MANTRA

I cannot begin to express my gratitude to all of my teachers who have given me their blessings and shown me the grace of yoga. I truly hope, from the bottom of my heart, that I can give you even more than what I received.

I have had many teachers along the path, but I feel most intimately connected to the teacher who gave me the mantra that vibrates in my heart, Svāmī Vidyanand. This lineage can be traced back to Svāmī Śivānanda Sarasvatī. Svāmī Vidyanand, who came from a family of Brahmins, had a vision of the divine mother that made him turn to the teachings of Śrī Aurobindo, the founder of Integral Yoga. Svāmījī was also a student of the tantric master Śrī Svāmījī of Peetambra Peeth, with whom he lived in the forest and received from him the unsurpassed joy of simple being. The two lineages of the tantric worship of the Mother and Śrī Aurobindo, along with the traditional Hatha lineage of Śivānanda, were fused together to form this teaching.

Śrī Aurobindo spent his final years deeply meditating within his chamber. He wrote of his meditative experiences and passed them on in his *Records of Yoga*, written entirely in his last years of contemplation. Śrī Aurobindo revealed our mantra in 1927 as one of the many blessings from the mother. His wife, Śrī Mā, the great Yogini, transliterated his writing as follows:

Oṃ

Ānanda-mayī

Oṃ – She, the Delight

(We invoke supreme bliss)

Chaitanyamaẏī

She, the Consciousness

(We invoke supreme consciousness)

Satyāmaẏī

She, the Truth

(We invoke supreme truth)

Pāramī

She, the Supreme

(Eternally)

All Nature dumbly calls to her alone
To heal with her feet the aching throb of life
And break the seals on the dim soul of man
And kindle her fire in the closed heart of things.

Śrī Aurobindo (81.24)

Important note: Because you own this book, you have the right to receive guidance and support by chanting these mantras and *bījas*, which radiate the spirit and love of this teaching. I have created a hidden section on our school's website where you can listen and learn the mantras mentioned in this chapter. For more, simply go to: *yogamatsya.com/mantra-downloads*

CHAKRA TRANSFORMATION

As mentioned previously, spiritual evolution – or evolution through consciousness – is the transformation of one's own desires. Desires are expressed through the chakras – especially the lower triangle, or the first three chakras. The transformation of desire thus includes a shift in the energy of the first three chakras into their corresponding higher counterparts. Or, simply put, the transformation of the lower triangle into the higher.

This transformation process is expressed as the transformation of a physical element into its governing deity. *Dhāraṇā* is the point of focus here. The mantra is placed below. The table below shows which mantras are placed successively in which chakras.

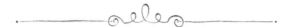

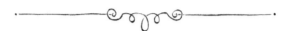

	Lower Form	Dhāraṇā	Transformed Form	Dhāraṇā
1st	*Oṃ pṛthvī Namaḥ*	*Mūlādhāra*	*Oṃ Mahāsarasvatī Namaḥ*	*Sahasrāra*
2nd	*Oṃ Samudrāi Namaḥ*	*Svadhisthana*	*Oṃ Mahālakṣmī Namaḥ*	*Ājñā*
3rd	*Oṃ Agni Namaḥ*	*Maṇipūra*	*Oṃ Mahākālī Namaḥ*	*Viśuddha*
4th	*Oṃ Vāyu Namaḥ*	*Anāhata*	*Oṃ Maheśvarī Namaḥ*	*Anāhata*
5th	*Oṃ ākāśai Namaḥ*	*Viśuddha*	*Oṃ Aditi Namaḥ*	*Suṣumnā*

Chakra	Installed Element Bīja	Purification Scala
Mūlādhāra	*Laṃ*	*Sa*
Svadhisthana	*Vaṃ*	*Re*
Maṇipūra	*Raṃ*	*Ga*
Anāhata	*Yaṃ*	*Ma*
Viśuddha	*Haṃ*	*Pa*
Ājñā	*Kṣaṃ/Haṃ/Oṃ*	*Dha*
Sahasrāra	*Śrī/Oṃ*	*Ni*

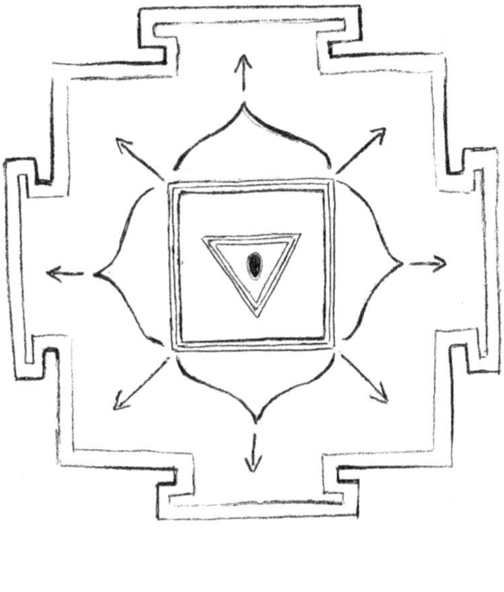

A TANTRIC OPENING

Tantra means to worship the Goddess as sound. It means to incorporate her sound body, to embody the divine body of sound.

This opening, that can be practiced at the beginning of each class, is a dance with sound. It is worshiping the Goddess as the energy of the six chakras and moving them through your being. It was passed down to me by my friend and teacher Rainer Neyer from the lineage of Dhīrendra Brahmacārī.

Step 1 – Fold the hands in front of the heart and chant from the core *Yaṃ Ying Yaṃ*

Step 2 – Bring the hands in front of your face with the thumbs tucked in under your chin, venerate the essence and chant *Haṃ Sāra*

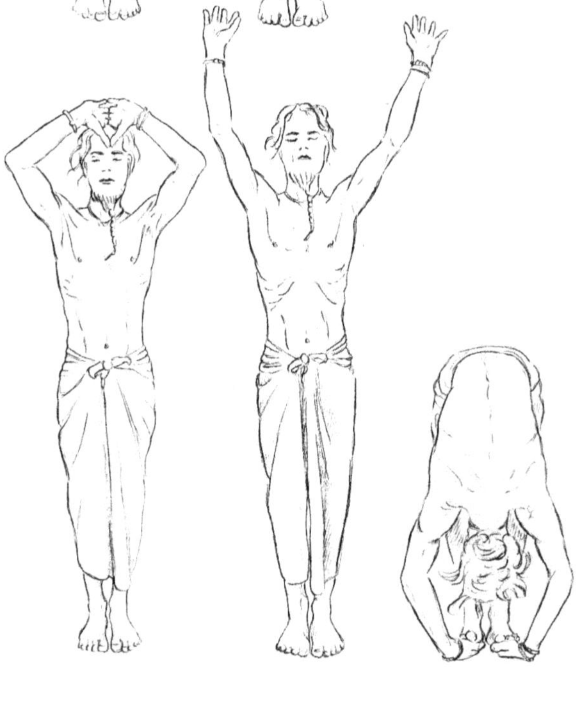

Step 3 – turn your hands backwards over your fore head with your fingers touching your eyebrow center. Chant the great fiery name *Oṃ Dāha*

Step 4 – inhale, elevate your arms over your head and bend backwards, sing *Oṃ* while bowing down in front of the one great existence.

Step 5 – Being bent forward, look inwards and bow down in front of the great temple of live. Chant *Laṃ Sanam*

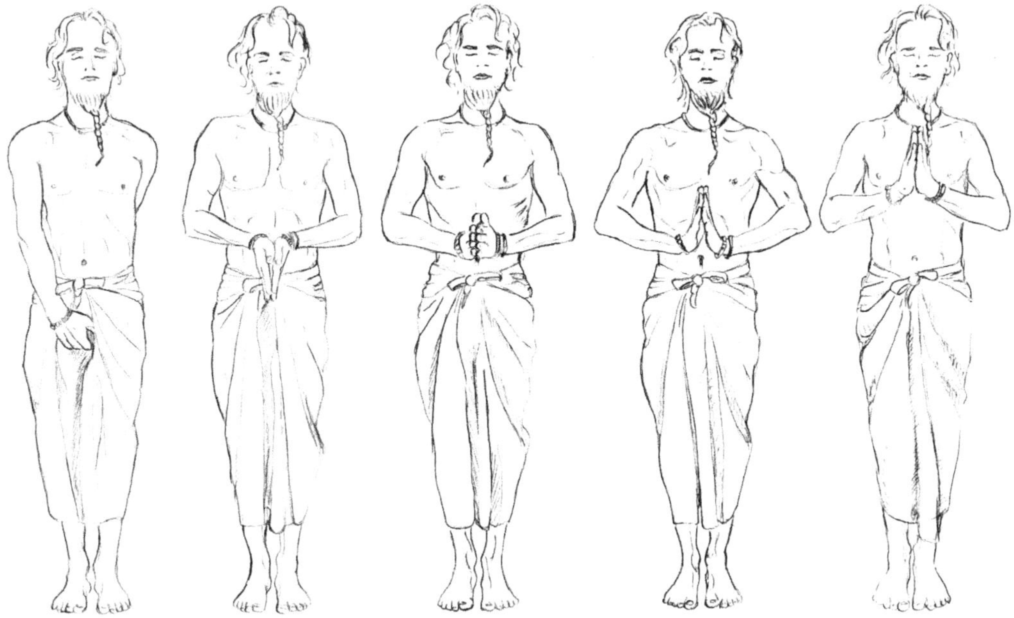

Step 6 – Elevate your body and touch with your right hand your genitals from the front, your left hand rests on the sacrum behind. remember the great creator and preserver of all things - *Vaṃ Bhojam*

Step 7 – Bring your hands in front of the navel center with fingers pointing downwards and chant the name of the powerful thunderclouds. Repeat this mantra two more times by moving the hands pointing forward horizontally and then upwards. *Raṃ Ghanam.*

Step 1 – Come back to your heart, the beginning and end. *Yaṃ Ying Yaṃ.* This in one round. Do as many as you wish.

1. I am the balance of things.

Yaṃ Ying Yaṃ

2. I recognize the essence.

Haṃ Sāra

3. I am bow in front of the burning light.

Oṃ Dāha

4. It is all that is.

Oṃ

5. I bow to the temple of the beloved.

Laṃ Sanam

6. I venerate the big and nourishing one.

Vaṃ Bhojam

7. I incorporate the flashing thunder clouds.

Raṃ Ghanam

OṂ

The *Yoga-Sūtras* of Patañjali tell us that Oṃ is *Īśvara*, the deity, the ideal of highest consciousness, or consciousness itself, the sound body of the highest deity. Oṃ is also *praṇava*, the seed that creates and projects *prāṇa* in emptiness. This means that it is the source, the consciousness out of which all other mantras emerge. Oṃ has three parts, or *kāras* (phonemes): A, U, and M . Oṃ must be uttered with the entire body, rising through the practitioner into the infinite. In reality, Oṃ has three and a half parts. This is reminiscent of how Kuṇḍalinī is coiled three and a half times around the *liṅga* in *mūlādhāra*. This last half step to liberation is the silent expansion into that which cannot be heard after the audible sounds are uttered. Inside the silence lies the final step into totality.

> *The three syllables are A, U, and MA. These three sound units consist of the guṇas sattva, rajas, tamas. Free from the guṇas and only accessible for the yogi another sound, a half measure is situated above these three. It is known as Gāndhāri and is the gāndhāra musical note. When Gāndhāri is chanted, it is characterized by a sensation of crawling ants in the head, in the same way. When Oṃ is chanted it moves forth into the head. And the yogi who is filled with the syllable Oṃ becomes imperishable in the imperishable. Prāṇa is the bow and the self is the arrow with which the supreme Brahman is pierced (...). The three and a half syllables should be known as the highest reality. The Yogi who practices them intently attains dissolution into Brahman (...). The first unit is short, the second unit is double, and the third unit is triple. The half unit in the end is beyond the vocal range. In this way the supreme, indestructible Brahman is known.*
>
> *Mārkaṇḍeya-purāṇa (39:1–14)*

BĪJA

Our school has a strong tradition of using *bīja* mantras to invoke the energy of the centres and their corresponding elements. *Bījas* are not just sung, they are first installed and then vibrated in the centre. When the *bīja* is sung, it should be tangible. It should be an object of sound that the student can sink into.

These exoteric elemental *bījas* are related to the elements whose energy they invoke. The invocations are short and strong, frequently uttered in one breath.

The Esoteric Bījas

In tantric yoga, *bījas* are uttered to stimulate the body from the bottom to the top so as to reflect and emphasise the rising energy. The *bījas* are considered to be Kuṇḍalinī and are treated as such.

In this form, the *bīja* is sung in one breath for as long as it can be held. The sound then rises through the body, carrying the practitioner with it. The sound is never closed so to allow the energy to expand into the infinite. Their correct form of utterance can only be taught in class.

Other Bījas

The five *kāranas* (causes) are highly secret and extremely powerful. They constitute the seeds of the known universe and the elements. The five causes are the five movements consciousness performs to create any given experience of reality. Everything that is must have first passed through these stages. Every thought, every object, everything is governed by them. Uttering them is uttering the world. They will be revealed in class..

> *Initially, having known the purification of form, one should recall the principle of the command (AIṂ). If, due to negligence, this vidyā is uttered by someone without consciousness, the transmission (krama) of such a one, devoid of the authority of the teacher, is empty.*
>
> *Manthana-bhairava-tantra (9:40)*

BIJA NYASA

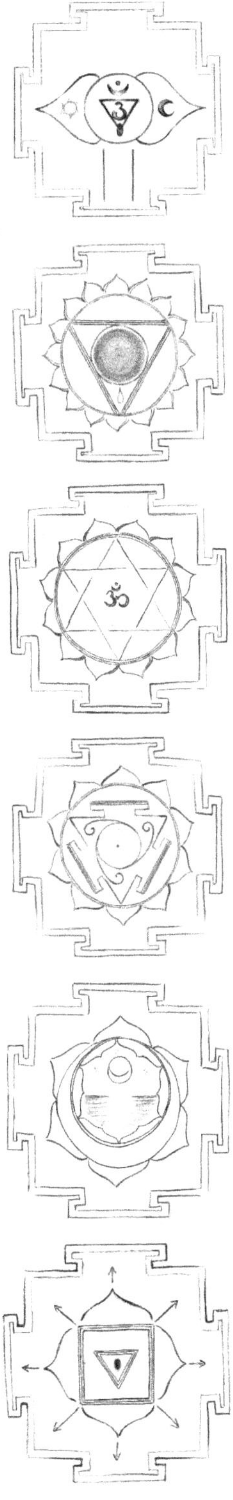

Placing the seed syllables can be an internal act, it doesn't require any posture, action or movement. One can even lay down on the ground, gently utter the seed syllables and make them vibrate in the body. This form here, however, is a dance of the arms and upper body, helping to support the flow of consciousness through the chakras.

Here the stimulation of the chakras is on the forefront. Every chakra is a doorway into the internal landscape of your own consciousness; when you walk through this door you can explore the secrets of your own powers within it. However, travelling through these doors is also an internal process, no gesture can do for you what only you alone can do. Also here, remember that this journey comes from the inside, starts at the platform of your imagination, supported by your belief, brightened by your heart, fired by your passion and guided by your surrender to the greater good. Travel this journey with an open mind, look deep and you will travel far.

Approximately 10 – 20 minutes.

First sit down in your favourite sitting posture and remember your heart, hold your hands in front of your centre and look deep inside. Utter the great *Oṃ*; the mother, the father, the friend, your home.

Interlace your fingers and bring your hands in your lab, palms facing downwards. Fold your feet in a way that you can bring your hands comfortably in the centre right in front of you. Apply slight pressure downwards and lengthen your spine, straighten the arms and look deep inside, feel the pressure that your hands apply towards the ground, pull *mūlabandha* and gently start to utter *dharā bīja* (*Laṃ*).

3x *Laṃ*; 3x *Oṃ Laṃ Ma*

Then open your hands and let the left hand rest on your right one, both of them open with the palms facing the sky. You venerate the silver crescent disc of the moon, look inside, relax all your body. Then utter the *bīja* of *Varuṇa* himself, the God of water, king of dreams, lord of passions.

3x *Vaṃ*

3x *Oṃ Vaṃ Ma*

Interlace your fingers, thumbs up and pull your elbows to the side, apply a gentle pressure between your fingers as if you would like to pull your hands apart. Open the chest and let the hands rest your belly. Feel the warmth of your fingers when they rest on the centre, this is the seat of fire, health, determination. Venerate the great *Raṃ*, shining, golden like the rising sun.

3x *Raṃ*

3x *Oṃ Raṃ Ma*

Bring your hands in front of your heart in *namaskāra mudrā*. Press the palms slightly against each other, and press the thumbs against your chest. Lengthen your spine and feel the sky. You are great, you are life, you are the wind. Venerate the great tree of life, that grows on a secret island, watery and tranquil. Recollect

it there, the wisdom that carries the triple teaching. Utter the great *bīja* of *vāyu*, carrier of life, that grows all fruits of your deepest desires.

3x *Yaṃ*

3x *Oṃ Yaṃ Ma*

Interlace your fingers and bring them behind your neck, thumbs downwards, both thumbs resting along your neck. Open your chest and pull your elbows to the side. Your head falls backwards, acknowledge the great sky above. See the white mountain ranges, the last sunbeams of the setting sun, making them shine like pure gold. See the open sky, right after sunset. Venerate the stars shining in the dark blue space. See the silver disk of *ākāśa* expanding in the night sky. Venerate the great *Haṃ*, carrier of what is beyond.

3x *Haṃ*

3x *Oṃ Haṃ Ma*

Bring your hands in front of your forehead, fingertips together. Thumbs resting at the root of your nose. Your fingers form a diamond shape. Open the elbows to the sides. There is a great light beyond, beyond the river of duality, the ONE light, the ONE place. Venerate the great *Kṣaṃ*, like a chain of brilliant lights.

3x Kṣaṃ

3x Oṃ Kṣaṃ Ma

Interlace your fingers and stretch them over your head, palms facing the sky. Balance the joy on your hands. Straighten your spine, lengthen your arms. Pull *mūlabandha.* Utter the brilliant *Śrī*, the *bīja* of the Goddess, carving the sky path.

3x Śrī

3x Oṃ Śrī Ma

Bring your hands to your knees, let them rest, contemplate the great *Oṃ*, you are home.

Oṃ

SVARA

According to the *Nāṭyaśāstra* (6:10 & 19:28), there are seven tones (*svara*), to be used in different sentiments, related to the seven chakras. The following list clarifies to which tones of our Western scale the *svaras* are related. N.B. The *svaras* themselves are not *bījas*, but tones in which they are sung. Their sonic vibration is said to purify and stimulate the chakras.

Svara (Long)	*Ṣaḍja* *(षड्ज)*	*Ṛṣabha* *(ऋषभ)*	*Gāndhāra* *(गान्धार)*	*Madhyama* *(मध्यम)*	*Pañcama* *(पञ्चम)*	*Dhaivata* *(धैवत)*	*Niṣāda* *(निषाद)*
Svara (Short)	Sa (सा)	Re (रे)	Ga (ग)	Ma (म)	Pa (प)	Dha (ध)	Ni (नि)
12 Varieties (names)	C (shadja)	Db (komal re) D (shuddha re)	Eb (komal ga) E (shuddha ga)	F (shuddha ma) F♯ (teevra ma)	G (panchama)	Ab (komal dha) A (shuddha dha)	Bb (komal ni) B (shuddha ni)

Sa (Ṣaḍja)	six-born peacock, *mūlādhāra*, (base of spine), Ganapati
Re (Ṛṣabha)	bull, *svādhiṣṭhāna*, (genitals), Agni
Ga (Gāndhāra)	sky goat, *maṇipūra*, (navel), Rudra (Śiva)
Ma (Madhyama)	middle dove/heron, *anāhata*, (heart), Viṣṇu
Pa (Pañcama)	fifth nightingale, *viśuddha*, (throat), Nārada
Dha (Dhaivata)	earth horse, *ājñā*, (third eye), Sadāśiva (the unmanifest)
Ni (Niṣāda)	hunter elephant *sahasrāra*

(crown of the head), Sūrya (sun)

Now I will explain something else, the most excellent secret concerning the five causes. The first is called the form of passion, which is the peak in the shape of the triangular water chestnut (AIṂ). The second is the seed of Māyā (HRĪṂ). It is the silent Goddess, the Gesture and the cave. The third is Rudra's divine seed (ŚRĪṂ), which is worshipped by the best of the Gods. The fourth is khecara's sacred seat whose form is (KHAPHAREṂ). The fifth is called Bhairava marked with the seed-syllable (HASARAUUṂ). This is said to be the secret name of the group of the five sacred seats in the kula scripture. I am their mistress; I am the Mahāntārikā Vidyā, the incantation of the great Saviouress. Decorated with a nondual form she both has form and is formless. She is gross. She is subtle. She is the inwardly moving energy of consciousness. She is Mahāmāyā who is the form of consciousness. She cannot be written about and yet she is all that can be written about. May the supreme Goddess play in the genitals, the heart and the mouth. She is conjoined with the peak syllable and with gesture and so she is stamped onto the body.

Manthana-bhairava-tantra (9:19cd–29)

HAṂSA – AJAPA JAPA

Haṃsa or *haṃ-saḥ* is a tantric mantra that was absorbed into the Haṭha tradition. When reversed, it creates the Vedic 'so' *haṃ*' which translates as 'I am He/That'. In Vedic philosophy, '*so' haṃ*' means identifying oneself with the ultimate reality. *Haṃsa* derives from '*so' ham*' and is the *ajapā gāyatrī* (unrecited *gāyatrī mantra*). It is the mantra that every being utters at least 21,600 times a day without even noticing. Each and every breath expelled from your body is the *Ha*, just as every breath which enters is *Sa*. Every being is thought to be a mirror of the universe. Therefore, every being must manifest, and be manifested by, the universe. *Ha* is your dissolution in the universe and *Sa* is your manifestation within it. Every breath transports this in and outflow of your creative consciousness between you and the whole world.

Haṃsa is your humble bowing in front of creation and its humble bowing in front of you.

MEDITATION

INTRODUCTION

In contrast to its modern perceptions, the Hatha Yoga of the past was mostly a path to meditation. This was due to the meditative state being one of introspection in which the truth about the world and oneself becomes clear. This search for final understanding of the world and the self has always been yoga's highest goal. Patañjali, who examined the foundations of yoga, clarified this as he laid out his eight steps of yoga that lead to meditation and, eventually, liberation.

Āsana is understood as a preparatory exercise for *prāṇāyāma*, which in turn is a preparatory practice for *pratyāhāra* (introspection). Indeed, *prāṇāyāma* and *pratyāhāra* are often understood in conjunction as the former ultimately leads to the latter, so the one is the technique for achieving the other. The observation of internal processes free from the influence of the senses (*pratyāhāra*) is the precondition of the mental fixation inside a perception. This fixation enables a complete alignment of one's own mental flow with the object observed. This is *dhāraṇā*. Oneness with this object, and dwelling within its characteristics, is deep meditation – *dhyana*. Meditative absorption leads to the loss of one's own form and the gain of a state of oneness with the actual nature of all objects. This state is *samādhi*.

Kuṇḍalinī is in mūlādhāra in the form of a snake. The individual self dwells here in the form of the flame of the lamp. The yogi should meditate on Brahman as made of light. This is the supreme luminous meditation. Between the eyebrows and above the mind is a light consisting OṂ. The yogi should meditate on it as joined with a ring of fire. That is the luminous meditation.

Gheraṇḍasaṃhitā (6:1–22)

Here, meditation is an integral process that flows from the internalisation of the senses to complete oneness with the highest goal. All meditation techniques favour one or other stage of this fluent process.

PRATYĀHĀRA (WITHDRAWAL)

Pratyāhāra means both the withdrawal of, and mastery over, the senses. When one can look, feel, and perceive inside of oneself, then the senses have been mastered. *Prāṇāyāma* leads to a control of the sensual mind, *mānas*. When this mind is controlled, so are the senses. One can then understand oneself as the cause of all perception.

> *He should practice unaccompanied breath retention kevala-kumbhaka once a day for three hours, either by day or by night, withdrawal will thus arise for the yogi practicing this way. When the yogi while holding his breath completely withdrawals his sense organs from their objects, that is called withdrawal. Whatever he sees with his eyes he should cause this to exists in his self. Whatever he smells with his nose, he should cause to exists in his self. Whatever he tastes with his mouth he should cause to exist in his self. Whatever he touches with his skin he should cause it to exist in his self.*
>
> *Dattāreya-yoga-śāstra (93–96)*

Pratyāhāra is already meditation in the common sense of the word. It is the sustained effort to internalise attention and restrain the outflow of awareness. Through this process, every hidden truth outside of time and space can become knowable.

> *Withdrawing in succession the sight and other senses as they move among their objects is called withdrawal. As the sun at*

noon withdraws the shadow, so the yogi practicing this third auxiliary gets rid of mental disturbances. Just like a tortoise draws its limbs into itself, so does the yogi withdraw his senses into himself (...). Whatever he sees with his eyes, beautiful or not, the knower of Yoga draws it in, recognising it as the self. Whatever the he smells with his nose, fragrant or not, the knower of Yoga draws it in, recognising it as the self.

Vivekamārtāṇḍa (103–10)

DHĀRAṆĀ (FIXATION)

Dhāraṇā (to hold), or fixation, is to lock the mind on one point. This point can be a body part, a mantra, a *bīja*, an image, or a yantra (a geometric representation of the deity's energy). This meditative stage generates great power, as oneness with the power of the object of *dhāraṇā* can be attained.

Now I shall teach a rapid method for someone who wants quickly to unite himself to this chariot (divine chariot of Brahman), intent on reaching the imperishable. He is performing yoga by means of yoga who silently performs all seven fixations (dhāraṇās), attains in sequence sovereignty over earth, air, space, water, light, egoism and intellect, gradually acquires sovereignty over the unmanifest, and possesses powers.

Mahabharata (12:228.8–15)

In the *Śiva Saṃhitā*, Śiva talks of the great powers obtained when one rigidly fixes one's attention each day (for two and a half hours) on the location of any chakra. Similar *dhāraṇās* are expounded in the *Vijñāna-bhairava-tantra*, where Bhairava teaches his consort to fix the mind uninterruptedly on any chakra (*dvādaśānta*) in order to manifest the highest goal.

> *By bringing the mind forcibly to dvādaśānta again and again, however and wherever possible, the fluctuations of the mind diminish day by day, so that each moment becomes an extraordinary state.*
>
> *Vijñāna-bhairava-tantra (51)*

Further *dhāraṇās* include *bīja* chanting (*bīja nyāsa*), any mantra meditation, *nāsikāgra dṛṣṭi*, *śāmbhavī mudrā*, and *vipassanā*.

DHYANA (MEDITATIVE ABSORPTION)

Dhyāna is the process of unifying with the object of one's meditation. *Dhāraṇā*, the preceding stage, is part of the same process where one establishes a pointed focus to this object. Meditation, which is in its greatest extension *dhyāna*, is thus not technically dissimilar from *dhāraṇā*. It is simply the full absorption within, or mental alignment with, the object of *dhāraṇā*.

A more advanced form of meditation is that over the formless. This is because the true ground of existence – or the deity's essential nature – cannot be understood by the power of one's own limited mind. In this technique, the yogi concentrates on anything that creates tranquillity in his consciousness, avoiding form, position, or size. This leads the yogi to rest in his own formless existence, which is that of Śiva himself. Classical meditations have always distinguished between these types of meditation, namely that with and without form.

Meditation is perception of one's own form by means of the mind. It can be with attributes (*saguṇa*) or without attributes (*nirguṇa*): *saguṇa* is said to have five variations, whereas there is only one meditation without attributes.

> *One, luminous, pure, omnipresent like space, firm, very clear, free from impurity, eternal, devoid of beginning, middle or end... having the form of the universe,*

formless... May I be Brahman and made of Brahman, this is the meditation without attributes...

Vasistha-saṃhitā, (4:21)

SAMĀDHI (COMING TOGETHER)

Samādhi literally translates as 'putting or joining together', and is commonly considered the final destination of being and the endpoint of the meditative process. It signifies a state of inner union with that which is beyond comprehension. As such, it is true yoga. According to Patañjali, *samādhi*, together with *dhāraṇā* and *dhyana*, forms the complete discipline of the mind, termed *saṃyama*.

This last stage, *samādhi*, is the complete cessation of the creation of mental impressions that lead to rebirth or bondage to the sensual reality. This conception is frequently thought of as being a death-like state in which the yogi neither perceives nor reacts to reality, but simply lives in an elevated state of superior existence. The yoga of Patañjali is closely connected to the ascetic traditions which held this view and who sincerely strove for the ultimate cessation of self and freedom from existence. The perception of *samādhi* as death-like may also have resulted from many yogis having allowed themselves to be buried alive for up to 40 days to prove their *samādhi's* strength. Even today, the astonishingly lengthy public burials of yogis is practiced in India.

When prāṇa is completely destroyed and the mind dissolves, then all experience is the same. That is called samādhi. When the individual self and the supreme self are joined and all conceptions are destroyed, that is samādhi.

Vivekamārtāṇḍa (160–69)

In the later Vedantic and tantric traditions, *Samādhi* is no longer understood solely from this perspective. *Samādhi's* goal is understood as being *mokṣa* or *siddhi. Mokṣa* is nothing but freedom and *siddhi* is the attainment (or accomplishment) of power. For the *Vedāntas*, *samādhi* is simply oneness with God and ultimate bliss. In tantra, the term *jīvan-mukta* is used to refer to a liberated soul within a human body. A *Jīvan-mukta* is not a dead block of wood existing without perception or effect in an empty world, but rather a liberated being who is free to exist from the highest place. This liberation is attained by oneness with one's personal deity and therefore divine grace.

Kundalini Yoga is intended to lead one to this state. Kuṇḍalinī shall rise, taking the soul (or *jīva*) and uniting it with the universal soul in the highest lotus. Freedom through Kuṇḍalinī, the goddess and mother of the world, is not freedom from the world, but freedom with the world.

> *Place the mind in the Śakti (Kuṇḍalinī), and the Śakti as light in the mind through meditation; then mind and Śakti become one. Awaken the Śakti by listening to the mind with the power of the heart and thus strive for the highest goal of samādhi. Making the ātman the centre Brahman, making the Brahman the centre of ātman, and making everything Brahman. Remain in samādhi without even a single thought. Within this void, outside this void; like an empty vessel in space, completely full internally, completely full externally, just like a pot in the ocean (...). Mind concentrated on the ātman becomes one with it like camphor with the flame, like salt with the water of the ocean.*
>
> *Haṭha-yoga-pradīpikā (4:43 & 59)*

TANTRIC MEDITATION

Different techniques were practised in the left-handed traditions of tantra, such as *bhāvanā*, which simultaneously means awareness cultivation, creative contemplation, or feeling what actually is. *Bhāvanā* comes from the root *bhū*, which means to bring something into being. *Bhāvanā* is multi-faceted and contains a great variety of meditation techniques, such as visualisation and imagination. In some, the deity is visualised in great detail and one is encouraged to fuse with its image. This refers to the creative aspect of meditation.

This very painting of the flow of existence has three realms, five destinations in five pigments, and exists on three levels (...). On that painting, the actions of the mind, like a painter, by engaging in sensuality, paint various images based on objects of consciousness of the sphere of sensuality, with the brush of the four meditations in the sphere of subtle materiality.

Sad-dharma-smṛty-upasthāna-sūtra (7:12 & 7:37)

Bhāvanā can also mean the contemplation of a pure thought (*śuddha vikalpa*), such as 'all things are fused with divine presence'. *Bhāvanā* appreciates reality as the playground of the one universal consciousness. As any object of contemplation is understood as being a manifestation of the true knower (the all-pervasive self), these meditations can be practiced on any object of the outer or inner world. This means that mindful contemplation over any object is in actual fact contemplation over the self. The knower and the known are one.

The awareness of knower and known is common to all embodied beings, but for yogis, this is the difference, they pay careful attention to their connection.

Vijñāna-bhairava-tantra, (106)

The Vijñāna-Bhairava-Tantra

In traditional understandings, the *Vijñāna-bhairava-tantra* has no author except for Śiva, i.e., consciousness itself. This is correct in the sense that consciousness is the one true agent. As such, viewing the *Vijñāna-bhairava-tantra* as not being a human creation does not mean that is has no human author.

According to the speculations of the 9th-century CE Krama master and lineage-holder *siddhā yoginī*, Keyūravatī could have authored the *Vijñāna-bhairava-tantra*. Keyūravatī was a woman held in the highest esteem by her devotees. She was simply and respectfully known as 'the Goddess K'.

Vijñāna means the knowledge derived from insight or consciousness, and Bhairava is a tantric Śiva. Bhairava is the fearsome one, or he who dispels all fear. He is the highest, most ultimate void. He has a frightening appearance and was formerly worshiped as the emanation of Śiva that would destroy one's enemies. Bhairava, in the tantric context, is he who destroys the true enemies – one's limited desires – by the power of ultimate consciousness (the highest void). In so doing, Bhairava bestows freedom from destruction and thus freedom from fear. In the *Vijñāna-bhairava-tantra*, Bhaivarī – the power of Bhairava or the highest goddess – is used as a means to achieve Bhairava, or freedom from fear. Bhaivarī is the power of consciousness, which is the Goddess Kuṇḍalinī, or Parā.

> *Śiva is also known as Bhairava because he brings about the awakening that makes us cry out in fear of remaining in the dreamstate (bhava-bhaya) and due to that cry of longing he becomes manifest in the radiant domain of the heart, bestowing absence of fear (abhaya) for those who are terrified.*
>
> *Kṣemarāja on Bhairava*

Have you ever been terrified by the world's darkness? By death and limitation? Read and practice this tantra with an open heart, and you will be set free.

Tantras are typically centre on rituals and performance. This makes the *Vijñāna-bhairava-tantra* somewhat unusual as it is entirely concerned with meditation. It describes itself as (in a highly henotheistic manner) the most secret and highest of all tantras. In my course I discuss the 112 *dhāraṇās* of the *Vijñāna-bhairava-tantra* as they are all forms of *bhāvanā*. They are highly precious and must be kept secret, just as you guard what is most intimate to you.

YOGIC LIFE

The Tao that can be told is not the eternal Tao.

The name that can be named is not the eternal name.

Tao Te Ching (1:1)

SECRECY

Yoga is not a guarded secret, nor can it harm oneself or others. Nobody can acquire magical powers through its use or commit acts of evil that one would not have been able to do without it. Yoga is an opportunity, and anybody with a sense of gratitude is able to learn it.

Yoga is still secret to the average person and must remain so to the ordinary world. This is because all yoga remains, and always will be, a secret. As yoga's nature is unspoken, how can it be otherwise? Any attempt to heighten its visibility would cloud its true invisible spirit. To define it as easily understood and practiced is to neglect that part of it which cannot be practiced. This neglection would destroy yoga for the practicioner and make it inaccessible for those who truly seek the path.

The yogi must acknowledge that which is formless. The deeper the yogi reaches down into himself, the more clearly he can see that true yoga – the great nameless – refuses all words, actions, and practices. The yogi bows down in front of it and remains silent about its silent nature.

The yogi prefers solitude in unity with the great. When with others, the yogi acts as they do. Once grasped, the great truth cannot be undone by any action, nor can it be acquired through special means. The yogi stays detached from all actions and remains invisible among the ordinary world.

Since the yogi carries this great secret in his heart, he neither preaches nor proselytises. He thus never disturbs the minds of the others. His secret is open only to those who humbly ask for it.

Words cannot express what the mind cannot grasp. The mind cannot grasp what the words try to say. Truth is always beyond all words. Truth cannot be revealed by anyone, but must be experienced alone. All must remain speechless in front of the great truth, the nameless, the great formless, and the great all-pervasive.

The ignorant act because of their attachment to action, but the wise act without such attachment, oriented towards the welfare of the whole world.

But the wise man should not disturb the minds of the ignorant, who are attached to action; Simply performing his own actions in the right spirit, with concentration on Me, he quietly inspires others to do the same.

Bhagavad Gītā (2:25-26)

SĀDHANA

Sādhana is your way, your commitment. Without *sādhana*, nothing would come into existence. Instead, everything would exist as a dream within the clouds. *Sādhana* is the materialisation of your commitment to the goal. All that is materialised is real, what is not remains unreal.

Sādhana is structured so as to allow you to attain something higher than what your individual mind can grasp. Without structure or regularity, your *sādhana* would be shackled to your moods. One day joyous, the next morose. Following your moods means following your mind. Following your mind means following your limitations. *Sādhana* must be a path to elevate one away from the mundanity of existence. Therefore, it cannot be shaped by your moods, but must stay stronger than what is bent by time and space. If you surrender to your *sādhana*, every day you will become ever greater.

Should you begin to think of your *sādhana* as boring, be honest with yourself. Become aware of how boring your alternatives to practice were!

Without following this sequence (krama) or methodology, if one practices yoga as per the dictates of likes and dislikes, such an approach will not give any benefits of Ashtanga Yoga.

Yoga-rahasya

FOOD

Food is vital. After all, you are what you eat. Every cell, fibre, and bone in your body is made out of food. Your body is nothing that is not food. This is why your body is called *anamaya kośa*, the foody layer. Again, you are what you eat.

Food changes your metabolism and consciousness, and influences your immune system. Food can heal, or destroy, you. The difficulty is that these effects do not occur suddenly, so they are mostly overlooked. Only long-term change in your diet can alter your body. Some changes need decades to manifest, others weeks. However, change your food and you can change your life.

A Yogi may eat rice or wheaten bread. He may eat mugo beans and masha beans and grain. These should be clean, white and free from caff. A yogi may eat cucumber, jackfruit, kakkola berry ad jujube. He may eat green fresh vegetable, black vegetables and the leaves of Patola (...). Eating thus sweet juices with pleasure and leaving the other half of the stomach empty is called moderation of diet.

Gheraṇḍa-saṃhitā (5:20)

Yogic food

A yogic diet is simple and uncomplicated. In fact, from my experience, I believe it to be the most comprehensive and healthy diet one can follow. It demands no unnecessary rules, and instead focuses upon the necessary ones. Since yoga is the science of consciousness, food is mainly categorised according to its influence on awareness and *prāṇa*. Bodily health is automatically established once the disturbing factors of improper food are removed. As such, food itself does not establish health. Instead, health is considered to be the natural state of the body and bad food is simply a hindrance to this state.

According to yoga, food is divided into three categories: *tamasic*, *rajasic*, and *sattvic* food.

Sattvic food:

Vegetables, fruits, grains, whole-wheat, and dairy from happy cows. *Sattvic* food creates clarity and openness, and tranquillity of mind, emotion, and body.

Rajasic food:

Acidic, onions, coffee, chocolate, eggs, fish, cigarettes, alcohol, drugs, salt, and spice. *Rajasic* food is exciting and addictive. It creates arousal and movement, and invokes passion, desire, and action.

Tamasic food:

Overcooked, ready-made, meat, and white bread – all in over abundant quantities is *tamasic*. This food is weakening and confusing, and causes lethargy, tiredness, indolence, and depression.

From a yogic perspective, food should be observed not only for what it is, but also as the underlying attitude or action from which it emerges. Actions that bring about food can also be *sattvic*, *rajasic*, or *tamasic*.

Food eaten out of truthfulness, personal conviction, integrity, and strength is *sattvic*. Food eaten from desire, lust, and excitement is *rajasic*. Food eaten out of weakness, laziness, and dullness is *tamasic*. A yogi should act and eat from a *sattvic* attitude. Once this attitude is adopted, the food chosen cannot be anything but *sattvic*.

Contrary to popular assumption, a yogic diet does not force one toward vegetarianism. Rather, being carnivorous undermines the full responsibility for the suffering of other beings or the fragile ecology surrounding us, therefore meat cannot be eaten by the yogi. The one who eats meat is not a yogi. Not because the food itself is a hindrance, but the negative mindset underlying this consumption would be corrosive to one's being. Therefore, one should choose one's food from an attitude of integrity and responsibility.

A *sattvic* attitude will automatically lead one to the consumption of *sattvic* food. Cultivating this *sattvic* attitude, rather than fussing over stringent rules, is therefore the key. In my opinion, the most important commandment related to yogic food came from my teacher:

> *The yogi should fill one third of the stomach with food, one third with water, and leave one third empty, to please lord Śiva the protector of all yogis.*

This means that the quantity is just as important as the quality of the diet itself. The body is believed to be able to digest every kind of energy when the *prāṇas* are strong. Both overeating and fasting can destroy the balance of the *prāṇas*, resulting in their inability to naturally manage and integrate various kinds of food into the body. Aside from the instructions relating to quantity and *sattvic* action, food must be considered moderate. Here, the Pradīpikā states:

> *The brahmacharin who, observing moderate diet, renouncing the fruits of his actions, practices yoga will become a siddha in the span of one year. Moderate diet means pleasant, sweet food, leaving free one fourth of the stomach. The act of eating is dedicated to Śiva. The following are considered as not being salutary: sour, pungent, and hot food; mustard, alcohol, fish, meat, curds,*

buttermilk, chicle peas, fruit of the jujube, linseed cakes, asafoetida, and garlic. It is also advisable to avoid: reheated food, an excess of salt or acid, foods that are hard to digest or are woody. Gorakṣa teaches that in the beginning the yogi should avoid bad company, proximity to fire, sexual relations, long trips, cold baths in the early morning, fasting, and heavy physical work. The following items can be used without hesitation: wheat products [bread, etc.] rice, milk, fats, rock candy, honey, dried ginger, cucumbers, vegetables, and fresh water. The yogi should eat nourishing, sweet foods mixed with milk. They should benefit the senses and stimulate the functions.

Haṭha-Yoga-Pradīpikā (1:57–63)

Natural Food

To understand natural food, let us first talk about bees.

Bees feed from the nectar of plants, which the plants serve them willingly. The plants themselves create beautiful flowers that mark the nectar and serve as landing pads for bees and flies. The flower needs the bee to transmit pollen. Without this symbiotic relationship, procreation between flowers would be impossible. The bee thus acts as part of the plant's male sexual organ to transmit precious semen. The body of the plant and the body of the bee are thus one and the same – they are life. One cannot live without the other, much like how you could not live without the organs necessary for survival or reproduction. This is a very basic example of the relationships between the life forms that surround us. Each appears as one distinct life form but, upon closer inspection, we can clearly see that they are simply different parts of a bigger body jointly enabling life.

Your human body is the same. You have evolved with countless microbes, plants, animals, and fruits that are vital to your body's function. In return, your body plays a key role in their lives.

Your body knows all of these organisms even if, consciously, you do not. In fact, your body and the body of these microbes comprise a unit. You rely on them as they rely on you. Non-natural food is unknown to the body. It is manufactured and appears to your conscious self differently than how it appears to your body. The body, being one with food, becomes confused.

It has been proven beyond doubt that processed or synthetic food is responsible for depression, obesity, inflammatory diseases, and the rise in allergies. As such, you must be careful. Eat only things that are natural. This way you can be sure that your body knows how to deal with them.

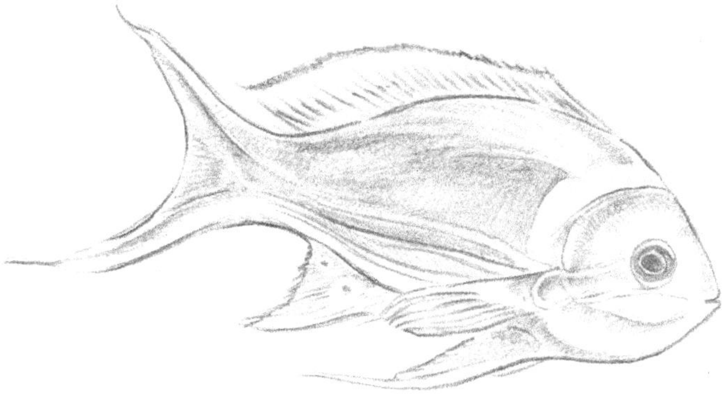

Veganism, vegetarianism, organic, and regional food

Veganism must be respected as an expression of compassion and responsibility towards our society's wrongdoing and insatiable greed. It is a form of dietary protest against our cruelty and blindness, and is therefore predominantly *sattvic*. While it is an expression of protest against wrongdoing (which is *rajasic*), it does not help practitioners strengthen their body for practice. However, as this subject is overloaded with emotion, an objective discussion is difficult. The human body evolved in a certain symbiotic relationship with all organic life around it. Veganism, therefore, not only severs this relationship to the animal kingdom, but declares symbiotic interactions to be impossible and always based on exploitation. Since the body has evolved with other animals, not consuming their protein while still maintaining one's health and strength is complicated. Of course, while it is certainly possible with synthetic aid or supplements, it is still a difficult process. Veganism is not a moderate diet and is therefore dangerous. In the long-term, it can lead to a loss of vitality and an increased chance of sickness. These symptoms usually manifest themselves years, or even decades, after practicing this diet, and are therefore frequently misunderstood.

Vegetarianism is the balance between a proper respect for the creatures of the world and the maintenance of a relationship with them. Spirituality, society, and diet are subject to a form of natural selection of modes of action. Different methods for creating prosperous and sustainable ways of living are in constant competition with one another, and the world itself eventually shapes their forms in the course of time. This process of selection, in which veganism has surely occurred in the course of history, has favoured vegetarianism as the most appropriate diet for spiritual and bodily progress. We can trust that Indian culture – with its 4,000-year history – to have given us the most suited tool for being healthy, happy, and holy.

Organic food is produced with the least invasive impact on the environment. Such food (*sattvic* in nature) is to be preferred. Non-organic food is that which is produced with substances lethal to the insect kingdom, which accelerate the evolution of dangerous bacteria, and have a devastating impact on plant diversity. These foods also contain substances that weaken our ecosystem and harm the human body. Humanity is too large and powerful to ignore its impact on the environment. We must all take responsibility.

Food should be regional. A great deal of suffering stems from people's ignorance of the full impact of their actions. The obfuscation of the effect in time or space (through distance) is greatly detrimental to understanding the consequences of one's actions. If one would at least consume those things of which one knows their origin, much suffering could be avoided.

BEING A YOGI IN THIS WORLD – PAY ATTENTION

My personal belief is that everyone should strive to make this world a better, brighter place. Liberation cannot mean isolation. Liberation in this life, *Jīvan-mukti*, must be liberation *grounded* in this life. This grounding is contact, embracement, engagement. It will always care for others and the world. The liberated cannot avoid aiding the liberation of others. The Dalai Lama once said: 'Enlightenment is the inability to see suffering and not try to change anything about it'. Liberation is part of the world and therefore must engage in it.

All of you who undertake yoga must therefore prepare for your personal engagement. How do you want to contribute to the reduction of suffering?

This world stands on a knife edge. Never have humanity and the world been under such strain. Suffering lies ahead. Economic, social, and ecological peril are advancing unchecked and threaten to destroy the world as we know it. This is a fact, evidence by:

The massive decline in biodiversity and bio-abundance.

The destruction of the soil.

The destruction of the oceans.

The change of the global climate.

The weakening of human bonds through technology.

The destruction of value.

These developments are most likely irreversible. They will continue until they have reached their maximum damage – this is in human nature. This is the age of Kali. And yet, we should not abandon all hope.

There is still a way to properly face this challenge. The question here is not whether one can change this suffering through one's own actions, but to ascertain which actions apply to you. The question is not 'can I change the world?', but instead 'can I change myself?' The question is not 'what should others do?', but 'what can I do?' It is unimportant if your actions change the world. It is far more important for you to determine which actions express your highest being. It is unimportant whether recycling can rescue oceanic life, but far more important to establish whether you are someone with the strength to recycle. One should act as a role model for everyone else, and then practice contentment.

Ask yourself what version of you is the greatest person that you can be. Be this person for the sake of your self-experience.

This is both your duty and the greatest possible contribution you can make.

EGO

Being a good person is hard, but harder still is being a yogi. Some say that the devil is inside each and every one of us. They say that this devil is your ego – the source of all evil. Some also tell you to avoid having a spiritual ego, as this ego is the worst of all. The spiritual ego is over-concerned with the pride and social recognition gained by your achievements. Fighting your ego may seem hopeless and countless people have failed – as seen in the many scandals that blemish the histories of many spiritual communities. Yet even if you can successfully fight it, you may end up dead and dry without knowing why.

What is this ego that people speak so badly of? What is this source of all evil, this secret attraction that we all have? *Sāṃkhya* tell us that the ego is a function of the mind called the 'I-maker', or *ahaṃkāra*. It is the very self, *puruṣa*, contracted into a singular point by the force of *tamas*. Ego is a mirror of the self. It is that function which can depict any experience to the self. Without ego, there would be no individual experience or perspective to life. There would be no individual self and no life to be lived. What gladdens the ego is the experience of joy, which it will depict as personal. What saddens it is experiencing suffering, depicted in the same manner. Yoga teaches us that the self is boundless joy, that beyond limitation the very nature of being is bliss. This is what the ego, as a mirror of the self, seeks when it strives for pleasure and flees from pain. It secretly hunts its greatest friend, its dearest love, the true and only self, the final satisfaction.

> *Whenever there is satisfaction of mind and the mind is held there alone, the true nature of supreme bliss may shine forth.*

Vijñāna-bhairava-tantra (74)

Fighting the ego on its search for love and joy of the true self would be like beating a begging dog who is desperately searching for food. The wise man gives it food, but there is a trick to doing so.

This true self, which is the sole aim of the ego, is said to sit in your heart. It is the eternal flame, *akhaṇḍa jyoti.* It is the unbroken sound, *anāhata-nāda.* It is consciousness, *cit.* The ego must not be destroyed, but rather fed by this very flame. When you love this hungry dog, you give it food. Could you imagine a wise man beating the dog, chasing it away because it is hungry? Could you imagine the wise man shouting at the dog, calling it a miserable slave of its ego? Could you imagine the wise man killing the world because it mirrors the limited self? Of course not. Then why do we do this to ourselves?

When astronauts orbit the Earth and look from their capsules at this blue wonder, they see life. They see a perfect sphere containing countless billions of lives. Each and every one is a carrier of the One Consciousness. They are astonished and touched, moved to tears. They love this place, even if it is created by this very ego. All of these singular egos mingle together in this one beautiful blue globe. It is a lovable place, and only this can be the answer.

What is the wise man's trick? How do we feed this dog? How do we satisfy this ego before its burning hunger kills us and lays waste to everything around it?

Settle yourself in this very flame in the bottom of your heart and all will be well. You will be home, where you have always been. Who can be afraid of their ego when it is loving? Who can be afraid of anyone else's ego when they are full of love? Life is here to be lived. The ego is here to be fed with the one food it is hungry for: the love of your own heart.

Patañjali says that union (yoga) can be accomplished when the qualities of the heart are cultivated. This is the answer to the problem of ego. Judging your actions is meaningless. Judge neither the world nor yourself. Do not try to discern what is ego and what is not – all is ego. The important question is: are you acting from the bottom of your heart? If you are, the ego naturally dissolves to leave only this one great joy of being.

The mind becomes clear and serene when the qualities of

the heart are cultivated:

Friendliness toward the joyful,
Compassion toward the suffering,
Happiness toward the pure,
And impartiality toward the impure.

Patañjali Yoga-Sūtras (1:33)

THE CHALLENGE OF TEACHING YOGA

Teaching others is first and foremost about teaching yourself. If you have not educated yourself sufficiently before you begin teaching, you will encounter yourself as the worst student you have ever had. Do not worry if this happens, instead be grateful and continue. Carry your suffering with honour and continue walking the path. The less you withdraw from your inner suffering, the stronger you will become. If you run and hide from your own imperfections, you will lose both the path and the magic. Do not be afraid. Remember that being allowed to teach is

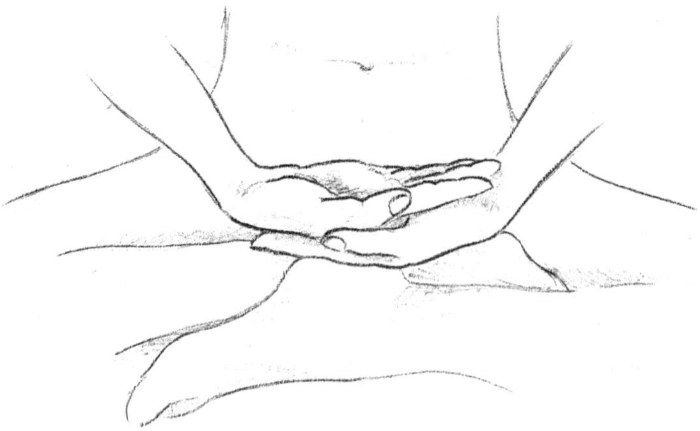

a great honour. Carry this gift bravely and humbly. Remind yourself that you are not the one teaching. The great teacher – the spirit behind all – teaches through you.

Ethics as a teacher

Yogi Bhajan, an influencal figure in Western Kundalini Yoga, taught his students a certain ethical standard. He emphasised the importance of full personal sacrifice for the position of a teacher. This is nothing less than the sacrifice of one's entire self for the pure spirit of the teaching. He vowed the following:

You are not a man.

You are not a woman.

You are not a person.

You are not you.

You are a teacher.

Sadly the man behind these words revealed himself to be a rapist, a liar, and not a true yogi. If famous teachers cannot live up to the ideals they hold high and the values they preach, what are they worth, and what can we believe in? When I completed the first draft of this book, I gave it to a friend, who told me: 'You see, unfortunately you are a man, you are also a person, and you are you, so you are not only a teacher. Denying that is a lie and lies are destined to fail'.

Therefore, perhaps it is best to aim for being a good person rather than something beyond. Maybe it is better to aim for being a person of honour and grace rather than something transcendental. Maybe it is better not to avoid being you, but rather being the best possible you. Perhaps only then we can become great teachers.

Life does not want us not to be, because we are. If we were to deny our being, others could not learn anything about their own being from us. When we deny our human existence, we cannot teach anything about life and the yoga within it. It seems highly likely that to deny our humanity would turn us into monsters, and this is not what our students should learn from us.

Therefore, ethical guidelines do not constrain you, but help to direct you to become a greater person who can live a greater life. This is what we have to teach, and so I say:

You are more than the man you believe yourself to be,

live up to it!

You are more than the woman you believe yourself to be,

life up to it!

You are a greater person than what you believe yourself to be,

make it real!

You are more beautiful than you know,

make it true!

You are a teacher.

If you can honestly aim for these simple guidelines, you will discover your greatness and beauty, and make them radiate within yourself. You will have achieved more than most do in their entire lives.

SEX, POWER AND MONEY

I was recently made aware of the fact that many high ranking teachers in Yogi Bhajan's community, and indeed the man himself, committed adultery with many of their disciples' wives. Furthermore, sexual harassment – in particular the exploitation of positions of power for the sake of sexual favours – became unfortunately commonplace in their communities.

Kata Singh, a lead teacher and student of Bhajan, was accused of having sex with many students who stayed at his ashram with their husbands and families. Singh's behaviour had a devastating effect on these women and their families. I stayed at Singh's ashram in 2012 – before these accusations were made public – and I recall a lecture that he gave. He, amusingly at the time, mentioned that he was still unmarried because (in his own words) he 'loves all the other women much too much'. This was greeted by laughter throughout the room – obviously no one was aware of what these other women and their husbands had to say about his statement. I remember his words because it made a strong impression on me. I suddenly felt that he was walking a dangerous path and I could not find peace with his words. They simply made no sense in the context of his teachings. Now I know why, but I think that somehow the answer of how to face this kind of problem was already in the air.

Brahmacharya

It seems to be that Sex is in its core the veneration of the beauty of live and the pleasures within it, that enable live to blossom. In this way rejecting sex is to reject life, and this is of course unacceptable for people who love to live. Sex is woven into the matrix of life just like breathing, eating and sleeping, denying it necessarily leads to breaking one's own vows. Celibacy only makes sense when one is living in an enclosed environment, solely focusing one's mind on the supreme, sacrificing everything. A community of men and women cannot, and should not deny their natural sexual attraction. However, in my opinion sexual attraction must be a key for personal growth.

When men and women build a sexual bond, they form a relationship. This relationship is in many ways similar to celibacy as it implies sexual exclusivity from the inside and celibacy to the outside. Both partners then celebrate their sexuality and love while concurrently practicing restraint and the containment of desire. As such, both needs are satisfied.

Furthermore, the animalistic desire to sexually consume the body of another is nourished through the excitement of something new. Whenever something new arises, so does desire. Once it has been sufficiently tasted, the desire subsides. By celebrating and gratifying desire within a stable relationship, the yogi protects himself from many dangers. Sex then becomes a binding force between people which helps overcome personal egoism. Moreover, the mere animalistic attraction that arises from contact with an unknown body must be refined so that sex can continue to be pleasing and inspiring. Sexual exclusivity thus nurtures willpower and creativity.

The most important thing to remember here is that, when one has chosen a partner to walk the path with, one is not wasting one's precious life anymore pursuing dead-end sexual journeys. One can instead deepen one's own path with a partner, follow it to the end, and finally reach the goal of true satisfaction. This kind of satisfaction is an expression of personal, not physical, accomplishment in life. One can rest happy in one's own being.

I believe this to be the best kind of *brahmacharya* one can reach in this world. I also do not consider it hard to be achieved. Many evils can be defeated this way. I believe that much suffering could have been avoided if Kata Singh or Yogi Bhajan would have just upheld this one type of vow.

ABOUT

THE WAY

I bow to the goddess who resides in the body of Bhairava's dancing form and plays within it like a lightning flash in a sky covered with dense storm clouds.

We believe in the beautiful goddess who is the creative intelligence of consciousness. She is the lightening flash of being that dances within all things. She is Kuṇḍalinī when striving for the totality of one's inner potential. She is the joy of pure being.

There are many teachers on this path. The first teacher is your own heart. It will answer your questions when your mind will not. It will protect your spirit when it wanders in the mist. The heart knows the space beyond your comprehension. It is a mirror of the one great heart at the centre of all things.

The second teacher is your practice, *sādhana*. It will show you the one reality through experience. Everything that is known first comes from experience. No knowledge can be acquired without it. One must practice. This is the world.

You achieve success because you know that you alone are its seed and goal. Even your diligent practice is fruitless compared to the light of your own solid awareness. You know that it is you, that it has always been you, you alone.

The goal is here. It is in your hands.

THE AUTHOR

I know nothing about Kundalini Yoga. If you were to ask me how to perform *mūlabandha*, I would look at you blankly. I cannot, nor can anyone else for that matter, comprehend the essence of this teaching. Yoga must unveil itself beyond your understanding. The goddess herself, just like you, does not know the way; she simply is the way. The way must repeatedly unfold each time according to the nature of your own heart. You are the one who must discover the way, new and full of life.

Life is a miracle and yoga is a part of it.

I grew up in Salzburg, Austria. When I was a little boy, I always yearned to see the magic that tantalisingly dwells behind appearance. I began practicing Tai Chi at a young age. At 16, I developed a love for sitting in the forest, trying to meditate or simply traveling in my dreams. I was alone in this in my village, with no teacher to guide me. Since I loved the forest and always wanted to protect the living world, I went to university to study environmental engineering and limnology. I worked as an engineer for several years, but in the end I felt drawn to settle down with the yoga that had always been my companion. I learned Kundalini Yoga from Svāmī Vidjanand, student of Svāmī Satyānanda. He showed me the way of the heart and gave me Kundalini Yoga from a completely new direction.
I continued to learn from my teacher and friend, Rainer Neyer, in the tradition of Dhīrendra Brahmacārī. I also studied the Kashmir Śaiva traditions from Mark Dyczkowsky as transmitted by the great master, Svāmī Lakshman Joo.

In 2016, I opened a yoga studio in my beautiful city of Vienna, where I live and work. I practice and explore the secrets of yoga with my students both in my studio and all over Europe. I am extremely grateful to be allowed to share these teachings with you.

May the great heart be with you.

SANSKRIT SPELLING

Vokals

अ [ə] a A
आ [ɑː] ā Ā
इ [i] i I
ई [iː] ī Ī
उ [u] u U
ऊ [uː] ū Ū
ऋ [ɹ̩] ṛ Ṛ
ॠ [ɹ̩ː] ṝ Ṝ
ऌ [l̩] ḷ Ḷ
ॡ [l̩]:ḹ Ḹ

Anusvara अं [^{n}] ṃ Ṃ
Visarga अः[h] ḥ

Diphthongs

ए [eː] e E
ऐ [aːi] ai Ai
ओ [oː] o O
औ [aːu] au Au

Unvoiced consonants

क [k] k K
च [c] c C
ट [ʈ] ṭ Ṭ
त [t̪] t T
प [p] p P

Aspirated voiceless consonants

ख [kʰ] kh Kh
छ [cʰ] ch Ch
ठ [ʈʰ] ṭh Ṭh
थ [t̪]ʰth Th
फ [pʰ] ph Ph

Voiced consonants

ग [g] g G
ज [ɟ] j J
ड [ɖ] ḍ Ḍ
द [d̪] d D
ब [b] b B

Aspirated voiced consonants

घ [gʰ] gh Gh
झ [ɟʰ] jh Jh
ढ [ɖʰ] ḍh Ḍh
ध [d̪]ʰdh Dh
भ [bʰ] bh Bh

Nasal

ङ [ŋ] ṅ Ṅ　　ञ [ɲ] ñ Ñ　　ण [ɳ] ṇ Ṇ　　न [n] n N

म [m] m M

Semi-vowels

य [j] y Y　　र [r] r R　　ल [l] l L　　व [v] v V

Sibilants

श [ɕ] ś Ś　　ष [ʂ] ṣ Ṣ　　स [s] s S

Voiced fricative

ह [ɦ] h H

GLOSSARY

Ādhāra -	Foundation, support, ground.
Ādhāra Mudrā -	Energy Gestures for the base of the body.
Āgama -	Corpus of tantric scriptures in Buddhism and Hinduism. The term literally means tradition or that which has come down.
Agni -	Fire, God of fire, fire of digestion.
Aham -	Meaning "I"
Aham idam aham -	"I am this, this I am" Emphasizing the undifferentiated and eternal nature of the absolute.
Ahaṃkāra. -	*Ahaṃ* is the "I" and *kāra* is "any created thing" It is that faculty of the mind creating the phenomenon of the ego, the limited perception of self.
Ajapā gāyatrī -	Continuous, spontaneous repetition of mantra; meditation practice in which mantra is coordinated with the breath
Ājñā -	Meaning "command". Sixth chakra of the human body.
Ākāśa -	Space, ether. The fifth element, also associated with Shiva.
Akhaṇḍa Jyoti -	The eternal flame. A light that shines from within without smoke.
Amṛt -	Nectar of immortality. Dropping from the thousand pedaled lotus.
Amṛteśvara -	Lord of nectar, Shiva.
Anāhata -	The unstruck, that what is unbeaten. The heart chakra
Anāhata Nāda -	The sound of the heart. OM. The imperishable sound, no beginning no end.

Anamaya Kośa - Layer of Illusion of food, the material body.

Ānanda - Bliss, the ecstasy of being

Ānandamaya Kośa - Layer of illusion of bliss, the body made from bliss.

Ānandāśakti - Energy of universal bliss, also identified with the Goddess herself.

Añjali mudrā- Gesture or seal of salutation, *Añjali* meaning offering.

Antaḥkaraṇa - Internal organ of Mind, the platform on which all mental faculties, like thought, ego and discernment play their parts.

Antarakumbhaka - Internal breath retention.

Anugraha - The grace of the divine.

Anusvāra - Marks a type of a special nasal sound.

Anuttaraśakti - Supreme energy, the unsurpassed Śakti.

Apāna prāṇa - Usually referring to the lower prāṇa, associated with inhalation (in early Tantra), excretion and fertility.

Aparā - The lower world, the manifest word. The impure

Āpas - Meaning water, or liquid.

Āraṇyakas - Later section of the holy Hinduistic Vedas that constitutes the philosophy behind ritual sacrifice.

Āsana - Seat, meditation posture and the 3rd limb of Patañjali Yoga.

Ashtanga - Meaning "eight points", can relate to Patañjalis yoga that highlights the eight steps of yoga.

Āstika - Are schools of Philosophy that accept the epistemic authority of the Vedas, the existence of *ātman* and the existence of *Ishvara.*

Aśvinīmudrā - Gesture of the horse, contraction of the anus or the external anal sphincter

Atharvaveda -	Knowledge storehouse of *atharvāṇas*, "the procedures for everyday life", also often called Veda of magical formulas.
Ātman -	Individual soul. Resting in the heart in the form of a flame.
Ayoni -	Unborn, meaning that which did not pass through the vagina. For example the imperishable self.
Bāhyakumbhaka -	Outer breath retention.
Bandhas -	Locks or gates, used in yogic practice to centre the energy in the body.
Bhairava Mudrā -	The gesture of the dispeller of fear, both hand are resting open in the lab,
Bhairava/Maheśvara -	The highest tantric deity/the great lord.
Bhakti Yoga -	The yoga of devotion, centering ones mind in the love for God.
Bhastrikā -	Meaning "little bag" and referring to the bellows of the blacksmith that fans the fire. Breath of fire.
Bhāvanā -	Contemplative meditation using imagination and visualization.
Bhrāmarī -	Meaning "like a bee". The humming bee breath.
Bhrūmadhya dṛṣṭi -	Gazing at the brow point. Belonging to the category of mudras
Bhūta śuddhi -	Cleansing of the five elements. This can be done with ritual or chanting.
Bīja -	Seed, usually referring to a seed sound.
Bīja nyāsa-	Placing seed sounds in specific parts of the body. Here referring to the central channel.
Bindu -	Meaning "point". Point of origination. Non dimensional

existence.

Bodhānanda - *Bhoda*- "insight, realization, awareness". The bliss of ones own awareness.

Brahmā - The creator God

Brahmacharya - Chastity, usually not followed by yogis and yoginis ;-)

Brahmāgranthi - Psychic knot of Brahmā, limitation in energy, when pieced by Kuṇḍalinī, energy is awakened.

Brahmamuhūrta - The hour of the creator. The time that starts 1 hour and 36 minutes before sunrise.

Brāhmanas - Parts of the Vedas meaning that what belongs to the priest. Often explaining myths and legends that are related to ritual.

Brahmarandhra - A point on the top of the head. The passage of Brahma, through which life can enter or leave. Also called *dvādaśānta*.

Bhrūmadhya - A point in the middle between the eyebrows

Buddhi - Intellect, a mental organ being able to decide and discern. The closest mental agent to pure individual consciousness, saturated by *sattwa* (luminosity).

Caitanya - Meaning "spiritual consciousness", awakeness. Being present.

Cakra - Wheel, referring to a centre of pranic energy.

Chinmudrā - Gesture of Consciousness.

Citrini Nāḍi - The innermost layer of the central channel. Being made from *sattwa*, reflecting consciousness.

Citśakti - Universal energy of consciousness. A power of God (*śaktiman*)

Citta - Field of the mind. Thinking, imagination, memory.

Cittavṛtti -	Modification of thought or mind. Thought patterns.
Dantien -	Energetic centre below the navel, well known by all north Asian traditions.
Devī -	The Goddess.
Dhāraṇā -	Th hold, meditative mental fixation on an object of focus.
Dharma -	Law, justice or nature. It is the law of the world, the way to go. The right moral conduct. The natural order of things.
Dhvani -	Acoustical sound
Dhyana -	Complete mental (internal) alignment with the object of *dhāraṇā* or fokus.
Dvādaśānta -	Meaning "the end of the twelve". Each chakra is depicted to be 12 fingers with apart from another. *Dvādaśānta* can refer to each centre or to the highest one, right over the head.
Gorakṣa -	Master Goraksha Nāth, who founded the *nāth* Yogi lineage, student of Matsyendra.
Granthi -	Psychic knot, that is to overcome to reach higher states of consciousness.
Guṇas -	The tree basic qualities of nature and the world. Pain, pleasure, and indifference. The best description of the three *gunas* can be found in the Bhagavad Gītā
Haṃsa -	The sunbird flying back and forth between to the universal and the limited, in each breath of live.
Hasta mudrās -	Gestures of energy being performed with the hands.
Icchāśakti -	Universal power of will, or desire. The will to be. A power of God.
Iḍā -	Meaning "nourishing", the left side channel of the yogic anatomy. Related to moon and introversion.
Indriya -	The sense organ.

Īśvara - Lord of the excellent. The personal God.

Jālandharabandha - Neck lock. *Jāla* is water, it is that lock that collects the heavenly waters. *Amṛt*, the nectar is collected there.

Jīva - Meaning "alive". The individual alive soul, resting in the heart, also identified with *puruṣa.*

Jīvan-mukti - The liberated soul, individual but free.

Jīvātman - Atman is the spirit, the breath of life. This is a term for the individual eternal being, the soul.

Jñānaśakti - The universal power of knowledge or gnosis, the knowledge about the absolute. A power of God.

Jñāna Yoga - The yoga of right knowledge. Contemplation about the truth.

Kaivalya - The ultimate goal of *Rāja* Yoga, meaning solitude, detachment or isolation.

Kalā - The covering shell (*kañcukas*) *kalā*, limited capacity for action and a limited knowledge.

Kāla - The covering shell *kāla*, the individual soul has become subject to time, past, present and future.

Kālīkula - The family of the black Goddess, north eastern *Śāktaḥ* tantric school.

Kalpa taru - The mystical tree that grants the wishes, it grows the fruits of live.

Kañcukas - Limiting shell. A power of illusion, limiting a universal power of God to an individual one.

Kanda - A point underneath the navel, considered to be equivalent to dantien, the centre of bodily energy.

Kandasthāna - Seat of *kanda.*

Kapālabhāti - Shining skull *prāṇāyāma.*

Kārana - The cause having an effect. In this case a bija that is the cause of existence.

Karma - Action, law of cause and effect. Destiny.***Karma Yoga*** - Yoga of action. Doing an action for the sake of the right action and not for the result. More about this in the Bhagavad Gītā.

Kaubjikā - Goddess Kubjikās tradition.

Kaula - Family, Group. Kulamarga were tantric groups worshiping the Goddesses Kuleśvarī, Kubjikā, Kālī and Tripurasundarī.

Kāya mudrās - *Mudrās* (gestures) performed with ones whole body.

Kevalakumbka - *Kevala* (alone). Spontaneous breath retention, occurring when the mind moves in the state beyond breath..

Khecaras - The skyfarers, the ones moving above.

Khecarī mudrā - The gesture of the skyfarer. In Hatha Yoga the backward curling of the tongue.

Khecarī vidyā - The knowledge of the skyfaring Goddess. Her body in sound form.

Kośas - Layers or bodies concealing ones true being.

Krama - Sequence. For the sequential way of energies leading to highest realization. School of tantric Shivaism, that could have written the Vijnana Bhairava Tantra.

Krama Mudrā - Mudrā of Sequence. A state of being in which the individual soul pulsates between the states of being unbound and limited.

Kriyā - Action.

Kriyāśakti - Universal power of Action. A power of God.

Kṣētraṁ - Place or temple, referring to anatomical points being especially related to chakras.

Kumbhaka - Holding of ones breath or breath exercises.

Kuṇḍalinī - Primal energy. The power of God. The Goddess in her coiled form. When active, the Goddess in full experience.

Līlā - The divine play, the play of Shiva moving between five acts of creation - maintenance - withdrawal - concealment - revelation.

Liṅga - Penis, referring to an ache typical form of Shiva, object of worship and symbol of consciousnesses, the seed of all.

Mahā prāṇa - The great prāṇa, the principal prāṇa, governing the chest.

Mahābhārata - The most important Indian epic, telling the story of bharats and containing the Bhagavad Gita.

Māyā - The Mother, illusion. She brings about all forms. Everything is born from her womb. If you know her, she is the stairway to freedom. If you are ignorant she will bind you.

Māyā's seed - HRĪM (M is sung with *anusvāra*, the nasal sound).

Mālāmantras - Lengthy mantras being a conglomerate of many bijas.

Malini - A name for the Goddess Kubjikā.

Mānas - The sensual mind.

Maṇḍūkī mudrā - The gesture of the frog, being explained in the section *mudrā.*

Maṇipūra - City of gems, one of the most important chakras for yoga.

Manomaya Kośa - Layer of illusion of mind.

Manonmanī - The place beyond mind. Knowledge beyond what can be comprehended individually.

Mantra siddhi - The accomplishment of mantra, the power being attained in mantra.

Mantrapīṭha -	Throne of mantras, tantric school of kashmir Shivaism, autors of *Svacchandatantra.*
Mantraśakti -	Power of mantra. Essentially Kuṇḍalinī, the inner vitality of mantra.
Mātṝkā -	Little mother, meaning the letter. The sound that creates the world.
Māyā -	Terrifying Goddess of illusion, mother of the *kañcukas*, mother of the world.
Meru -	The holy mountain. The spinal cord, *suṣumnā.*
Mīmāṃsā -	Also *Pūrva-Mīmāṃsā*, School of Indian Philosophy. Concerned with justifying Vedic Ritual.
Mokṣa -	Liberation.
Mudrā -	Gesture, seal or the Goddess herself. That what draws forth delight. That what melts away what has been sealed.
Muktikā -	Rescue. Referring to the collection of 108 principal Upanishads.
Mūla Prakŕti -	A Sāṃkhya term referring to the first and primal nature of all things. The powers of nature in perfect equilibrium.
Mūlabandha -	Support lock, the master key of *Hatha* Yoga practice.
Mūlādhāra -	Seat of the support, first chakra of the Kuabjika tradition.
Nābhi chakra -	The navel centre. Often understood as manipura, the house of gems, sometimes understood as kanda.
Nād Anāhat -	The sound of the heart, see *Anāhata Nāda.*
Nāda -	The first sound, the primal vibration, Oṃ.
Nāḍis -	Psychic energy channels, transporting prāṇa.
Nāḍiśodhana -	Psychic network purification, alternate nostril prāṇayma.

Namaskāra Mudrā - Gesture of gratitude also known as anjali mudrā.

Nāsikāgra dṛṣṭi - Gazing at ones nose tip. Important practice to still the mind and connect to ones own energy.

Naṭarāja - King of the dance, referring to Shiva dancing the play of life and death.

Nāth - Lineage of early *haṭha* yogis.

Nidrā - Yogic sleep, earlier understood as samadhi.

Nirodha - Complete peace and clarity of consciousness, the stilling.

Nirvāṇa - Term referring to the state of liberation in emptiness.

Niyama - Restraint, ethical rule of behavior. Second step in the eight step Patañjali Yoga.

Niyati - Meaning destiny and is one of the limitations of the universal. Being bound to cause and effect and therefore possessing destiny.

Nyāsa - Placing something within.

Nyāya - Meaning rules method or judgment. School of Indian philosophy being concerned with logic.

Pañca bhūta - The five gross elements. Earth, Water, Fire, Air and Ether.

Parā - The supreme. The pure. Also the supreme Goddess, who is said to be white like cows milk.

Parā Kuṇḍalinī - Supreme Kuṇḍalinī, the Kuṇḍalinī that is beyond any limitation she cannot be experienced individually

Paramātmāṇ - Supreme soul. Identical with Brahman.

Parāśakti - The energy of the supreme. The highest energy, identical with Bhairava.

Paśu - The fetters soul, the individual being, the animal.

Piṅgalā - Right sided primary energy channel, forms with iḍā and *suṣumnā* the three main energy channels. Transporting the solar energy of extroversion, objectivity and wakefulness.

Prakāśa - The one light of consciousness, the source of all as nothing exists independently from it.

Prakṛti - Nature, representing everything apart from individual consciousness, which is the created world.

Prāṇa - Energy of breath. Breath of live.

Prāṇa mudrā - Gesture or attitude of *prāṇa*, an exercise highlighting the balance of *prāṇa*, also called *śānti mudrā*, the gesture of peace.

Prāṇāmaya Kośa - Layer of illusion of *prāṇa*. Ones limitation within the sphere of *prāṇa*.

Prāṇāśakti - Energy of *prāṇa*, referring to *prāṇa*, but also to the universal power behind *prāṇa*, the Goddess.

Praṇava - The syllable Oṃ in Vedic context or in the tantric context any other *bija*. That what projects *prāṇa* into emptiness.

Prāṇa-Vāyus - Winds of *prāṇa*, referring to the vayus that govern the body like *apāna, mahā, samana, udana* and *vyana*.

Prāṇāyāma - Breath regulation. Yogic discipline of controlling vital energy. 3rd step in Patañjali Yoga

Pratyāhāra - Withdrawal of the senses. Internalization of attention. Being the 4th step in Patañjali Yoga.

Pṛthvī - Earth, the first *pañca bhūta* and last tattva 25 according to Sāṃkhya.

Pūraka - Means filling, referring to the yogic inbreath.

Puruṣa - Individual consciousness, highest and first tattva according to Sāṃkhya.

Rāga -	Desire, *kañcuka* limiting ones bliss and therefore creating the desire for fulfillment.
Rajas -	One of the three *gunas* or primary constituents of all creation. Representing movement, indifference and desire.
Rāja Yoga -	Royal Yoga, the path of Patañjali Yoga through the eight steps.
Recaka -	Emptying. The process of yogic exhalation.
Ṛgveda -	Oldest of the four Vedas, consisting like the others of four main parts.
Rudra -	The roarer. A Rigvedic deity and later identified with Shiva, the destroyer God.
Rudra's Seed -	HRAUM (M is sung with *anusvāra*, the nasal sound). Also (HRĀM HRĪM HRAUM)
Rudragranthi -	Knot of Rudra, an energy blockage located at *ājñā cakra*, if transcended non dual consciousness can shine.
Rūpa -	Form.
Śabda -	Sound.
Śabda-brahmaṇi -	God in form of sound.
Saccidānanda -	Truth, bliss, consciousnesses. The attributes of God consciousness.
Sadāśiva -	Highest tantric Paraśiva (supreme Shiva). He is the omnipotent, subtle, luminous. He is grace, the blessing of the absolute.
Sādhana -	The way to the goal, a means of accomplishing something. Ones daily practice.
Sādhana Pāda -	Patañjalis second chapter of the Yoga-Sūtras. The way of practice.
Sahasrāra -	Thousandfold, referring to the highest chakra on the top of

the head.

Sahitakumbhaka - Conscious and willful holding of the breath.

Śaiva Siddhānta - Conservative movement within Kashmir Shaivism with a more dualistic view on reality.

Śāktaḥ - Doctrine of energy or power, the eternal Goddess. traditions worshiping the Goddess.

Śakti- Energy, the Goddess, or the Goddess energy,

Śakti-cālana-mudrā - Gesture of the rising of energy. A Kundalini Yoga contemplation

Samādhi - Bringing together. Last step in Patnajali Yoga. The place where one meets ones self.

Samāna - One of the five principal *prāṇas*. The energy of the digestive fire. The energy of one-pointedness.

Sāmaveda - Song. Is the Veda of melodies and chants.

Samavṛtti - Equal length in movement. Same duration in and outbreath in *prāṇāyāma* practice.

Śāmbhavī mudrā - Gesture of the friendly Shiva. Gazing at the brow point.

Saṃhāra - Annihilation or withdrawal or the world. One of the five acts of Shiva.

Saṃhitās - Put together, joined, union. Textual corpus that is a collection.

Sāṃkhya - Meaning counting. One of the six *āstika* (conservative) schools of Hindu philosophy. They form the basis for Patañjali Yoga.

Saṁmukhī Mudrā - Gesture of the six mouths. A Seal that emphasizes the closing of the body's gates in order to withdraw into the inner sound.

Saṃkalpa - Intention, mindset, goal:

Sattva - One of the three *gunas* or basic constituents of the manifest world. Lightness, transparency, pleasure.

Siddha - An accomplished person:

Siddhi - An accomplishment, like a magical power.

Śītalī - Meaning cooling or soothing in Sanskrit, is a cooling breath exercise in traditional Hatha Yoga.

Śiva - The auspicious one, the highest deity; the way, the goal. The holder of dharma- the law. Also the destroyer God.

So'Haṃ - Meaning "He is me." Vedic Mantra that also influenced tantra. Emphasizing the oneness with God.

Śramaṇas - One who labors, toils, or exerts themselves for some higher or religious purpose. An early yogi living in the forest.

Śrīvidja - Meaning auspicious knowledge, *Śāktaḥ* tantrism's most influential movement. Its central symbol is the the *śrī cakra* also known as *śrī yantra.*

Sthiti - One of the five acts of Shiva, the preservation of the moment of reality.

Sthūla - Meaning dense, gross, solid. Gross appearance of any object.

Śuddha Vidyā - Also *shuddhavidyātattva*. Pure knowlege/whisdom. The 5th of the 36 tattvas of Śaivaism.

Śuddha vikalpa - Pure thought construct. A modification of thought patterns, mirroring a divine truth.

Sukhopāya - The sweet and easy way. A tantric way of meditative contemplation. Also introduced in the *Svabodhodaya-*

mañjarī.

Sūkṣma - Subtle, referring to the subtle sound that is not audible by the gross ear.

Śūnya- Zero, nothing, empty or void. Being the place that is eternal and unchanging.

Suṣumnā - The central nadi. The channel of the observer. The channel of the soul. Associated with the element of fire.

Sutras - Thread. Is a text usually being composed out of short verses. Guiding one on the path.

Svādhiṣṭhāna - One's own seat. Second chakra of the Kuabjika tradition.

Svāmī - A Yogi.

Svaras - Tones in Indian traditional music. A svara is a note within successive steps of the octave.

Sva-rūpa - One's own form. The essential nature of something.

Svātantrya - Meaning Self-dependency or free will.

Svātantryaśakti - The universal power of true self-dependency and free will. A power of God and one of the properties of *prakāśa.*

Tamas - One of the three *gunas* or basic properties of nature. Darkness, heaviness, dullness, pain.

Tattva - Basic category of reality in which a living being can subsume the experiences within it.

Trimūrti - Three forms. Hindu triad of Gods. Brahma the creator, Viṣṇu the preserver, and Shiva the destroyer.

Tirodhana - Disappearing, concealing. One of the five powers of God by which he conceals the reality.

Trika - Trinity. One of the tantric schools of Kashmir Shaivism.

Uccāra - Utterance, expression. A form of Mantra and bija recitation.

Uccārayoga - Yoga of projection/uttering forth a state of consciousnesses. Described in Tantrasara.

Udāna - Upward moving *prāṇa*, one of the five principal *prāṇa*s, also identified with Kuṇḍalinī

Uḍḍīyānabandha - The upward rising lock. A yogic exercise emphasizing the movement of *prāṇa* though the abdomen till the heart.

Ujjāyī - The invincible breath. A form of yogic *prāṇāyāma*.

Unmeṣaśakti - The universal power of awakening. The power that opens ones eyes to the truth.

Upadeśa - Teaching or instruction.

Upaniṣads - Scriptures close to the teacher. Part of the Vedas, dealing with meditation, philosophy, and spiritual knowledge.

Vāgbhava - AIM (M is sung with *anusvāra*, the nasal sound). Brahmas mantra, that is especially connected to the earth element. It is the sonic form of the goddess Kubjikā (Kuṇḍalinī) residing in the centre of the Goddess mandala.

Vaiśeṣika - One of the six *āstika* schools of Hindu philosophy. It was an independent philosophy with metaphysics, epistemology, logic, ethics, and soteriology

Vajrolī Mudrā - Gesture of the thunderbolt, Yogic psychic seal to preserve sexual energy.

Vakrā - Crooked, bend. A Name for Kuṇḍalinī or Kubjikā.

Vāma - The left. The female breast. One of the schools of left handed tantra.

Vāyu - Wind, one of the five gross elements or referring to *prāṇa* or life force.

Vedānta - The end of knowledge. One of the six *āstika* schools of Hindu philosophy, dealing with the philosophy of the Upanishads.

Vidyā - Divine Knowledge. Can also refer to mantra or *bija* that is the knowledge of the deity in seed form.

Vijñāna - Consciousness, life force or mind.

Vijñānamaya Kośa - Layer of illusion of consciousness, or state of mind.

Vikalpa - Modification of thought patterns, imagination and fantasy.

Viṣamavṛtti - Different length in movement. Different duration in inhalation and exhalation in *prāṇāyāma* practice.

Viṣṇu - Meaning preserver. He is one of the Hindu triad (*trimurti*), Viṣṇu is revered as the supreme being in Vaishnavism.

Viṣṇugranthi - Knot of the preserver. A psychic knot underneath the heart, signifying the attachment to feeling.

Viśuddha - The pure wheel, 5th chakra of the Kaubjikā, situated in the throat.

Vyāna - One of the five principal *prāṇas*. The pervasive breath. According to Abhinava Gupta it is the energy of the pervasive state of consciousness.

Yajurveda - *Yajus* meaning worship. The knowledge Veda of worship. Containing primary mantras for ritual worship.

Yama - Self control, restraint. The first step in Patañjali Yoga.

Yāmala - The couple, very intense early left handed tantic tradition, famous for its transgressive rituals.

Yantra - Machine, contraption. Geometric symbol, being a manifestation of the deities energy.

Yoga - Yoga is the unification of the many pairs of opposites.

Yoga Mudrā - Gesture or seal of union. A bowing down in front of all.

Yogācāra - Meaning yoga practice. Buddhist tradition dealing with yogic practices, very important or early tantra and therefore for *haṭha* as well.

Yonimudrā - Gesture of the womb or source. A famous hand *mudrā*.

Yuga - Meaning epoch or era. A complete *yuga* cycle is fourfold. The *satya yuga, treta yuga, dvapara yuga* and in the end *kali yuga.*

BIBLIOGRAPHY

Secondary Literature:

A. G. Mohan - Yoga Yajnavalkya, Svastha Yoga (5. Juli 2013), ISBN-10: 9810716486

Arthur Avalon, Sir John Woodroffe- Mahanirvana Tantra Of The Great Liberation (Englisch) Kessinger Publishing, LLC (10. September 2010), ISBN-10: 1169319823

Arthur Avalon, Sir John Woodroffe- The Serpent Power: The Secrets of Tantric and Shaktic Yoga (Englisch), Dover Publications; Auflage: Revised ed. (1. Juni 1974), ISBN-10: 0486230589

Bettina Sharada Bäumer - The Yoga of Netra Tantra:: Third Eye and Overcoming Death, D.K. Print World Ltd (7. Januar 2019), ISBN-10: 8124609667

Brereton, Joel (1999). "Edifying Puzzlement: Ṛgveda and the Uses of Enigma". Journal of the American Oriental Society.

C. G. Jung - The Psychology of Kundalini Yoga: Notes of the Seminar Given in 1932, Princeton University Press (12. Januar 2012), ASIN: B0073X0GJC

Christopher Wallis- Tantra Illuminated: The Philosophy, History, and Practice of a Timeless Tradition, Mattamayura Press; Auflage: 2 (15. August 2013). ISBN-10: 0989761304

Christopher Wallis- The Recognition Sutras: Illuminating a 1,000-year-old spiritual masterpiece (English), Mattamayura Press (1. Mai 2017), ISBN-10: 0989761371

Christopher Wallis- Chakras Illuminated, handouts given at a course of Dr. Wallis in 2018.

Dory Heilijgers-Seelen - The System of Five Cakras in Kubjikamatantra 14-16 (Groningen Oriental Studies), Published by Egbert Forsten Pub, 1994, ISBN 10: 9069800594

Gautam Chaterjee - Abhinavagupta - Tantrasara: Text with English Translation, Dilip Kumar Publishers (1703). ASIN: B01NBPL4D0

H.N. Chakravarty - Abhinavagupta - Tantrasara, Translation from Sanskrit and

Introduction by , Edited by Boris Marjanovic. Published by Rudra Press

HarperCollins Publishers; Box Lea Edition (3. März 2011), Holy Bible: King James Version (KJV) (Bible Kjv), ISBN-10 : 9780007259762

Jaideva Singh - Siva Sutras: The Yoga of Supreme Identity (Englisch), Motilal Banarsidass; Auflage: New edition (30. Oktober 2012), ISBN-10: 8120804074

Mark S.G. Dyczkowski - Manthanabhairavatantram, Kumarikakhandah 12 Vol. The Section Concerning the Virgin Goddess. (Englisch) Paperback – 2009. ISBN-10: 8124604983

Saraswati Satyasangananda - Shri Vijnana Bhairava Tantra: The Ascent (Englisch) Taschenbuch – Motilal Books UK (1. Dezember 2003), ISBN-10: 818633632X

Sir James Mallinson- Roots of Yoga (Penguin Classics) (Englisch) Paperback, Penguin Classics; Auflage: 2017 (11. April 2017), ISBN-10: 9780241253045

Sri Aurobindo - Savitri: A Legend & a Symbol, Herausgeber : LOTUS BRANDS INC; U.S Edition (4. Juni 1998), ISBN-10 : 9780941524803, ISBN-13 : 978-0941524803

Stephen Mitchell - Bhagavad Gita: A New Translation Taschenbuch, Herausgeber : Harmony; Reprint Edition (27. August 2002), ISBN-10 : 0609810340, ISBN-13 : 978-0609810347

Stephen Mitchell - Tao Te Ching New Edition: The book of the way, Taschenbuch – 19. Mai 2011, Herausgeber : Kyle Books (19. Mai 2011) ISBN-10 : 0857830155, ISBN-13 : 978-0857830159

Swami Lakshmanjoo - Kashmir Shaivism: The Secret Supreme, CreateSpace Independent Publishing Platform (6. August 2015). ISBN-10: 1548539899

Swami Lakshmanjoo - Vijnana Bhairava The Practice of Centering Awareness (Englisch) Paperback – Januar 1, 2007. ISBN-10: 8186569359

Swami Ranganathananda (1991). Human Being in Depth: A Scientific Approach to Religion. SUNY Press. p. 21. ISBN 0-7914-0679-2

Traditional sources:

Gerard D. C. Kuiken, Śiva sutra- The Shiva Sutra of Vasugupta, Publisher: OTAM Books, ISBN 978-90-78623-07-6

Richard Sheppard- 108 Upanishads (The order as given in the Muktika Upanishad) With commentary on the first 10 Upanishads by Swami Nirmalananda Giri, International Gita Society.

Vladimir Antonov- Vyasa, BHAGAVAD GITA Edition of the Bhagavad Gita and commentaries by, Translated by Mikhail Nikolenko,Vladimir Antonov, 2002 ISBN — 978-1-897510-23-0

Rai Bahadur Srisa Chandra Vasu- Gheranda Samhita, Sri Satguru Publications 1979, No ISBN.

Chip Hartranft- The Yoga-Sûtra of Patañjali Sanskrit-English Translation & Glossary, published by Chip Hartranft, The Arlington Center 2003.

Swami Vivekananda- PATANJALI YOGA SUTRAS Sanskrit text with Translation and Commentary, open ebook.

HATHA YOGA PRADIPIKA Foreword by B K S Iyengar Commentary by Hans Ulrich Rieker, Translated by Elsy Becherer, This edition published by The Aquarian Press 1992, 13579108642

Hatha Yoga Pradipika- Muktibodhananda Swami, Bihar School of Yoga, 17.03.1999, ISBN 978-81-85787-38-1.

Rai Bahadur Srisa Chandra Vasu, THE SIVA SAMHITA, published by the Panini Office Bhuvaneshwari Ashram Bahadurganj, Indian press 1914,

The Yoga Rahasya of Nathamuni, Krishnamacharya Healing and Yoga Foundation;(1. April 2018), ISBN-10: 9382470042.

Christopher Wallis aka Hareesh - A translation of the Vijñāna-bhairava-tantra, 2018, open version

Christopher Wallis & Alexis Sanderson, Vīranātha- Svabodhodaya-mañjarī, open version.

Mark Dyczkowsky - The Vijñānabhairavatantra an English Translation, open version

Goraksha Shataka of Gorakhnath, (translated in English by Yoga Nath), open version

Shri Purohit Swami- The Sage Vyasa, The Bhagavad Gita, open ebook.

Yoga Nath (translator)- Goraksha Shataka of Gorakhnath, open ebook

INDEX OF CITATIONS

Translation 21, 94

Gorakhnath - Goraksha Shataka (translated in English by Yoga Nath) 25, 254, 259

H

H.N. Chakravarty - Tantrasara of Abhinavagupta, Translation from Sanskrit and Introduction by H.N. Chakravarty 47, 58, 168

J

Jaideva Singh - Siva Sutras: The Yoga of Supreme Identity 55, 278–279

M

Mark Dyczkowsky - The Vijñānabhairavatantra an English Translation 19, 152

Mark S.G. Dyczkowski - Manthanabhairavatantram, Kumarikakhandah 12 Vol. The Section Concerning the Virgin Goddess 73, 89, 165, 252, 260, 281, 289, 295

N

Nathamuni - The Yoga Rahasya of Nathamuni, Krishnamacharya Healing and Yoga Foundation 29, 236, 241, 310

R

Rai Bahadur Srisa Chandra Vasu- Gheranda Samhita, Sri Satguru Publications 171, 238–239, 310

Rai Bahadur Srisa Chandra Vasu, THE SIVA SAMHITA 27, 101, 116, 136, 148, 266

Richard Sheppard- 108 Upanishads, With commentary on the first 10 Upanishads by Swami Nirmalananda Giri 17, 67, 97–98, 103, 105–107, 110–111, 128

S

Saraswati Satyasangananda - Shri Vijnana Bhairava Tantra: The Ascent 57, 132, 301, 317

Shri Purohit Swami- The Sage Vyasa, The Bhagavad Gita 67

Sir James Mallinson- Roots of Yoga 272–273, 288, 299–302, 304

Stephen Mitchell - Bhagavad Gita 14, 33–37

Stephen Mitchell - Tao Te Ching: A New English Version 308

Interpretive translation according to: Swami Muktananda - Kundalini Stavah, SYDA Foundation,U.S. (1. Januar 1980). As well as Hymn to the Kundalinī from the later recension of the Tantra of the Divine Couple, translation Christopher D. Wallis. And also Chit Kundalini Stava from the venerable Sri Kamakoti Mandali. 190

T

Tantraloka course - Trinity Goddess handouts- Mark Dyczkovsky 326

The Bible - King James Version (KJV) 279

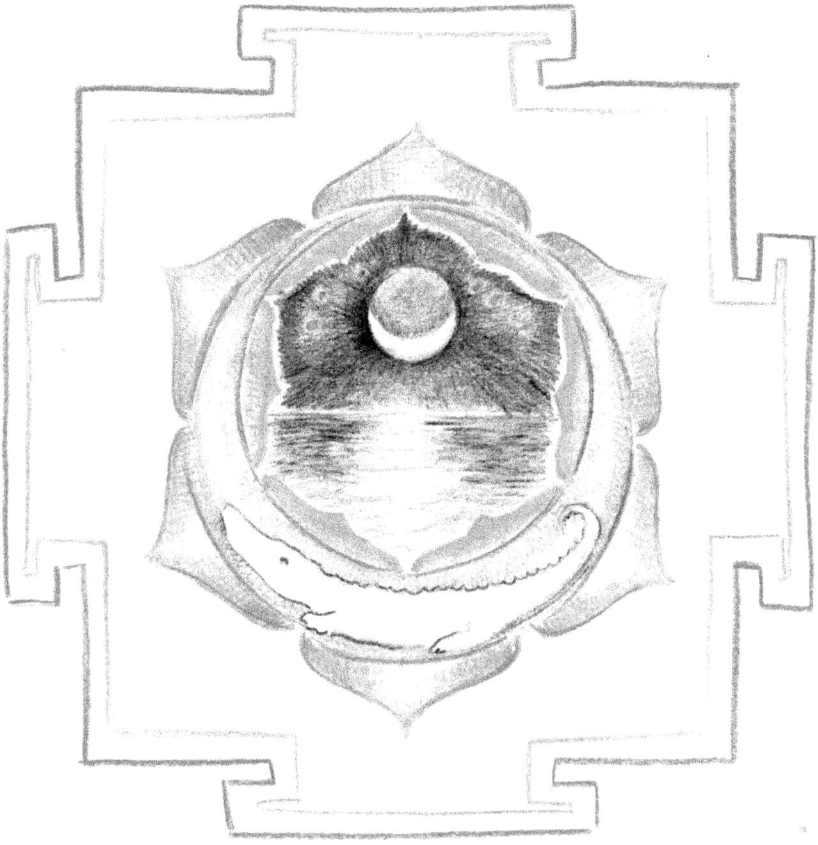

CPSIA information can be obtained
at www.ICGtesting.com
Printed in the USA
LVHW060935181222
735478LV00011B/596

9 798543 949061